Strangers
in my Sleeper

Strangers
in my Sleeper

Rail journeys and
encounters on the
Indian subcontinent

PETER RIORDAN

First published in 2006 by New Holland Publishers (NZ) Ltd
Auckland • Sydney • London • Cape Town

www.newhollandpublishers.co.nz

218 Lake Road, Northcote, Auckland, New Zealand
14 Aquatic Drive, Frenchs Forest, NSW 2086, Australia
86–88 Edgware Road, London W2 2EA, United Kingdom
80 McKenzie Street, Cape Town 8001, South Africa

Managing editor: Matt Turner
Editor: Anna Rogers
Design: Nick Turzynski, redinc.

National Library of New Zealand Cataloguing-in-Publication Data

Riordan, Peter.
Strangers in my sleeper : rail trips and encounters on the Indian
subcontinent / Peter Riordan.
ISBN-13: 978-1-86966-145-8
ISBN-10: 1-86966-145-1
1. Riordan, Peter—Travel—India. 2. Railroad travel—India.
3. India—Description and travel. I. Title.
919.540453—dc 22

1 3 5 7 9 10 8 6 4 2

Colour reproduction by Pica Digital Pte Ltd, Singapore
Printed in China at Everbest Printing Co

The publishers would like to thank Samit Roychoudhury of the
Indian Railways Fan Club (www.irfca.org) for his assistance.

For Steph and Tim

Contents

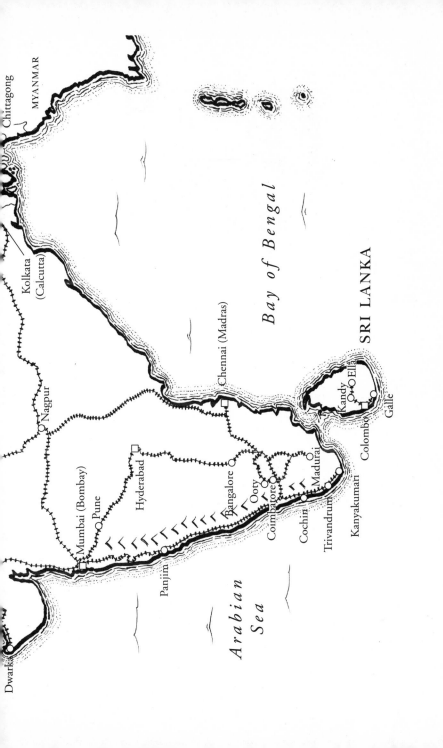

Auto-rickshaw to Chennai Central Station.

Introduction

THE LONG PLAINTIVE SCREECH of an Indian locomotive horn. No sound on the subcontinent, to my mind, is more evocative. The memories tumble out: all those paddy fields and baked plains passing endlessly before my eyes; the string of rust-red carriages curving out of sight to either side of my window; the bearer pausing at the compartment entrance to enquire droningly: 'Chai? Chai? Chai?'; the smell of cheroots from the coupling; the rush of tinder-dry air through the window grilles; the passengers with whom I idled away the hours.

A train journey on the subcontinent is always life-enriching, never merely a convenient means to get to one's destination. It can be full of disappointments, discomforts, tedium, disagreeable passengers, free-loaders, but also absorbing company, a kaleidoscope of sights, kindly conductors with clipboards in hand to guide you through applications in triplicate, and the perpetual commotion of the platform ('that perennially ravishing show', as Mark Twain observed).

The railway is a subtle and complex organism, built by the British and now thoroughly made over to Indian (in the pre-Partition sense) purposes. The lifeblood of the Raj is now an inseparable part of modern India, hauling the freight wagons of industry, speeding passengers in air-conditioned comfort between the principal cities and running third-class-only services in the dusty provinces. I say 'modern India' because the first 33 kilometres of track were opened for traffic only in 1853, and that, by the standards of this ancient land, is very recent indeed. Even so, the vast web of tracks, bridges and stations, from humble to foolishly grand, whether on branch or main line, feels as though it has always belonged, that it is as rooted in the land as the mouldering ruins which dot the countryside.

There can be no doubt the railway is one of the greatest legacies of British rule, a dazzling technical achievement built to connect, and thus secure, the empire's prize colonial possession. A product of the age of steam, it is simple and sound – an old solution to old problems. Monsoon floods, outbreaks of disease, communal violence, hartals, border clashes or political agitation: tragedies may strike the subcontinent in a multiplicity of guises and with all the destructive rage of the goddess Kali herself, but the trains can always be relied on to run, and to schedule, too.

The railway is the great constant, the tie that binds the vast region encircled on three sides by mountain chains and impenetrable hills once known as the Land of Nod ('wandering'). That tradition persists. Sadhus, itinerants, salesmen, traders, pilgrims, holidaying families, politicians, military men taking up postings, the great masses – for nearly all, their first thought is not the roads with their potholes and tooting, sagging, unruly traffic but the railway.

One day in 2003 when the consolations of writing for newspaper barons felt particularly meagre, I asked myself: What better way to discover the Land of Nod, to do some wandering of my own, than by train? It was sociable. It was relatively comfortable. And it was practical, allowing the traveller to lope across great distances without the wrenching distortions of aeroplanes or the exhaustion of the long-distance bus. There was no better choice for someone like me intent on sedentary, not high, adventure.

Pakistan and Bangladesh, parts of that far-flung network in British times, were also on my itinerary, and Sri Lanka, too. With independence, they had evolved distinctive traits, which inevitably imprinted themselves on their railways. With luck and patience I might get to peek behind the train schedules and into the psyche of each country.

My plan was to cross the length and breadth of the subcontinent, to go to the end of the line, to see who lived and worked and travelled aboard this sprawling, indispensable and now fragmented institution called the railways of the subcontinent. For my purposes, the longer the ride the better. I would take sleepers, settle in and let the world's greatest railway show come to me.

Downtown Ooty.

The Nilgiri Express to Ooty

MY FIRST TRAIN JOURNEY was as brief as it was unexpected – a scant half-hour. But Mr Ramaswami, a banker from Bombay who, like me, was just off a plane, approved of my impulse decision.

'You are wise to be taking the train,' he said. 'Here you will be safe, but not with that lot.'

Behind us, not five minutes' walk away, taxi drivers and disreputable-looking touts swarmed over the other groggy midnight arrivals at Madras Airport.

'Take the train,' some kind-hearted soul outside the terminal had said, seeing my blinking confused face. 'It's just over there.'

So I zigzagged through the car park, crossed a road teeming with lorries, bought an 8-rupee ticket and joined Mr Ramaswami on the platform. The suburban station was unlit so we stood in companionable darkness chatting until the rattle of a train interrupted us.

'Here it comes,' he said. 'Quickly, platform four.'

He picked up his one piece of luggage, a briefcase, and made for the underpass. I followed, grateful for having been taken in hand by this stranger.

When six empty carriages, all battered wrecks, pulled up I felt a trace of disappointment. This was not quite the glorious machine I had envisioned would set me off on my journey. The walls were grubby and peeling, the slatted wooden seats burnished to a dull glint by a million suburban backsides, the bars across the windows looked as fixed as any in a prison cell, and above my head metal handgrips like old-fashioned manacles rattled and swayed in perfect unison as we trundled off into the low unremarkable suburbs of Madras – or Chennai as it has now become known. The city's lights, so conventionally patterned from the plane's window, were revealed as a free-for-all of fluorescent tubes and bulbs clustered on lampposts, walls and balconies, each clump crowned by a bramble of power lines to form a sort of sagging electrical undergrowth around Madras's flats and tower blocks.

We stopped at a station. Gaunt figures lay asleep beneath puddles of light. A pariah dog stopped, sniffed and limped on. A truck growled past without its lights on. Overhanging everything, thickening even the air itself, was grey dust, a dust that had been shifted from doorstep to doorstep by centuries of sweepers. The grimness of it all was a shock to my jet-lagged eyes.

Mr Ramaswami was unnaturally chirpy for such an awful hour although he had reason enough to be: he was home for two weeks' holiday. And life was good. He was manager of an American-owned bank, and his son and daughter were both doing well in their studies in the United States. Would his children try eventually for green cards? 'Many do – there are more opportunities – but no, they will come back after a year or so. Here there are so many people and so much competition for jobs. Too many people,' he said in a matter-of-fact tone that made plain no comment was required of me. Even so, I couldn't resist a smile; barely an hour had passed since my arrival and already someone was bemoaning India's population problem.

'Reservations are there, too,' he resumed.

'You mean caste reservations?'

He nodded. 'Merit is there, yes, but only a percentage.' He drew a thumb and forefinger together until they almost touched.

We slowed for another station and Mr Ramaswami indicated to an ill-lit side street: 'My house is down there.' It seemed a modest address for a successful banker. He rose, pumped my hand and vanished into the night.

The shabby suburban train gathered momentum again. Despite the late hour it was still very hot, and the roof-mounted fans whirred away without offering any relief. I felt suddenly quite alone, jet-lagged and overawed. But three stops on I took my rucksack and descended at Egmore Station.

That was it. I had taken my first small step by train across the subcontinent. It had been almost accidental, and certainly undistinguished. But, I told myself, if Mr Ramaswami was any guide I was not likely to lack for good company.

Indians have a penchant for bureaucratic obfuscation and flowery titles, and at Chennai Central Station, as at all the country's main stations, this bent is given full expression. Drifting around the warren of cavernous halls and foyers, I came upon the besieged Current Reservation Counter (anyone can buy a ticket for a particular train though it is worthless without a reservation) and the deserted Platform Ticket Counter (a ticket of a few rupees being theoretically necessary to enter the platform areas). I also found waiting rooms graded according to gender and ticket class; and refreshment stalls divided according to vegetarian and non-vegetarian requirements; and the Excess Fare Ticket Counter ('Are you busy?' I asked the idle clerk. 'Oh yes, very!' he exclaimed.).

And side by side in the main concourse were to be found the 'May I Help You?' booth for general enquiries, the Military Police Assistance Booth and the Railway Police Assistance Booth. ('Aren't you doubling up?' I asked the duty sergeant at the second. 'No, no, they are looking after civilians, we are responsible for all military personnel – air force, army, navy and so forth.') Nearby were the Passenger Grievance and Suggestion Box and the Complaints Box Against Eve Teasers (as lecherous tit-and-bum feelers are so delicately referred to), a sign beneath which vowed to act without exception on all complaints. I found, too, the blackboard for Word for the Day – Memorable Maxim (no entry) and the office of the Bomb Detection Squad (its one occupant engaged in reading the day's *Times of India*).

Upstairs, I passed the overseer of the retiring rooms, officially designated the Matron, whose scowl betrayed her indifference to travellers' opinion of her. She had the all-important power to release or withhold rooms according to whim or a consideration. Outside her office door, chalked on a board, were room occupants' particulars, and next to that a numbered line of blue light bulbs, each corresponding to a room. The light bulbs lit up when the occupants were in.

Back downstairs I came upon the notice detailing porterage fees, based on number of items and weight, and an admonition to hire only officially sanctioned porters, who were identifiable by their red jackets and a brass authorisation tag strapped around one arm. As I noted this, a porter staggered by with three suitcases balanced on his head, the biggest on the bottom, the smallest on top in a tiered, wedding-cake-like effect. He also carried two kitbags, the handles looped around his upper arms, raised to brace the pile of luggage.

The public address system rattled off a stream of arrivals and departures, reminding me that I had a train to catch. But first I had to eat. I swerved through the principal concourse where crowds sweltered miserably in the heat and inspected the Railways-licensed vegetarian refreshment room. It was a grubby, standing-only outlet and unpatronised. I settled on another that was jam-packed and, with my fingers, tucked into a masala dosa, a spicy pancake with chutneys and South India's pre-eminent snack. Indians prefer to eat with their fingers, a habit I, too, enjoyed. But the duty manager instructed a waiter, a surly youth, to fetch me a spoon, which he wiped on his cuff and put on my plate. I removed it. He put it back. I removed it again – and this time held on to it. He gave a pained look and left, only to return later and hover after presenting the bill. He wanted me gone: more customers were arriving and all the seats were taken.

An elderly customer leant over. 'Take your time,' he said. 'Take as long as you like.'

'Thank you,' I said. 'He seems to want me gone.'

'No, no, take your time. Do what you want! This is India.'

Every time I saw some apparently unfathomable act of selfishness or stupidity I remembered those gleeful words: 'Do what you want! This is India.'

❂

Blue was a fitting livery colour for the Nilgiri Express, which was about to sweep me away from the stickiness of Madras towards the cool heights of the Nilgiris, the Blue Mountains. The sight of so many perspiring brows and damp collars had convinced me the heat was a trial for Tamils, too. Many were limbering up for their overnight journeys, wrapping sarong-like lungis around their waists, dropping their trousers, swapping their shoes for chappals. But my ticket was not merely an escape from the plains; I relished the notion of the squat mountain train that would be flexing its muscles at the foot of the Nilgiris in anticipation of our arrival and the steep haul up to the hill station of Ooty, 2,267 metres above sea level.

I stood there, a hand against coach A1, catching my breath after a mad dash along platform eight, having dodged between wooden crates and great lumpy sacks and consignments of machinery parts, past food stalls and milling passengers, until finally I caught sight of the Nilgiri Express, my overnight connection to Mettupalaiyam, where the mountain train waited.

I boarded with four minutes to spare, a margin that drew disbelieving looks because Indians, by long habit, arrive hours in advance of departure. At 8.30 pm, right on schedule, we drew out. A bedroll attendant set to work passing blankets, pillows and freshly laundered sheets among the passengers, who promptly prepared for bed, adjusting themselves into their starchy white cocoons. Soon the carriage was transformed into a gently rocking dormitory, all rustling sheets, dimmed lights, drawn curtains and the murmur of drowsy voices.

I felt cheated. I had caught a mobile chamber, not a train. But I turned out to be lucky. The only other passenger in my four-berth compartment was himself in no mood to turn in. Mr Mathrubhuteswaran, who described himself as a tea scientist, spoke guardedly at first. ('I thought you were an English tea planter,' he confessed later.)

Tea was his life, his guiding passion, so I talked tea. I mentioned reading about a British study into the best way to make a pot of tea. Pre-heat the pot then add a teaspoon of tea for each person and one for the pot, add water brought to a rolling boil, stew for three minutes, place milk in the cup first and pour. The delight on Mr Mathrubhuteswaran's face grew with each stage I enumerated. In fact he was almost hopping for joy.

'You put in milk first, yes?' he exclaimed.

'That's right.'

'And after three minutes?' he egged me on, his voice having ascended in tone with each fresh question.

I had no answer for that. I shook my head.

'What about after three minutes? Yes, at three minutes fifteen seconds when you are pouring second cup? And three minutes thirty seconds for third cup? And at three minutes forty-five seconds for fourth cup? You must *decant.*'

I thought a moment. 'Ah, my teapot has a strainer beneath the lid. After the first cup, the tea leaves are left high and dry so the rest of the pot doesn't stew.'

I even sketched a cutaway on the back of my ticket, but he pursed his lips as though he'd bitten on a particularly bitter quince, took my pen and drew his own solution: No. 1: a pot. No. 2: a narrow-necked decanter, refuge from the scourge of overbrewing; and No. 3: a cup and saucer, the cup with a lid to retain heat as long as possible.

'That is best way. Time-consuming, yes, but best. I am selfish person so I am only making tea this way once a day.'

I nodded solemnly. I found it hard to imagine this softly spoken grey-haired scientist had a selfish bone in his body. An infatuation with tea, yes. But that was probably the most heinous of his vices.

In bed I lay for a long time staring vacantly out the window. There was nothing to see – South India passed in total darkness – but there were a million impressions to digest. The strangeness of everything around me, from the vinyl-trimmed berth I was lying on to the smell of the laundered sheets, the continuous rush from the air vents, the eager rhythm of the wheels, Mr Mathrubhuteswaran's peaceful breathing – all of it exclaimed to me that I was finally on my way.

❈

'Mettupalaiyam! Mettupalaiyam!' called out a voice receding down the aisle. I rubbed my eyes and looked at my watch: it was just after 6 am. Then I listened for a sound, any sound, but there was none. With a start I realised I had overslept and everyone was gone. Outside, the dawn was deliciously cool. A crow squawked mechanically in the silence. Directly ahead the moon was sinking over the Nilgiris, which at this distance were no more than a mist-shrouded and delicate-blue row of protrusions beyond the jungle clearing of the station. And what a station! With its little casement windows and steeply pitched tile roof it more nearly resembled an oversized cottage. Only a single track either side of it, one broad gauge, the other narrow, and a couple of blackened loco sheds gave the game away.

I walked along to the wooden coaches on the narrow-gauge line. They were so low and skinny and insignificant – you had to stoop to get aboard – that my first thought was: these are ludicrous, like jumbo toys. Incredibly, they performed a real job – and a tough one, too.

Everyone from the overnight service had already taken their places in anticipation of leaving, though the coaches were going nowhere without an engine. I found a seat in the very front coach. After a while our steam-engine emerged from a shed belching smoke and hissing madly. The coal bunker was topped to overflowing. Despite its ancient appearance – it looked as old as the coaches themselves, which had gone into service in the 1920s – I never doubted its reliability. It reversed past us, scattering goats from the track, locked onto the rear coach and there it remained for an hour while everyone waited patiently in their pew-like wooden seats.

The leading brakeman appeared and took his place in the open gallery. He squeezed the rubber bellow of his horn, which emitted a throaty sort of noise, and we moved off, trundling past thatch huts whose roofs were strewn with bricks and broken chairs and worn bike tyres, and towards villagers squatting on the track for their morning defecation. The bowels of India were on the move. The brakeman pumped the bellow in a series of exasperated blasts as the toilet-goers ignored his warnings, sloping off with the greatest of reluctance and only as we bore down directly on them.

Beyond a bridge we stopped, and when we resumed our progress was by a series of jolts synchronised to the snorting of the unseen steam-engine. With speed the jolting faded. The incline increased. We chugged past a sawmill, a school, banana trees, a plantation of slender betel trees and palm trees of every sort. Fronds slapped the sides of our coach. The sensual rhythmic jolting resumed. Dampness and mildew and creepers cloaked everything. Greenery overlaid greenery in a vegetative riot.

My confined compartment had the protective feel of a wheelhouse with its much-dented woodwork, thick layers of paint and sticking louvred windows. Six of us sat along two facing benches, almost knee to knee, in enforced intimacy. A breeze blew through the front windows and brushed against our faces, though it was hardly more than a caress since any half-fit runner could have kept up with our leisurely pace. Not an arm's length away, with his back to us, was the brakeman.

Opposite me, turned almost cheek to cheek to face out the front window, sat a couple who smooched and giggled in the most unself-conscious way. It was the first, indeed the only, time I saw such affection in public. Same-sex displays – an innocent holding of hands, an arm rested on a friend's shoulder – that was commonplace, unremarkable. This was extraordinary. I kept sneaking glances, like some peeping Tom. They were both Tamil, perhaps thirty. She wore a salwar kameez, a long loose shirt over baggy pantaloons, and dabbed constantly at her runny nose with a handkerchief. Like nearly all

Indian males capable of growing one, he had a moustache, and wore a T-shirt, jeans and loafers.

At the hamlet of Kallar we halted while the rack-and-pinion system was engaged to prevent slippage on the steep inclines ahead. There was nothing to look at except some oily old sleepers heaped up like a funeral pyre, but passengers still got off and snapped away with their cameras. They were nearly all Indian holidaymakers. A signal warned brakemen: 'Stop here if main signal at danger.' Another warned passengers: 'Footboard travel totally forbidden.'

We trundled on, the toothed 'rack' rail plainly visible between the running rails. Maximum speed for this section was 13 kilometres an hour because of the severity of the gradient, which averaged 1:12 between Kallar and Coonoor. As we began up a steep incline there was more thrusting, an almost violent and climactic jerking of the coaches that made the three other passengers, a couple and their teenage daughter, giggle in embarrassment. The daughter had big almond-shaped eyes and sat cross-legged in the far corner spooning bhuja from a bag. She ate in a slow sensual way, almost massaging rather than chewing each mouthful, and whenever she laughed, which was frequently, she would raise a slender hand over her mouth in a coy and exaggerated display of politeness. Altogether, she made a transfixing sight.

By now we had gained some altitude. The Nilgiris, once so flat and indistinct, became three-dimensional things. Jungle-choked ravines fell away beneath us as we climbed along a series of bridges, curving insubstantial structures with rickety sleepers and tapering metal legs like delicate stick insects. Excitement rippled through the carriages and then hoots of delight and claps and cheers as we entered dank curving tunnels, before emerging onto curving bridges that spanned deep chasms in the hillsides.

Tunnel, bridge, tunnel, bridge – one followed the other in rapid succession, the tunnels drawing claps and cheers, the bridges a momentary awed silence as passengers gaped at the drop below, then more clapping and squeals of delight. I could hardly imagine a more atmospheric and less train-like journey. And along the way there were glimpses of the plain below, while immediately around us the jungle released ladybirds and butterflies through the windows.

As the sun rose, the mist began to clear on the highest hilltops. I couldn't have been happier: I had breakfast at hand, a bag of nuts, the soft jungle light was slanting into the carriage, the engine was making a slapping sound like a horse in full stride, and even the track ahead had been softened by a carpet of weeds that left only the rails visible.

The lovers had resumed their caressing, she running a finger distractedly back and forth along the neck of his T-shirt. It was a preoccupied action, but a proprietorial one nonetheless. Then, unprompted, he turned and remarked to me, 'Because it is so *steepy*, there are five brakemen to apply the brakes evenly – one man on each carriage.'

I was a little taken aback at this unexpected overture. 'You are very knowledgeable about trains.'

'I am working for Indian Railways,' he said, and he went on to explain the operation of the mountain train. The leading brakeman was for all intents and purposes in charge. With his forward view he could, with a wave of his red or green flag, stop the train or send it on its way. The whistles we heard were from the engine driver communicating orders to the five brakemen operating the wheel and rack brakes of each coach.

I never learned his name but he said he worked in the human relations department of the coach-building factory in Madras. Its 13,000 workers turned out 1,000 coaches a year.

'That many!' I whistled.

He smiled. I knew India was self-sufficient in rolling stock and locomotives, but it was only later I learned how elephantine some of the statistics were: 7,566 locomotives, 37,840 coaches, 22,147 freight wagons, 700 repair shops, 300 yards. And that was not to mention the stations (6,853), the workforce (1.54 million employees) or the track network (108,706 kilometres).

Having offered some information, he wanted some in return. What was my job? What was my native place? Was I married? Something prevented me from asking whether he also was married.

He let slip that he was taking a three-day holiday in Ooty. The woman beside him went unintroduced, unexplained. On we climbed, in full stride, through almost continuous cuttings into hillsides. Beyond the 14-kilometre marker (height: 900 metres above sea level) we passed beneath an overhanging cliff, like an immense unbreakable lump of coal, and then crossed bridge number fifty-five, replaced after being washed away two years earlier by heavy rains (there are 250 bridges on the 46-kilometre track). Landslides during the monsoon often damaged the line so it was inspected daily. And elephants could also be a hazard: some station buildings along the line had been attacked, forcing their closure.

At Hill Grove ('Look, a lady signalman,' cried a voice from the next compartment) a green all-clear flag waved us through and at Runneymede the first tea garden, Glendale Estate, appeared. Before long tea plants covered most of the hills, which were speckled with huge boulders and silver oaks and tea pickers' huts. But there was no sign of life bar a few trackmen who were hemmed in by ferns and lantana that grew thick as hedges. It was much cooler now – we were at 1,500 metres – and as we climbed higher banks of mist brushed the treetops, while below skeins of mist lay draped in the terraced valleys.

Coonoor loomed into view, a shabby agglomeration of tin-roofed houses and church spires that crept up the head of a ravine into the mist. With one look I decided against getting off. But the granite-built station building was sturdy and friendly looking. Coonoor played second fiddle to Ooty, even though it was noticeably warmer and less wet. The mild climate made it, in the words of my Murray's *Handbook*, that ancient font of wisdom on the subcontinent stretching back twenty-two editions to 1859, a favourite resort for 'persons of delicate health'.

With our old smoker retired to the loco shed, and now under diesel power, we made smoother, faster progress. Rack-and-pinion assistance was no longer necessary. Outside town we made a lengthy stop beside a graveyard. What inscriptions the elements hadn't erased from the gravestones were now concealed by the rampant lantana. At the tiny station of Wellington we waited again. Eucalypts rustled peacefully in the wind. We curved through grassy hills and forests of eucalypt and fir trees. The forest floor was thick with dried leaves, while the branches were draped with the hives of wild bees.

Along this section of track the Indian urge to catalogue was unmistakably evident: stocks of spare sleepers and rails were individually numbered; trees abutting the line were numbered; every work gang stopped to hold up a numbered paddle, like a metal table tennis bat, as we passed by. Inside the compartments it was the same: every fitting was stencilled with some tortuous reference number. The extent and complexity of this compulsion to enumerate and categorise was both awe-inspiring and exhausting to contemplate. Yet it was not exclusive to Indian Railways. Whether the caste system with its multiplicity of subdivisions or the forms of yoga and consciousness or the avatars of the gods or the love positions of the *Kama Sutra* or the astrological calculations necessary to set a wedding day, in India every waking moment could be found a slot within some cosmic register.

Now we had no more hills to climb. Instead we edged our way around ridges, the distant hilltops rolled smooth and at the same height as us. The lovers took out some snacks. 'Here, have a home-made sweet,' he said, passing over a tin of ladoos.

I took a bite of one. 'Delicious. Who made it?' (I was still fishing for their relationship.)

'*She* did,' he replied, pointing in her direction.

❂

Four kilometres before Ooty we halted at Lovedale, a sprinkling of houses set in a forest. The trio in our compartment detrained, to be met by two women wearing cardigans over their saris and a frail man with a tweed cap and a walking-stick. A cold breeze whipped through the windows as we made the final leg into Ooty and its pretty cottage-station.

Beyond the station it was not so pretty. The tranquil resort so favoured since the days of the British Raj, when it doubled as the summer headquarters of the government of Madras, was no more.

Yes, the tattered carcass was there – the lake with its hire boats, the racecourse, St Stephen's Church (its considerable roof timbers reputedly pillaged from Tipu Sultan's palace at Srirangapattana after his defeat by the British during the Mysore Wars), the Ootacamund Club (where snooker was invented), the Maharaja of Mysore's grand Fernhill Palace Hotel, the Botanical Gardens and former Government House – but the spirit of the place had long departed. Its charms had been eclipsed by concrete hotel blocks and litter and an ungodly symphony of vehicle horns. All the government tourist hoardings in the world, with their claim 'QUEEN OF THE HILL-STATIONS', could not persuade me otherwise.

On Commercial Road, the main thoroughfare through the bazaar, I watched students in blazers and ties stream out the gates of the Breeks Memorial Anglo-Indian Secondary School. Two sway-backed horses cropped the overgrown grass. Higher up the hill I found the original school, a red-brick range with a sharply inclined iron roof and a clock tower capped with a spire. This former private school was now the District and Sessions Court. In an alcove the size of a telephone box I came upon a plaque: 'The Breek Memorial School erected to the memory of James Wilkinson Breeks of the Madras Civil Service, First Commissioner of the Neilgerry Hills.'

'*Kneelgery Heels*,' giggled a voice behind me.

I looked around. Two men hovered outside the alcove.

'We saw you reading it,' said one. 'The plaque, I am meaning.'

'Yes, it's an odd spelling,' I agreed, and then mimicked their pronunciation.

That drew a laugh. They introduced themselves. Mr Kumar and Mr Dinesh were advocates. The former, a big stooping man with a tight-cropped beard and bloodshot eyes, cut a formidable figure, while Mr Dinesh was short and plump and had a ready laugh. Together, they made a sort of Little John and Friar Tuck of Ooty's legal fraternity. We compared our respective legal systems. Yes, in the antipodes judges and barristers had now dropped wigs and black gowns, as in India. We had four principal levels – district, high, supreme and appeal courts – whereas India, unsurprisingly, had about a dozen. Mr Kumar rattled them off on his fingers, which fell before his count like shooting targets in a fairground alley.

When I asked them about Madras's name change they declared most people were happy with the original. (Chennai is simply the Tamil word for Madras.) Mr Kumar shrugged his shoulders and raised his palms to the skies. Politicians, politicians, his gesture declared, their capriciousness is as certain as the monsoon.

'But Madras High Court has stuck with its name,' Mr Kumar went on, with a note of triumph in his voice, confirming that judiciaries everywhere were bastions of conservatism. The pair were waiting for a judge to reappear, and when he turned up they adopted the absurdly fawning demeanour of schoolboys before a tyrannical headmaster. But once he had left they fell back into chummy behaviour.

'You've been drinking, haven't you?' I teased them. Their breaths smelt unmistakably of alcohol. They gave a giggle of embarrassment before Mr Dinesh spluttered, 'Only the one.'

'Let us go outside,' suggested Mr Kumar.

We walked out into a courtyard. In its centre, beneath a tree, was a stone image of Ganesh, slopped with offerings and candle wax. Ganesh must have been close to Mr Dinesh's heart because he subjected me to a lengthy explanation of how the god came to have an elephant head on a human form. It was no mere regurgitating of mythology but the retelling of an event that really took place – and not so distantly either, judging by the animation in his voice. Condensed to its essentials, it seems Ganesh's head was mistakenly chopped off by his father Siva, who vowed to replace Ganesh's head with the first living creature that came by, which happened to be an elephant.

'Ganesh is god of truthfulness,' ended Mr Dinesh, although a more popular association was good fortune.

'A fitting attribute for lawyers, then,' I said.

They both gave a titter.

Their reticence only emboldened me. 'Which is more likely to win in a court of law,' I asked, 'truth or making a living?'

Once more neither answered, though I could have sworn a knowing look passed between them. They did not strike me as particularly shining examples of rectitude or incisiveness, two qualities essential in a defence lawyer in India's courts, whose legal logjams are legendary and whose accused have been known to languish in jail for years awaiting trail.

'Well, it is only right that Ganesh is so close by,' I said. 'After all, justice proceeds at an elephant's pace.'

'Indeed, you are right,' Mr Dinesh agreed.

Leaving Coimbatore, third-class carriage.

The Coimbatore–Madurai Express

IN A CRUSH OF KNEES AND ELBOWS I descended by bus to the plains. All the way down I fretted about abandoning so early on my resolution to catch only trains. But the mountain train's schedule would have dumped me late at night in the industrial city of Coimbatore. I had no wish to stay overnight there so I chose convenience and caught an early-morning bus. Besides, it was only a few hours of unfaithfulness. The bus was overcrowded in the Indian fashion, seventy or so aboard a vehicle intended for forty and not one willing to entrust his luggage to the roof rack.

But the ticket collector made the journey memorable. After gathering the fares he sat next to me in the back row and overhauled his principal tool, his whistle, which he held while on duty by a ring around one finger. With a needle he prised out what looked to be bits of snot. 'Dust,' he explained when he caught me observing him. With the job completed to his satisfaction, he spent every remaining moment sorting and discarding papers buried in the zip pockets of his satchel. He attacked the job at a frenetic pace, examining and refolding the frailest scraps, screwing up some, reassigning others. These pieces had been creased a hundred ways in a process that had taken place countless times before. Old lottery tickets, cryptic notes, news clippings, reminders, fragments so small I couldn't recognise despite sitting shoulder to shoulder with him – all passed before his scrutiny for recataloguing or discarding. Then on the home run into Coimbatore he did a stocktake of his tickets and made annotations on an inventory. With his boundless energy he could have run the Tamil Nadu State Transport Corporation rather than occupied one of its lowest rungs. For twenty-one years, he told me, he had made the twice-daily run to Coimbatore and back. And there was every likelihood that in ten or twenty years' time he would still be at it.

The only daytime train to Madurai was an unreserved third-class service, renamed 'second-class seat' though the new nomenclature fooled no one; it still had the wooden-slat seats of old. I bought a ticket and boarded. It confounded my anxieties. Not only was it nearly empty, it was clean, the floors were swept and the ceiling fans hummed away discreetly. I put my feet up, pleased with my luck, as the diesel loco gave a deep, solemn rumble and we pulled out.

Despite its name, the Coimbatore–Madurai Express is a slow train. It takes six and a half hours to cover 229 kilometres. But in less than five minutes we reached the edge of Coimbatore, a city of almost one and a half million people and an awful lot of cotton mills and factories. The remnants of the Nilgiris were visible as a band of widely spaced bumps, rather like the beautiful hills of Guilin in southern China.

Soon fields of sugar cane twice the height of a man pressed against the track, but in an hour it was all expanses of wasteland blowing with plastic litter. Although it was the beginning of August, the monsoon rains were no more than a taunt here in central Tamil Nadu. Against so bleak a backdrop, a kingfisher with electric-turquoise plumage perched on a wire made an astonishingly dazzling contrast.

The plains became broader and starker and the wind grew in strength, tugging determinedly at the feathery fronds of columns of graceful areca palms. Gradually the rubbish, in a thousand variations of bag, wrapper, bottle and cup, came to dominate the landscape. Shopping bags snagged on weeds shrieked a noisy rebuke at us. I gulped at the scale of this folly. Yet where were the humans responsible for it? No signs of life were to be seen bar a skein of foot tracks that led from nowhere to nowhere.

Early in the afternoon we halted at a tiny station. It portended a hundred more like it. Kinattukkadavu consisted of a signboard bearing its name, a banyan tree like a giant unfurled umbrella, a low station building thirty paces long and edged by flowerboxes, a drinking fountain and a concrete bench beneath which a pariah dog slept. A signalman in a stained white uniform peered from the gentle arches of a verandah.

It was very peaceful. Eucalypts shook rhythmically in the breeze, like waves lapping on a sandy beach. The heat and stillness made me dozy. After a while indignant voices down the corridor roused me. I caught the gist of their exchange: news had broken that traces of pesticide had been found in Pepsi soft drinks sold in India.* The manufacturer had been pumping contaminated bore water straight into its bottling plant. There was much tut-tutting. An *American* company trafficking this poisonous beverage! But the more remarkable fact, it seemed to me, was that the water was so heavily contaminated in the first place. Having fouled their environment Indians were now reaping the karmic consequences. The blizzard of indecomposable plastic was an obvious debasement, the overuse of pesticides a more insidious version.

A third-class service clattered through and after a protracted blast of the diesel's horn the carriages lurched forward like collapsing domino pieces and we moved off. Soon the land became noticeably more fertile as the line struck south adjacent to a gap in the Western Ghats. Through this corridor swept remnants of the monsoon rains that deluged coastal Kerala. Palm oil plantations, squares of sugar cane and vegetable plots sprouted from the lumpy red soil, along with a sea of coconut palms, regarded as 'green gold' by South

---

* The pesticide level was reported to be 0.36 per cent.

Indians, who can put every part of the tree to some use. And next to thatched huts were tied bullocks with brightly painted horns.

At the town of Pollachi we stopped and my solitary ride ended. Three students joined my compartment. All were studying towards an MA in English literature and they travelled each day between Pollachi and Udumalpet, 29 kilometres away. My express was a glorified commuter.

What was my view of globalisation, one asked. It was an unexpected question but I replied that it was leading the world to blandness. Followed to its ultimate conclusion, we would all be wearing Levis, snacking at McDonalds, drinking Coke and driving a Toyota or Ford. 'It's a fine theory – open markets, free trade – but it seems to be just a way for rich countries to exploit poor countries.'

That drew no sympathy, not even a response, but his friend said, 'They don't want our technology, they only want to sell us theirs.'

'You mean rich countries?'

'Yes.'

'Can you give an example?'

'See that neem tree, it is growing like a weed but it can cure smallpox. Ayurvedic treatment is to grind leaves into paste and put on skin or swallow. Now America pharmaceutical has found active ingredient and is starting a court battle. Over *our* ancient cure!'

'I see your point. America and India don't get on so well, do they?'

'America does all the talking. It doesn't listen. No listening.'

'The world's policeman!' added the third enthusiastically.

'Policing its own interests,' corrected another.

All three were clean-shaven, well mannered, enthusiastic – perfect students. They studied hard too, they told me. My apparently aimless wanderings baffled them. Or, more specifically, how I could afford such an indulgence.

'We live from hand to mouth,' said one, putting his closed fingers to his lips as though about to flick in a moistened ball of rice.

I fudged a reply to hide my discomfort.

'You have ancestors?' asked another.

'Relations, yes.'

'And you must give them money?' he asked. 'In India we have many obligations.'

'We also, but they are not so strong.'

That was only barely true. On the whole our help was discretionary and token, while theirs brooked no exceptions and was substantial.

The Western Ghats, an opaque-blue chain streaked with splashes of brown, reared up in wonderful irregular shapes that hooked the passing clouds.

'Beautiful, aren't they?' I said.

They looked out indifferently. 'In your own country, you know …' one trailed off.

We passed yellowy tamarind plantations and then a line of palmyra palm trees from whose branches hung the black pots of the toddy men. The sweet sap dripping from incisions in the branches would ferment in the heat to become frothy and intoxicating. Crows, I learned, were extremely fond of the juice and were known to sit motionless for hours in a state of intoxication.

'Have you drunk it?' I asked.

None of them had.

'And you?' the closest asked.

'No, I'd rather have a cold beer.'

He pumped my hand at the audacity of drinking alcohol.

Their stop came, there were more handshakes and they left. I watched them disperse across a common ground so awash with plastic litter that their ankles were lost from view.

I was alone again, staring vacantly at stubbly fields pock-marked by termite mounds. At Palani, a pilgrim centre whose famous hilltop temple was visible from my window, a dozen schoolboys invaded my compartment.* They crowded around me so tightly, each face lit up with curiosity and unbridled enthusiasm, that the compartment visibly darkened. Each time my pen touched the page there was a collective breathless concentration. I abandoned my note-taking.

---

* The temple is dedicated to Subrahmanya, an aspect of Shiva, whose image is composed of nine types of poisons formed into a wax-like substance.

They were headed for Dindigul, scarcely 30 kilometres away. Over the hubbub I asked each what he wanted to be. 'Engineer,' yelled one. 'Teacher,' cried another. 'Army,' a third. 'Collector.' 'Policeman.' 'Doctor.' 'Teacher,' repeated another, and so forth. Only one said, 'Artist.'

'Does no one want to be a farmer?'

Silence.

'Too hard?'

Another silence.

I pointed to the litter strewn across the landscape. I wrote the word down: L-I-T-T-E-R. What did they think?

Blank.

Finally one called out, 'There is no fine.'

'But it's ugly and unhealthy.'

'Sweeper will come,' suggested another.

'I think sweepers are beyond that job,' I said, waving my hand towards the plastic-strewn plain. At Dindigul they disembarked and at six o'clock, after a half-hour wait under a grey sky, we creaked out of the station, the five business types beside me looking like reluctant third-class passengers. They read their newspapers and talked among themselves. But one, a young customs officer called Mr Kamalakannan, was in the mood to chat. Smartly turned out in slacks, checked shirt and boat shoes, he was something of a man of the world. Although a modest-salaried public servant and married to boot, he was saving for a month's holiday in Israel the following spring. Hard as I pressed him, he would not openly take a side on the Israeli-Palestinian conflict.

'What about Kashmir?' I asked instead. 'What's the answer there?'

I'd seen Indians lose their composure at the mere mention of the word Kashmir but here, too, I failed.

'Actually, India is a collection of many nations,' he began. 'In Europe they have the EC; we have India. And we must find a way to live like a family of nations, peacefully.'

'Should India implement the UN resolution for a plebiscite by Kashmiris?'

He dodged the question with a meander through the byways of the intractable dispute before finally declaring that Kashmiris wanted autonomy, not a merging with their co-religionists in the Land of the Pure. I pondered that a moment. Maybe he was right. After a time he said to me, more brightly: 'How are you liking India?'

His four companions, who had grown bored with our political discussions, pricked up their ears. It was a big question. I wanted to say: It's beautiful, it's unlike any other country, but it's being spoilt by too many people. I wanted to mention the misery of the jobless millions, their idleness and wasted lives, the strain on the environment. But instead I reeled off the regular tourist drawcards: the diverse peoples and landscapes, the cultural and religious heritage, the culinary splendours.

Mr Kamalakannan paused and said, 'In India so many competing influences are there. What is strange in one country is normal in another.'

Those words, written down coldly on paper, seemed risible in their triteness, but spoken in his honey-smooth voice in that darkening coach, the mosquitoes biting at my ankles, my backside aching from six hours on a wooden seat, the glow of lanterns punctuating the flashing shadows of trees and hamlets, they seemed to salve the outsider's hot indignation.

'Our problem, you understand, is people. We have too many.'

'I can see that is a problem. What's to be done?'

'Communists and others are stirring up the old idea that children are wealth.'

'But they're not?'

'Not wealth, responsibility.'

'How many children do you have?'

'One.'

'And you?' I asked, turning to the companion sitting beside him.

'Two,' he replied. 'Your country is short of people, yes? Lots of land and few people?'

'Maybe.'

The outskirts of Madurai now came into view and as we neared the station Mr Kamalakannan put a peculiar question to me. 'What is the one message you have for us to take away?'

Flummoxed, I stalled for time: 'You first.'

'You must have more people so each older generation can be looked after by the younger ones.'

So now he was flying his true colours. Wasn't that precisely the children-as-wealth argument?

'And my message to you is also about population. Slow down!'

That brought hoots of laughter from all five, not, I knew, out of any cleverness on my part, but at the utter impossibility of the idea.

Hindus have no squeamishness about making a buck on holy ground. Madurai's main attraction, the Great Temple, draws some 10,000 visitors a day, and where there are visitors there are vendors. Within its precincts is a sprawling bazaar. To the Hindu mind, there are no doctrinal dilemmas in being simultaneously in the service of Mammon and Ganesh, Hanuman, Durga or any other favourite deity. Life is seamless. Work, prayer, procreation, eating, sleeping are all happily indivisible aspects of daily existence. Why fuss yourself unnecessarily with segregating them? Relax, enjoy yourself. As the bumper sticker on a passing Tempo van reminded everyone, 'Smile, God loves you.'

Hindus have a pantheon of 330 million gods, whose favourites they worship as they please, but they are all manifestations of Brahman, the one impersonal Being who, to the Hindu mind, pervades everything, expressed in the trinity of Brahma, the Creator; Vishnu, the Preserver; and Siva, the Destroyer and Reproducer, not unlike the Christian Holy Trinity of Father, Son and Holy Ghost.

The most striking thing about Madurai's Great Temple is the tapering towers over each of the four entrance gates, and in particular their riotous decoration. Every centimetre is a medley of sculpted animals, humans, fierce eye-bulging monster faces, divinities and various celestial beings. They are luridly painted, too, and soar skywards for 50 metres. The temple's interior is also eye-catching.

There is a columned hall called the Viravasantaraya Mandapam, 75 metres long and packed with merchants. Dealers ply their trade from stalls that overflow with religious trappings: 'holy' powders that look like mounds of paprika and chilli powder (to make the tilak mark on the forehead); turmeric bulbs ('for the *skeen* on lady's face,' advised one stall attendant); marriage threads and posters and lockets of deities (fat jolly Ganesh was the top seller). These spiritual aids share shelf space with more prosaic merchandise including plastic dolls, binoculars, garlands, face masks, chess sets, rolls of photographic film and tambourines. The combination of modern-day baubles and fifteenth-century architecture is, to say the least, incongruous.

In the Pudu Mandapam, another columned hall, I found Madurai's tailors hard at work. They had their heads down over treadle sewing-machines which clattered away ceaselessly, like a swarm of agitated bees.

The temple's custodians are not immune to a little commerce themselves. A sign before the innermost sanctum, the shrine of the god Sundareswar, declares 'Photo tickets available. Ticket rate Rs. 30/- (per camera)'. In strategic places are positioned candle sellers, and in another pillared corridor called the Minakshi Nayaka Mandapam there are kept elephants whose principal purpose is apparently to suck up through their trunks the loose change of passing pilgrims in exchange for a tap on the head from the same vacuum nozzle (the coins being disgorged into the obliging hands of mahouts).

Admission to the Hall of 1000 Pillars (though the total number is put variously at 985 and 997) is 2 rupees, with an additional 5 rupees for photography. Its conversion to a museum is a distraction. The pillars, each different in some slight way, are the attraction and they form a tightly compacted mass, like the descending aerial roots of an enormous banyan tree, to create a hall that appears to consist more of supports than of useable space.

The temple can claim no special holiness but it is hugely popular, crowded day and night with pilgrims. And for gawking foreigners, it conveniently distils India into a space 250 metres square. It contains

Hindu ritual and decoration in their most complete and baroque-like form: brooding, smoke-blackened stone corridors; the flicker of many oil lamps; the sentinel-like aspect of the lion brackets bearing the suspended roof beams; the surge of pilgrims in various states of spiritual ecstasy, the most fervent supplicants prostrating themselves full length before deities, the more common or garden variety – the mums and dads and kids of Madurai – contenting themselves to push and shove from shrine to shrine with the boisterousness of bazaar shoppers; the intoxicating compound of incense and babbling unintelligible voices: taken together, it forms an appealingly earthy and individualistic form of worship, especially to those, like me, raised on a childhood diet of damp-smelling churches, stern-faced parishioners and insufferable amounts of kneeling and standing.

I liked Madurai for its temple, its friendly crowds, its relaxed Tamils with their wonderful broad faces, frizzy mops of hair and toothy white smiles – and its South Indian food. Late one morning I sloshed through the old city's streets and found a place to eat. After the overnight downpours it was now very hot and sticky. A group of customers arrived, among them a garlanded and heavily bejewelled woman in an apple-green sari. She was very beautiful and somehow she had made it through the muddy puddles and the crush of traffic without so much as a speck of dirt soiling her garment. She was absolutely spotless. But so, too, I realised as I looked around, were all the other sari-clad women. I wiped the sweat from my brow and pondered how they managed to look so unblemished. Sitting there, plump and wreathed in fine cloth and feted by their skinny menfolk, they stirred in me an image of a lotus flower, sweet serene beauty resting on and nourished by a pile of watery muck.

I ordered and waited, watching the human and mechanical tide that swept through the narrow streets adjoining the temple. The inventory began with lowly pedestrians, the undifferentiated mass of labourers, sweepers, shoppers and hawkers who gave way to everything because they were at the bottom of the might-is-right pyramid. The list progressed up through the cyclists, bicycle-rickshaw riders and scooter riders to the auto-rickshaw drivers and the men straining at the pedals of bicycle-rickshaws converted to carry cumbersome loads (lengths of plumber's piping, empty oil-cooking tins stacked as much as 3 metres high and somebody's surplus charpoy). Next in the hierarchy were the coolies pushing handcarts burdened by fantastically big loads, then a jeep or two, a private car or two, a chauffeur-driven Hindustan Ambassador (a half-century-old replica of a Morris Oxford) conveying a state government Member of the Legislative Assembly home for lunch, and lastly two Tata lorries creaking by with builder's gravel, and perched on top the coolies who would unload it shovel by weary shovel. Everyone with a horn or bell used it, not maddeningly but merely habitually, as they heaved, swerved, darted and laboured towards their destinations.

This unpredictable vein of movement was obstructed by the beseeching beggars, the street sellers' carts, the parked motorbikes, the sacred cows which chewed on accumulated piles of rubbish or sat with regal indifference in the middle of the road, forcing the traffic to bend around them, the bicycle-rickshaw riders who parked their machines two deep at the roadside, the street hawkers flogging armloads of second-hand books, plastic combs and buckets, sunglasses ….

'You are thinking,' a voice broke my thoughts, 'that we Indians are masters of unruly driving.'

I turned to face the man at the next table. 'Why yes. Don't you find it a little frightening?'

He smiled. 'We get used to it. And actually you will, too, in time,' he said, before resuming the attack on his mound of mushy rice.

Porter balancing luggage, Bangalore City Junction.

The Tuticorin–Bangalore Express

SOON AFTER I BOARDED the overnight service to Bangalore the old man in the bunk opposite passed wind. Not furtively but long and loud, like a policeman blowing his whistle. My awkwardness was brief, though. His face, dry as parchment and overlaid by an intricate web of lines, registered not the slightest trace of embarrassment. Nor did the indiscretion draw any reaction from his wife, who busied herself clearing away the tiffin tins spread across their seat.

Madurai slipped into the night. The old man, replenished after the meal taken en route from Tuticorin where the train originated, now let out a long satisfying burp. A little later he raised a buttock off the seat to ease out another fart, also long and apparently satisfying. In an adjoining compartment a toddler, her head shaved and her eyes heavily underlined with kohl, began to cry, at first intermittently and then continuously. Then farter's wife began to develop a rasping cough – in between wide, wide yawns. Sleep seemed a welcome escape, except it wasn't yet nine o'clock.

At Dindigul Station, a man of military bearing with a fantastically, almost implausibly, generous handlebar moustache came aboard. A mobile phone hung from a cord around his neck. It was my first hint of Indians' love affair with cellphones. Having endured for decades the overloaded land lines and sticky fingers of a state-run monopoly, they were now understandably bedazzled by the novelty of instant communication.

My new companion began to read a book, *The Politics of Crime and Corruption*.

'Good?' I enquired, eventually.

'Actually it is very disturbing,' he replied.

Mr Pai took almost no prompting to elaborate on the book's main threads. Nirmal Kumar Singh, the author and a former senior Central Bureau of Investigation officer, had experienced at first hand the rise of criminal elements in politics and the galloping spread of corruption. These twin evils, according to the author, were the root cause of India's backwardness.

'Politicians, they are all corrupt – it is the way of things,' sighed Mr Pai. 'India is a very big country, so hard to manage.'

In his view corruption flourished whenever there was great competition for limited public services. It was a simple supply-and-demand imbalance. But corruption had been around a long time, well before the subcontinent's population explosion. About a decade before the country's independence from Britain, Mahatma Gandhi had expressed anger at the jobbery and nepotism in India's oldest political party, the Indian National Congress, declaring he would 'go to the length of giving the whole Congress organisation a decent burial, rather than put up with the corruption that is rampant'. He even argued that the cancer of corruption, if unchecked, would destroy everything.

Singh suggested a way out: a radical reform of the police, judiciary and electoral system. But he was a straight-shooter in a world of bent pennies. After Indira Gandhi's return to power in 1980 he was squeezed out of his job and took up writing to earn a living.

I was tired and got into my bunk. But Mr Pai kept his reading light on for a long time, absorbed by the corruption of the body politic, while the old man, from beneath his blanket, continued his corruption of the air.

About ten o'clock we approached the temple town of Tiruchirappalli on the southern bank of the Kaveri. This river, which soon after passing Trichy (as the town is more conveniently known), fans out across a broad fertile delta, is capable of supporting three rice crops a year before draining into the Bay of Bengal. We did not stop at Trichy, however, but maintained our night march north, climbing towards the Deccan Plateau.

❁

At dawn the coach was a sea of sheets, blankets and feet overhanging bunks at drunken angles, giving the impression we had passed the night in a storm-tossed ship. A few passengers got up, rubbed the sleep from their eyes and went to the toilet, but most stayed put until we neared Bangalore City Junction.

As our twenty-three coaches drew in, knots of red-shirted porters scurried alongside to congregate at the doors, anxious for any business. But business was light and getting lighter by the year. Most passengers preferred to carry their own small quantity of luggage, having been persuaded it was no longer necessary to take half their household belongings on a train journey. Where once they hauled about great metal trunks (generally containing favoured saris, a selection of pots, plates and utensils, meals and snacks prepared in conformity with caste rules, bedding, religious bits and pieces and various personal necessities and superfluities) so as to be able to set up home at a moment's notice, now most made do with one or two hard-shelled suitcases; these could be chained by their handles beneath a bottom bunk and forgotten for the duration of the journey. But in an exception to prove the rule I was overtaken by three porters, each with a mountainous pile of suitcases atop his head, who kept up a steady trot along the congested platform. The owners of the suitcases, a middle-class couple, struggled to keep up with the straight-backed porters.

The steadily growing pit-a-pat of disembarking passengers stirred a man who had passed the night on a ledge of the overbridge. He yawned and stretched, adjusted his dhoti, but did not see us. In the cavernous waiting room a masala movie blared from TV monitors; beautifully costumed women gyrated and sang against a backdrop of Himalayan splendour, but their syrupy screeching failed to elicit any signs of life from the formless bundles asleep on the floor. We were blundering through a giant improvised bedroom. But Indians have learnt to turn a blind eye to what is beneath their noses, and the crowd marched on without a thought.

Outside, with dirty grey clouds hanging low over the city, it felt almost cold after the humidity of previous days, a mildness guaranteed by Bangalore's position 1,000 metres above sea level.

It was Independence Day, the start of a holiday break, and it seemed sensible to book an onward ticket at once. The reservations office, like the station itself, exactly resembled an office block. And this was no surprise because in India every station is a microcosm of its town or city. Bangalore is a city of office workers bent on bringing the computer age to India. It is the country's high-tech capital, the home of software writers and venture capitalists and a magnet for foreign multinationals eager to exploit the pool of cheap graduates.

The reservations hall itself, a large neglected shell, looked decidedly pre-computer age. I fell into the rear of the queue of applicants at counter fourteen, designated for 'Freedom Fighters, Handicapped Persons and Foreign Tourists'. The queue at counter thirteen ('Ladies Only') was an exemplar of serenity and orderliness. Every other line, mine included, became pear-shaped near the counter as applicants could resist no longer the urge to shove and strain and listen in to someone else's business or offer the booking clerks an unsolicited piece of advice.

During my wait I concluded that personal space would forever be a foreign concept on the subcontinent. The man behind me pressed intermittently against my rucksack, his little nudging motions steadily irritating me more and more until finally I turned and snapped, 'Stop it, will you!'

'But look at all the space you are leaving,' he whined.

In the end all my queuing was to no avail. The best I could manage was to get on the waiting list. The clerk suggested applying to the Assistant Commercial Manager (ACM) for a place in the emergency quota.

Mr ACM, tall, thin, taciturn and bearing a remarkable resemblance to Pakistan's founder, Mohamed Ali Jinnah, minus his trademark imitation astrakhan hat, was located in a far-off building. I completed an application form while a sweeper, bent low with a grass broom, passed among the desks stirring up a considerable dust storm. Mr ACM took my form without comment. Would I get a reservation, I asked. Naturally he could not say. 'Come early, an hour at least. Then you will know.'

❈

Mobile phones are de rigueur in Bangalore. It is especially noticeable along the principal thoroughfare, the ubiquitously named Mahatma Gandhi Road, which is flanked on one side by Carippa Memorial Park and on the other by coffee shops and food outlets and shopping malls. In one café three women, their hair fashionably bobbed, their figures revealed to fine effect in tight denims, blew the froth from their cappuccinos. Each had her mobile phone on the table in a show of credentials, much as a posse of gunslingers wouldn't dream of showing their faces in a saloon without packing their sidearms.

There was a lot of preening and strutting among Bangalore's new young things who wore a unisex uniform of jeans, T-shirts and sunglasses. An underwear hoarding on MG Road depicted a young man and woman reclining artfully on a bed in a state of undress that would have had the mob howling for its removal in Lahore, and probably in Lucknow too. What made this sideshow mesmerising was that it took place against a backdrop of overcrowding, struggle and decay so overwhelming it ought to have instantly punctured any pretensions. How were you to imagine yourself in some sophisticated foreign metropolis when beggars were clawing at your dialling fingers or you almost toppled over in your high heels at every third or fourth step because the pavements were so full of gaps and irregularities?

It struck me that these pretenders, with their yearning to ape foreign ways, were doing themselves a disservice. They were balanced between two stools, one their own worthy traditions, the other the mirage-like allure of the West. Could they get both feet onto one stool without falling? Who was to say. But I saw more bickering among Indians in ambitious Bangalore than anywhere else on the subcontinent. And that raised a baffling point: how a billion Indians managed to endure the conditions of daily life with such equanimity, conditions that would have had the rest of us tearing at each other's throats.

❂

'You're not in computers too, are you?' I said to the clean-cut young man who sat at my table.

He stared back at me blankly.

'Everyone else seems to be,' I added.

'Actually, I am in business.'

'What sort, may I ask?'

'Printing. It is a family concern.'

Mr Moorthy apologised if he seemed a little distracted; he was feeling tired after being out late celebrating Independence Day with some flag-flying along MG Road on his motorbike, and later some prayers.

'What about partying?'

'Oh no,' he said, 'I would never do such a thing.'

I told him I'd been asleep on a train during the fateful moment of freedom at midnight. Then I asked, with genuine curiosity, 'Are you happy the British have gone?'

He hesitated. 'Yes, they stole everything.'

'*Stole*? Like what?'

'All our sources of wealth, our minerals, our gold, things like that. They took our raw materials, which we then had to buy back as finished goods.'

Mr Moorthy seemed to have a pretty good grasp of the mechanics of colonial exploitation.

'Did the British leave anything good behind?' I asked.

'English,' he answered emphatically. 'In this communication age it is vital. In Pakistan no one speaks English, only Urdu. That's one reason why more tourists come to India.'

He continued: 'People here can speak many languages. It is not uncommon. I myself speak six: English, Hindi, Tamil, Kannada, Telugu and Malayalam. I know lots of others who can do the same.'

The coffee shop was really filling up now, mostly old men who slurped from thick white porcelain cups. They suited the place. The Coffee House, an outlet of the Indian Coffee Workers' Co-operative Society, had been trading in its present shape since the 1940s.

I said to Mr Moorthy, 'I remember this place when I first came to India seventeen years ago. I don't think it's changed a dot. I don't suppose the fashionable crowd would be seen dead in here.'

He gave a wan smile. 'Too traditional, I think.'

It had the same fragile wooden tables and chairs, the same green-and-maroon coat of paint on the walls and, I could have sworn, the same waiters wearing a five o'clock shadow and soiled white livery, complete with embossed red-and-gold cummerbunds and elaborate headgear.

I mentioned having visited one of the city's abundant bars. It mimicked a nightclub in the West with depressing precision: the stroboscope and dim lighting, the jarring electronic music, the exorbitant prices and the coolly appraising eyes from circular cubicles. 'I don't suppose you go to such places?'

'At night sometimes,' he conceded, then added: 'We are very much following American ways here in Bangalore. What do you think?'

'The truth?' I asked.

'Yes.'

'Bloody awful.'

'So do I,' he said with unmistakable relief.

'Forget American ways, stick to your own ways,' I said. 'They're worth hanging on to. A simple example: look at all these men here, all in polyester pants and shirts and plastic shoes. What's happened to your home-spun, your khadi, your traditional garments? Surely they're more comfortable in the heat, too.'

'We wear such clothes, kurta, churidar and dhoti, for puja, for weddings and funerals, but frankly, if I wore them any other time people would laugh at me as old-fashioned.'

'Have you ever been to Pakistan?' I asked him. I'd told Mr Moorthy that I was going to Pakistan so decided it was a good line to smoke out Indians' attitude to their most important, and frostiest, neighbour.

'No.' His reaction was unexpectedly sullen.

'India and Pakistan may be on the verge of half-normal relations again. I see in today's papers that your prime minister has extended an olive branch to Musharraf.'

He shrugged his shoulders. 'I think we will always be enemies. Pakistan doesn't want peace, though I think Pakistanis do. They have been fighting for so long *against* something they've forgotten how to work and struggle *for* something.'

Mr Moorthy had a point. He was, of course, talking about Kashmir, which had always been Pakistanis' collective obsession. The country's rulers defined their relations with India by this issue, making Kashmir a rallying call to mobilise populist sentiment, a lightning-rod to dissipate disenchantment with the regime and, on two occasions (and almost three), literally a war cry.

Mr Moorthy went on: 'I will tell you this. Pakistan's claim to give no more than moral support to Kashmiri fighters is nonsense, one hundred per cent nonsense. Pakistan's politicians have been telling that lie for so long I think they believe it themselves now.'

Pakistan has clung tenaciously to a half-century-old United Nations resolution calling for a plebiscite in Muslim-dominated Kashmir. India equally vigorously has resisted the proposition, seeing it as a recipe to divide India on communal lines a second time. Some months later, Pakistan made a clean break from its entrenched position when its strongman General Musharraf pledged not to permit his country to be used as a haven for terrorism, and Indian Prime Minister Atal Vijpayee promised to seek a solution to the Kashmir dispute.

Mr Moorthy said he had to go, but the man who took his seat minutes later *was* in the computer business. Thinking back, I can hardly separate them in my mind. Both were young, both wore jeans and loafers and both had neatly clipped hair. Garg Viswanathan had started out four years ago with his software firm doing a nine-to-five job. Hard work and talent had taken him to the top of the corporate dung heap. Right now he was putting in sixteen-hour days to finish an important project. He had even done a stint in the United States. The most talented, he said, went there, lured by the salaries and prospects.

'I've got a taste and want to go back,' Mr Viswanathan admitted. 'Traffic runs smoothly, people do as they promise, cities are orderly ...'

'Other countries can offer that, too.'

He wasn't swayed. 'US is number one destination, no question about that. I'll try to go back. Maybe five years, six years. I can always return here, retire here ...'

Mr Viswanathan's mobile rang. He looked at his text message. 'Gotta go, work's calling.' And in a blink he was lost in the torrent washing along MG Road.

❂

If Mr Viswanathan was the new Bangalore, Air Force Colonel Singla (ret.) was the more agreeable, fast-vanishing old Bangalore. On the Sunday I was out strolling along Rest House Crescent, a leafy question-mark-shaped lane lined by low-slung bungalows, when I stopped before a huge rusting sign. Planted squarely in a flowerbed, it declared that a luxury residential tower would soon be taking shape on the site. Other apartment blocks already dotted the lane.

'Can I help?' asked a voice beside me. It was the colonel, out for his early-morning constitutional.

'These bungalows are so lovely,' I remarked. 'It seems a shame to knock them over.'

'Oh, there's no need to worry on that score,' he said. 'The sign has been there for as long as I can remember – twenty years at least, I should think.'

He scratched his thinning grey hair, as though to stimulate his memory. 'All tied up in the courts now. What was it? A dispute between the planter owners, I think.'

And looking more closely through the gardens, I could see the bungalow had two distinct halves. Weeds sprouted from the masonry of one half, but the other was in good repair. One party wanted to sell, it was clear, the other to stay put.

'Land this close in must be expensive,' I said.

'Oh yes. I bought in '68. Today I could never afford to.'

The colonel was tall and thin almost to the point of emaciation, though he held himself perfectly erect in his slacks, open shirt and running shoes. His face was cross-hatched with deep lines, but his eyes were youthful and enquiring.

'May I join you?' I found myself asking him.

'Of course,' he replied.

So we strolled on together in the cool air and dappled shade as watchmen, seated on their little wooden stools, observed our passing with supreme boredom. For once the sound of vehicle horns, a perennial nuisance in India, had subsided.

But the truth of India's cities soon reasserted itself. We reached Church Street where the gutters and verges were thick with litter. On a vacant corner lot that had become a de facto tip, a gang of municipal workers dug their shovels into a waist-high mound of decaying matter and heaved the sinewy stinking results onto the back of a truck. They were joined in their task by crows hopping about delightedly in this freshly turned treasure trove of filth.

'The authorities try their level best,' observed the colonel, 'but as soon as they clear one spot, up pops another.'

However, none of this urban decay had checked the city's real estate boom, he said. 'These computer people and the American companies are the cause. Servants, houses, food – all of it is going up, up, up. Young graduates, they get their computer engineering degree and at age twenty-two or twenty-three are commanding salaries of 30,000 rupees. That's more than I was earning when I retired, after thirty-five years of service, for goodness sake!'

We kept up a steady pace along the footpaths, the colonel hopping dexterously over the many obstructions in our way – here a ditch, a tree root or split paving stone, there an unfinished street repair, chopped-off utility pipe or squatter's hut. I marvelled at the vitality of this seventy-two-year-old retiree. The area we were ambling in, all 35 square kilometres of it, he informed me, had been the Cantonment in British times. We reached a State Bank of India compound that swallowed up an entire block and, after talking to the watchman, were admitted through the wrought iron gates.

'Behind here somewhere the British resident lived. There was a maharajah then of course, but the resident was the real power.'

And there, set among neglected gardens stood a two-storey mansion topped by a turret ('They could watch from there for trouble') and with a grand half-circle portico for receiving guests. This former residency, with its weedy lawns and air of abandonment, was now a guesthouse for the bank's top executives. It had once been surrounded by army barracks, parade grounds and officials' quarters, but successive residents had bequeathed large parcels of land for schools and churches.

And sure enough our walk next took us past a succession of such buildings. On Residency Road we passed Bishop Cotton Girls' School and Sacred Heart Girls' High School with its forbidding castellated façade and St Joseph's College, which was crowned by an observatory; and around the corner on Museum Road we came to the immaculately maintained Jesuit House and another college where an extension was under construction. ('Parents with American money.')

We reached Convent Road, where the colonel lived.

'Your next stop is?'

'Hyderabad.'

He gave a little sigh. 'Hyderabad was lovely once. Now it is gone.' There was a deep sadness, almost pain, in his words, as though speaking of a family member who had died long ago but whose loss was still felt keenly. 'Yes,' he repeated, 'now it is all gone.'

Visitors to Golconda Fort, Hyderabad.

The Nizamuddin Rajdhani Express

BANGALORE LOOKED SOGGY and grey as the super-fast Nizamuddin Rajdhani Express pulled out at 6.30 pm. The rain began to pelt down as we passed through a shanty town on the outskirts, row upon row of tarpaulin-and-thatch huts divided from one another by pathways filled with muddy water, a kind of deranged man's version of Venice, and dimly illuminated by fluorescent street lights spaced at such vast distances among the low hovels they gave the impression of a string of lighthouses in a dark convulsing sea of human misery. But at the end of one lane, beneath a solitary strip light, five or six children danced and played, unconcerned by the deluge or their surroundings.

Darkness fell as piped music rose to make itself heard, bland and soothing like hotel lobby muzak. My mind's eye conjured up a cocktail bar sprinkled with businessmen in a celebratory mood, but my eyes saw the jostle and shuffle of Indians padlocking their suitcases and shaking out their bed sheets. I sat there, absorbed by this incongruous chorus of piped music, droning ceiling fans, the rhythmical clunk-a-clunk of bogie wheels, the unbroken sighing from air-conditioning vents and the no-less-unbroken to and fro of three Tamils bemoaning the difficulties of doing business in Karnataka. ('Local business is not *wesponding* to greater purchasing power ... *wustomer* is king ... government is there, private is there, too .... One hundred lakhs it is costing and still they are not hurrying!')

When, much later, I took to my bunk, it was for a night of inexpressible discomfort. The interior layout of each class of coach is unvarying: in two-tier air-conditioned class the aisle runs off-centre down the length of the coach, with bunks arranged in groups of four on the wide side and in groups of two on the narrow side. The fours, the so-called 'inside' berths, are at right angles to the aisle so you sleep with your feet at the aisle end and your head at the window end. Together, they form a spacious cabin which can be closed off from the aisle by a curtain. The bunks themselves are wide and long, the backrests lifting up at night to form the top bunks. The two 'outside' bunks are a different matter. They run parallel to the aisle and for space reasons are very narrow. They are cramped by day, when you must sit knee to knee facing the passenger opposite, and by night, when the two seats fold down to form the lower bunk and you take your place top or bottom. Every inconsiderate person passing through the aisle knocks or bumps you unless your arms and legs are folded out of the way, and at night those same inconsiderate individuals bump and wake you. Drawing your curtain at night for privacy only heightens the powerful sense of claustrophobia.

So I lay in my top coffin, which was neither wide enough nor long enough for my frame, as my right shoulder strained against one of the support chains fastened to the ceiling and my feet pressed hard against the cubicle wall. I rolled onto my side and tried to arch my body in order to poke my feet over the edge. But the other support chain made that impossible. My tiredness was exceeded only by my impatience to get to sleep, which was of course impossible. Tossing about, I vowed never to be caught like this again.

Dawn unveiled the timeless beauty of the Deccan, the rolling treeless plateau of Central India, which here was studded with small pale lakes, themselves sprinkled with islets formed of enormous boulders piled up with casual abandon. In my absorption I soon forgot the hellish night.

My knee-to-knee companion over breakfast was Mr A. K. Parikh, who described himself as 'in government service'. He expressed great optimism about India's future. 'Who knows,' he ventured, 'in ten years we may be a developed country.'

That struck me as an exceedingly optimistic prediction. As he himself had pointed out, the country's annual population growth of 20 million ('Another Australia every year, isn't it!') swallowed up gains as fast as they were made.

'Yes, what to do?' mused Mr Parikh. Indians, I had noticed, had a habit of talking about the country's population explosion as though it were a remote, impersonal and insoluble problem.

❁

A cluster of Muslim gravestones subsiding in a watery depression gave the first hint of Secunderabad's approach. Confirmation came in the shape of scores of evil-looking factories and smokestacks and men squatting on their haunches to defecate beside the line. Secunderabad's station was in ruins, and the city itself was squalid and crowded; Hyderabad, to which I fled, seemed little better. Colonel Singla had not exaggerated. Battered municipal buses terrorised the roads, and their oppressive horn blasts were inescapable. I felt deflated and overwhelmed by India as I trudged about under a broiling sun, dust and petrol fumes in my face and seemingly a billion Indians blocking my every step.

Hyderabad's history, so long and splendid, was hard to appreciate walking the congested streets. Muslims dominated it in more recent times (adjoining Secunderabad was a British creation, becoming in time their main military station in Central India). For 400 years a courtly culture flourished, its physical reminder the city's many mosques, palaces, arches and gates, including the landmark Char Minar with its four corner minarets rising to a height of 56 metres.

Today the capital of Andhra Pradesh, Hyderabad was once the centre of the independent dynasty of the Nizams, whose princely state was forcibly incorporated into the Indian Union shortly after independence in 1947.

A good deal of the wealth for which the Nizams were known throughout the world came from neighbouring diamond mines (the Koh-i-noor was unearthed there), and the gems were cut and sold at Golconda, now an abandoned city, 8 kilometres to the west of Hyderabad. In its time Golconda had an international reputation as an emporium of the diamond trade. Today the attraction is Golconda Fort, an immense citadel built on a rocky outcrop rising above the surrounding plain. With its own water supply, fed by an elaborate hydraulic system to the upper levels, and a three-tiered ring of massive walls that rose to an average height of 18 metres and were built of blocks of granite frequently weighing more than a tonne, Golconda Fort had been a formidable nut to crack. For the occupiers, there were additional defences: eighty-seven rounded bastions at the angles of the crenellated walls, plus the usual reinforcements around the arched gateways, and huge iron spikes embedded in the gates themselves to repel the battering of elephants. Holed up in this fine example of military architecture, the last king of the Kutb Shahi kingdom, Abul Hasan, was able to withstand a nine-month siege in 1687 by Emperor Aurangzeb's powerful army; the fort fell only through treachery within the defenders' ranks.

Seen in the flesh, the fort, with its great blackened slabs of granite rising in folds up the hill, presents a squat and menacing face rather like that of a pug-dog – graceless but virtually unbeatable in a skirmish. I wandered the ruined halls and steam baths and mosques and pavilions with their vaulted roofs and stink of bat droppings, and climbed the steep steps wishing for the imaginative powers of a Rose Macaulay to bring forth life from these weathered stones.

But if the fort itself left me feeling somehow unsatisfied, the journey there did not. Physically it was strenuous. Masood, my auto-rickshaw driver, seemed to seek out every potholed lane between my hotel and the fort, each scarcely wide enough to overtake the cyclists and scooter riders who everywhere blocked our path. All the way I clung to the flimsy cab of this three-wheeled scooter, bouncing up and down while simultaneously being flung from side to side.

However, Masood's route gave me a close-up inspection of what could only be described as village India. All the minor tradesmen were there: the bicycle-repair wallah, and a little way beyond him the puncture-repair wallah (implements: one foot-operated pump, one bowl of water, three cannibalised tubes to be used as repair patches, tubes of glue and a box of hand tools); the vegetable seller with a handful of aubergines, twenty thin-skinned potatoes and a couple of scoops of stunted tomatoes; the housewife who sat cross-legged at a doorway sifting through lentils in a flaxen tray; Ahmed's Silverware Makers and his neighbour Ajanta Scooter Works, whose employees, all boys of apparent school age, squatted on the verge beside oil-leaking machines in various states of dismemberment; the shoeless but smartly uniformed schoolchildren who clutched a plastic satchel with one hand and with the other the hand of an older sibling as they were led along the still-perilous edges of the laneways; and the elderly men who congregated to watch the passing traffic and enjoy one another's company, and sipped from an occasional thimble-sized terracotta cup of tea dispensed by the char-cum-pan-wallah, himself perched on a minuscule roofed platform raised high off the ground.

There was also the tin fabricator who, like most tradesmen – and indeed workers of pretty much all occupations on the subcontinent – turned out astonishing results with the most primitive tools (in this case several hammers and cutters of varying sizes, plus a bit of empty floor space); and beside the fabricator's shop was the suitcase merchant who gave his stock a regular thrashing with a long-handled feather duster; and abutting the suitcase trader was the butchery, an open cubicle with the dimensions of a very large portmanteau, the pride of place being taken by a solitary leg of meat suspended by a hook and drawing the attention of every fly in the neighbourhood, the modest shop front being given a semblance of grandiosity by a finely wrought and vividly painted sign mounted on the roof: 'ALI'S BEEF'; and the kitchenware vendor whose shelves, stocked entirely of stainless steel items, glistened enticingly, like the contents of Ali Baba's cave, beyond the dust kicked up by the jostling crowds; and the barber who, with a cut-throat razor, mirror, shaving-brush and shaving-soap could remedy a five o'clock shadow in a jiffy; and the street hawker whose one product line was the astonishingly versatile remedy Zinda Tilismath (Trade Mark No. 577), 'one medicine trusted by millions over 85 years and a cure for many common ailments, including cholera, cold, headache, stomach disorder, cough, toothache and malaria'.

Not to be forgotten was the seller of sugar-cane juice, whose machine, a fearsomely complicated cast-iron contraption of cogged wheels actuating two rollers, squeezed the life out of his assembled lengths of sugar cane, much as the washing-machine wringers of my childhood days would transform waterlogged garments into stiffened planks of cloth; or the two boys who, with the jocular demeanour of true street urchins, collected up the discarded lengths of sugar cane, along with other food scraps and vegetable matter, and tossed them onto their creaking wooden-wheeled bullock-cart, thereby providing a sort of unofficial municipal collection service.

For sheer simple ingenuity there was the knife-sharpener, who conducted his trade with the aid of a bicycle: with the stand in place he would pedal furiously, his exertions driving a sharpening stone fitted behind the handlebars and driven via a chain connected to the chainwheel. As his legs pumped and the sparks flew, he would chat merrily to the knife's owner.

And finally there were the Muslim ladies who strolled the dusty margins of streets in twos and threes with a comportment as regal and dignified as that of any high priest or regent, and who were swathed in black from head to toe except for tiny rectangular eye slits.

But last of all there was twenty-two-year-old Inder, to whom I chatted while Mahood vanished somewhere on business midway through the return journey. Inder ran a roadside ironing business. With his coal-powered iron, and by flicking water on to each garment 'for steam effect', Inder continued a business conducted by his father before him. After eight years' experience he could expertly whip his cast-iron monster of an appliance over a business shirt (Rs 3/-) or 'pant' (Rs 2/-) or shawl (Rs 3/-) and earn a reasonable living – except during the rainy months when more often than not he would be forced to pack up and go home early. But this process was easy enough, he said: he stowed the padded sheet covering his table on the carrier of his bicycle, together with the iron, the water bowl and his modest supply of coal, and he was on his way.

'A good job?' I asked.

He grinned broadly. 'Yes, no boss.' And with flicking fingers he imitated someone jabbering orders in his ear.

He had a very good point.

❁

'PRESENT, PAST, FUTURE', promised the seer's pavement sign. I slowed my pace, intrigued by the succinctness of the claim, and the possibilities of those three words. Traffic tore along Tankbund Road, the freeway abutting the eastern shore of Husain Sagar, Hyderabad's broad artificial lake, but the seer-cum-godman sat cross-legged and coolly composed on the footpath. Not even the blazing sun bothered him; his big black umbrella lay folded at his side.

His appearance was highly arresting. His face was framed by a wild hennaed beard and a mass of hair tied in a Gautama-style bun. Across his bare chest he wore a large breastplate, rather like that of a general in ancient Rome but dabbed with ochre paint and featuring a bas-relief image of Siva. He sported the usual assortment of necklaces, rings, bangles and body smears, but, unusually, wore vine-like coils around his upper arms. Spread before him on a mat were various charms, sticks, books, bottles, battered tobacco tins and several shapeless substances I couldn't identify even as I drew alongside. Ranged on either side were three associates, not nearly so elaborately done up. He was the peacock, they the drab females.

A portly young man who looked dressed for the office sat on the seer's right. 'Come, come, sir, please sit,' he called out. Behind this little band, protected by a high fence, stood Hyderabad's Secretariat buildings, home of Andhra Pradesh's politicians and senior babus.

'Please, sit down,' the earnest-looking man repeated, 'he will tell your future. He knows only Hindi and Telugu, but I know a little English. Tell me what you want and I will tell him.'

What the hell, I thought and squatted on the pavement.

'First, give him 20 rupees.'

'I can only give 10.'

They conversed. 'Okay, okay, 10.'

I handed over a 10-rupee note.

'Now, what do you want?'

I smiled. 'Nothing.'

'You must. You have problems? Sex problems? Financial problems? An enemy who wants to get you …?'

'No, none of those things.'

The seer, meanwhile, was yapping in his ear.

'He says, give him 51 rupees.'

'No, that is too much,' I answered, wondering idly about the significance of the number. I was growing impatient. 'Give me back my money and I'll go.'

At that the godman decided to proceed. He picked up some wooden strips, each about the length and thickness of a school ruler, and made me insert the 10-rupee note between any two of them. That done, he laid flat the strips enclosing the money and began to interpret the symbols engraved on their surface.

'He says you are looking to get married.'

'No,' I laughed, 'I'm already married.' More muttering among themselves.

'Then he says you will be seeking another's hand in marriage.'

'No,' I laughed again, 'I'm happily married.'

More muttering.

'Then he says you will be helping someone else to get married.'

'Maybe, but I doubt it.'

Further examination followed.

'He says you are desiring to travel the world – that is your great life's ambition.'

'Well, that's not hard to guess,' I replied. 'Look at me, a tourist in another country.'

They ploughed on, undeterred.

'You are having a friend you help out financially and he is not returning the money.'

'No.'

'He says you are about to start a new business.'

'No.'

'He says you are looking to build a house.'

'Now *that* may be true.'

More muttering.

'How much will you be spending on your house?' asked my self-appointed helper.

I thought for a moment. The whole idea was just a vague possibility. 'At a guess, maybe 200,000 dollars.'

'In rupees please.'

I did a rough calculation. 'About 6 million rupees.'

'Don't tell him that,' he scolded. 'He will want more money.'

'Well, tell him whatever you want then,' I snapped back.

More conferring followed. The godman produced a canister from which he selected a twig. It was dusted with some sort of reddish powder.

'He says if you carry this you will always have good luck. Do you want it?'

'Why not,' I answered, naively.

'He says, give him 300 rupees first.'

This had to be the sharpest businessman in Hyderabad.

'No,' I lied, 'I don't have that much on me.'

The consultation suddenly was over. The godman pocketed the magical twig and began to pick up the tools of his trade, aided by his three silent assistants. But as he did, he babbled to the translator. 'He says you are a good man – you will have a good life.'

'What do you do, by the way?' I asked my helper.

'I am civil engineer. I am going off with this man now. I have a problem.'

'What is your problem?'

'It is very complicated. It will take many hours to explain.'

He reached into a shopping bag and withdrew some sheets of paper. They contained detailed astrological information relating to his life. I noticed his date of birth, 18 September 1972.

'Look,' he said, flicking through the pages. 'Complicated, very complicated.'

There were planetary charts, the moon here, Mercury there.

'See,' he said, 'this is Ravi, the sun.'

More charts, extraordinarily complex-looking, like a doctoral thesis in some arcane branch of astrophysics.

'Here,' he said, pointing to the last page, which contained some sort of inventory, 'here is every year up to 2059. With this, each year can be foretold.'

The seer was by now packed up and ready to go.

'I will go with this man to his house,' he went on. 'He will do a puja and some things and it will clear the blockage. You see (and here he pointed to an intersection of life lines on his left palm) Venus is in opposition to Saturn at this point. He will unblock it and fix my problem.'

So the godman, as well as being a seer, was also a sort of spiritual plumber.

A waiting auto-rickshaw driver bundled the godman and his acolytes into the back seat along with their assortment of belongings. It was a terrible squeeze. My helper managed somehow to get a little purchase on the edge of the driver's seat. The godman was still grappling with his long umbrella, trying to find a means to tuck it out of the way. He blathered away to the civil engineer again.

'He says, come back in two days' time. He will have many answers for you.'

And with that they receded from view in a trail of bluish low-octane fumes.

Bridge over Mula River, Poona.

To Victoria Terminus

'I'M GOING TO HAVE SOME FUN in Mumbai before I get married,' said Hussein. His two bachelor friends, who had come to see him off, nodded approvingly.

'Did you like Hyderabad?' he asked.

'Well,' I said and paused, wondering whether to tell the truth and then losing courage, 'it's very busy and dusty. But then it's a city of, what, four million?'

Hussein shook his head. 'No one knows its population. Or India's actually. We are having no proper census. And no one is practising family planning.'*

'What exactly is family planning?' I asked.

The question produced only an embarrassed titter, so I went on: 'Indians must have smaller families, I think. Even two children per couple will just be marking time.'

Hussein might have been a bachelor, and a young one at that, but

* India's state-sponsored family planning programme began in 1952. Its population continues to rise inexorably, with one commentator predicting India will 'stabilise' at between 1.5 billion and 1.8 billion citizens by 2050.

it seemed he had already formed firm ideas about the manipulative nature of women. 'You should try telling that to a wife,' he declared. 'Women, they are the cause of this craving for big families.' Once more, it seemed, the root cause of overpopulation lay at someone else's doorstep.

Hussein and I were both awaiting the Hyderabad–Mumbai Express, but I was getting off early, at Poona (aka Pune). When the diesel loco and its twenty-three carriages drew into Nampally Station we parted company and the clammy stillness was ruffled by the heaving and shoving of the waiting hundreds. At 8.45 pm we drew out and the now familiar rituals were enacted: the issuing of bedrolls, the tentative greetings, the storing and locking of baggage, the unfurling of sheets and blankets, the inspection of tickets, the brushing of teeth, the pulling of curtains. With no company or friendly faces, I turned in and opened my book, *Years of Endurance*, Arthur Bryant's study of revolutionary Europe. Like every book I carried, it was tatty enough to discard without a moment's hesitation. Soon mine was the only reading light on. Then out of the blue a passenger turned up and the compartment was engulfed in a musky sweetness like betel-nut. Where he had come from I had no idea: the last halt had been a long way back. A porter carried his luggage, a taped-up cardboard box, a plastic shopping bag and a suitcase in a canvas wrap. He paid off the porter and prepared for bed, ignoring me.

I dubbed him Mr White for the simple reason that everything he wore was white: his shirt and trousers, his singlet, his shoes and his night garments, which he eventually got into after meticulously folding his clothes. This folding was quite a thing. Using his suitcase as a convenient hard surface, he removed his business shirt and folded it into a crisp perfect rectangle. Tentatively it was lowered into the suitcase, along with the pants – which were accorded the same painstaking treatment – and then began the scrupulous business of adjusting his lungi and nightshirt to his satisfaction.

All this I observed out of the corner of my eye as I pretended to read. Finally Mr White covered himself in sheets whose spotless whiteness would certainly have met with his approval. There was something almost effeminate about his fussing and his preoccupation with his appearance, which ran to heavy rings, bracelets, a necklace and watch, all of gold. He was a reminder to me of how little kerfuffle Indians made while travelling. Undoubtedly Mr White would have disapproved of my methods: the clothes I wore by day were the same crumpled clothes I wore overnight on trains, making them still more crumpled by next morning.

❂

The first sight to greet me when I opened my eyes in the morning was Mr White's natty shoes. He had propped them against the side of the compartment as though fearing the soles might be contaminated if left overnight on the floor. He himself was an inert molehill beneath his top sheet, pulled over his head to extinguish the world.

Drawing back my curtain revealed field upon field of sunflowers drooped forlornly awaiting the first flush of sunlight. We were now somewhere in Maharashtra state. In the stillness of early morning a wonderful placidity hung over everything: the mirror-like rivers we crossed, the motionless Brahminy bulls, the silent fields of sugar cane and plots of vegetables, the pellucid sky. The work of ploughs revealed a rich clumpy red earth, like bean stew. Gradually, though, the land lost its vitality and more and more ground went uncultivated. A gently sloping hill would swell out of the plain and subside from view, exhausted by the effort.

Breakfast arrived, an omelette and tea, followed by an attendant who had been called to mop up a condensation leak that had dribbled from a window and collected among the luggage. The attendant, shoeless and dressed in khaki, was indistinguishable from all the others in India who wore the dull-brown uniform of the menial worker: those who spent half their waking moments on their haunches moving crab-like beneath restaurant tables sweeping and mopping the floor; their upright co-workers who collected plates and wiped tables; the exhausted hotel attendants who draped themselves about the stairwell landings day and night awaiting the buzzer that signalled a guest wanted water, tea, tiffin, another towel – and straightaway, thank you very much; the janitors, the lift operators, the night watchmen, the municipal bus drivers, the auto-rickshaw drivers – every one was dressed in a shapeless shirt worn loose over slightly flared trousers, and set off by a long dirty scarf wrapped about the neck for mopping the brow, and by bare feet whose soles were deeply cracked and whose toes were splayed out from a lifetime without shoes.

All this mopping and shifting about of suitcases made no impression on Mr White. He dozed on throughout the morning, denying me the pleasure of the next instalment of his routine, so I talked to Khrishnaraj, who had stirred from the bunk above. He was an engineer and sold 'universal-joint shafts' to steel manufacturers. He was making a whistle-stop in Poona.

He was not the first person I had met selling impossible-to-comprehend machinery parts. That honour went to a sales manager at Ooty bus station who said his line of 'filament-free cooking elements' had been acclaimed as leading-edge technology. Was it convection cooking, I ventured. 'No, not convection, not microwave – it is in category all of its own. Unique! Filament-free, you understand.'

Khrishnaraj's next stop after Poona was Bombay (Mumbai), which he described as a very 'happening place'. 'It is only city in India that goes round-the-clock,' he said, 'but Bangalore is a very happening place, too.'

Khrishnaraj believed in the transforming power of technology. He and another passenger brimmed with enthusiasm as they discussed advances in cellphones, which they waved about in the air to underline their point, but that zeal drained away when I wanted to talk about rural India where three-quarters of the population lived in half a million villages. Eventually he conceded that the recent liberalisation of India's economy had produced few benefits yet for India's voiceless millions. (But then things always changed slowly in India.) He also agreed government services were not reaching into the countryside and that neglect, incompetence and corruption were taking a heavy toll on funds allocated to rural improvement.

Khrishnaraj did not want to dwell on these uncomfortable facts. He said cheerily, 'This area is famous for sugar cane.' The window was indeed now an almost continuous green blur. But there was no sign of a single modern labour-saving machine to aid villagers. Crops were planted and weeds held at bay not by tractors and steel farm implements but by fingers and stooped-over backs. The one sign of the modern age was satellite dishes, which could be seen atop the humblest huts. Cable television offered at least one small escape from the rigours of daily life.

As for Mr White, he preferred to avert his eyes from the glare of reality beyond the window. He remained in bed, tossing and snuffling beneath his sheet. With his fastidious ways and callus-free hands and his gold rings and bracelets, he was a thoroughly urbanised fellow and, I guessed, an owl of Bombay's nightlife. I got down at Poona, certain he would not be rousing himself until he had returned to the embrace of India's biggest metropolis.

The Deccan Queen, pride of Central Railway, waited at platform one. Despite the watery morning light, the red, white and blue livery gleamed as if reflecting the midday sun. The locomotive, emblazoned with its name, prepared to go, and at 7.15, on time to the minute, we slipped out of Pune Junction Station.

The Deccan Queen's passengers expected such punctuality. They were commuters, in spite of the 192-kilometre journey to Bombay. Sky-high real estate prices in the country's economic powerhouse, together with growing commercial links with Poona, lay behind their daily trip. Poona was in transition from pleasant city to Bombay outstation. A six-lane expressway under construction would make sure of that. (At 549 metres above sea level, Poona has a climate infinitely preferable to muggy Bombay, which was why the British took themselves and their administrative machinery there during the monsoon months.)

Inside my carriage it was, seat for seat, all businessmen, many of whom would repeat the three-and-a-half-hour journey that evening.

The man at my shoulder huffed and puffed his way through the *Economic Times* before losing patience and attempting to doze. He occupied more than his share of space, monopolising the armrests with his elbows, or spreading his legs wide while I was forced to sit with my knees firmly together. But it was a short journey and for once I held my tongue.

Breakfast arrived as we finally shook off Poona's outskirts. It consisted of a small thermos of tea and vegetable cutlets, actually deep-fried vegetable fritters which, squinted at with one eye, might be said to have the outline of mutton neck-chops. So I flipped down my seat tray, nibbled at my cutlets and stared in wonder at the pathless wilderness of jungle crowding to the very edge of the electrified lines. Trees and palms of every height and shape and shade of green struggled for space, each festooned with ferns and creepers and flowering vines and clumps of moss.

Then we cleared the jungle and I saw well beyond us hillocks, little more than gentle bumps, scattered among ponds and paddy fields. Pylons strode across these tropical downs. It was an exceedingly beautiful sight, made more so by the fog that clung to the horizon and the mist-shrouded sun that transformed the parallel track into two immensely long gold bars. Among all this verdure there was not the slightest trace of Maharashtra's scarlet-hued earth; it lay beneath the jungle and paddy fields and swollen, brown, motionless rivers beside which stood wiry Mahrattas, equally motionless, striking slightly whimsical poses.

An hour on, Lonavla appeared. It was listed evocatively on my map as a hill station, though in the drizzling rain it looked exceedingly drab. In less than a minute we were on our way again, back among the riot of trees and undergrowth.

I turned to my paper. The *Times of India* is an English-language publication, although, like its rivals, it is often a baffling read to the non-Indian English speaker. It demands an insider's knowledge. I soon found this small piece, under the headline 'Final Kumbh Mela shahi snan today'. It began: 'Nasik: The district administration is gearing up for the third and the final shahi snan on Sunday at

Trimbakeshwar, 29 km from here. As per jahirnama issued by the police, mahants, sadhus belonging to Shri Shambhu Panchdashnam Juna Akhada will arrive in a procession for the royal bath at 4 am, followed by avahan, agni, niranjani, anand, mashanirwani, atal, bada udasin, naya udasin and nirmal akhadas.'

This was in fact describing one of the high points of the Kumbh Mela, or Grand Pitcher Festival. This festival rotates among four holy sites and was being held this year in the twin temple towns of Nasik and Trimbakeshwar, some 200 kilometres north-east of Bombay. In the festival's climax, thousands of sadhus and other devotees bathe in the Godavari River (only slightly less holy than the Ganges) to wash away their sins in the first shahi snan, or royal bath. Such is the auspiciousness of bathing at this precise time and such are the huge numbers of holy men attracted to the festival, in particular the naked sadhus, or nagas, of the militant monastic orders, that the order of immersion in the Godavari assumes great importance. Hence the detailing of the order of precedence for taking a dip.

Like so much Hindu mythology, the festival's origins are highly fanciful. Nasik is said to be one of the four places where the nectar of immortality fell to earth after spilling from a kumbh, or pitcher, as gods and demons fought over the vessel. The Kumbh Mela normally lasts six weeks, but a rare alignment of the stars made the Nasik festival a year-long event. The biggest Kumbh Mela, which takes place every twelve years in the northern city of Allahabad, drew – according to my guidebook anyway – 30 million pilgrims when it was held in 2001. A later check of newspaper reports produced numbers of up to 100 million descending on Allahabad. But when the numbers reached those proportions, did it really matter? One thing was for sure: the strain on the services of Allahabad, a city normally of 2 million, must have been insufferably heavy.

My morning paper did, however, carry two decipherable articles, and of great interest they were, too. The first contained figures that put in perspective the furore over the Pepsi contamination scare, a story that continued to flare up in the press like a bushfire. The story noted that relatively few could afford to buy the foreign soft drink in the first place and that, though the contamination was regrettable, it paled into insignificance compared with the quality of the drinking water the overwhelming majority of Indians were forced to consume. Six out of ten households didn't have water on tap, it reported, and three out of ten didn't even have a safe water supply nearby. Another 5 million households (or 25 million people) relied on rivers and ponds for their daily water intake. As one government minister admitted, 'We cannot forget that more than 80 per cent of our population is made to drink contaminated water that would be declared unfit for even animals in the West.'

The other article revealed the tangle of issues complicating population control. A study had found that 37 per cent of brides were below the legal minimum age of eighteen. And in states where population growth rates were high, the underage percentage was also high – 58 per cent of brides in the case of Bihar state. In such states the Child Marriage Restraint Act was but an academic scrap of paper. Nothing new in that, some might say: poor people everywhere have more children and start at it early, too. However, there was also a religious dimension to the population planners' headaches. Economically disadvantaged Muslims were responsible for the biggest population rises in states such as Bihar and Uttar Pradesh. In fact, proportionately, Muslims were the fastest-growing religious community, adding 5 million a year to India's population compared with 18 million extra Hindus. The difference was not solely the consequence of wealth or poverty. There were politics and mistrust stretching back to Partition. The Muslim leaders of the 1940s who urged the creation of Pakistan, a separate state for those areas of British India with a Muslim majority, cut adrift Muslims who were in a minority elsewhere in India. Partition reduced what would have been a sizeable and influential minority in a united India to a shrunken and defensive community who saw their best hope in flouting the family planning programmes Hindus, Christians and Jains were signing up for.

I laid my paper aside. The mist had closed in, swallowing the tangle of trees and vines in its velvety maw. This sea of rankness was easily enough explained. We were crossing the northernmost extremity of the Western Ghats, a spine of hills running just inland from the sea all the way to Cape Comorin, aka Kanyakumari, at the southernmost tip of the subcontinent. Reaching as high as 2,000 metres in places, the ghats absorbed the monsoon-bearing clouds sweeping in from the south-west. In essence, they were a 1,600-kilometre-long hothouse.

We now entered a series of tunnels, a sign we were starting to bore through the top of the ghats before making our descent. Office workers holding big black umbrellas tiptoed along the parallel track on their way to work. The sun briefly reappeared, but the light was so watery and diffuse that the day reverted to a sort of second dawn. Beneath the main cloud banks, wisps of mist clung to the jungle hills.

Like a pedantic trainspotter I had taken to counting the tunnels, and at number eleven the train buried itself into the longest yet, emerging to begin an appreciable descent. At one point, looking down into a valley, it was as though a colossal army camouflage web had been tossed artfully over the treetops, so thoroughly did creepers cloak the topmost canopy.

Out of the clouds we plummeted, into a sprinkling of paddy fields, cows munching on tufted grass and the sprawling yards of a railway engineering workshop. The paddy fields grew more numerous until they entirely dominated the landscape, extending to the horizon and, one presumes, beyond. Like a foil to this immensity of endeavour, two boys stood in a pond playfully scrubbing a water buffalo, while behind them a farmer stood among his crops, simply daydreaming. In its intensity of cultivation and palpable aura of fertility, this world of shin-deep water and tender jade shoots might have been the Indonesian island of Bali.

But what soon took its place was the beginning of the vast ugly conurbation called Bombay. Tenement blocks bore the scars of the relentless humidity. Mildew blackened their brickwork and gnarled plants grew in the mortar of those walls permanently in shadow. At ground level, shanty towns had been thrown up out of flattened cardboard, lengths of tin and thatch, their roofs plastic sheeting held down with bricks, worn-out tyres, bits of wood and broken pots, as if the medley of rubbish would prevent these homes from blowing away. A lucky few could boast shingle roofs. A river flowed by, but its waters were infested with rubbish, its muddy banks a battlefield of tree stumps.

Rain began to fall more heavily and every station we passed was a sea of umbrellas. Eventually it fell in torrents, and through my window umbrella and tenement dissolved into a weeping palette of black, grey, red, yellow and blue.

Inexplicably, the jungle returned. It was as impenetrable as that cloaking the ghats. Trees strained against the grip of tenacious tendrils and the suckers of distant plants. The heat and moisture had combined to produce conditions quite as luxuriant and inexhaustible as those in a rain forest. But soon after the Deccan Queen roared out of tunnel sixteen, apartments rose up around us again, along with their ever-present shadow, the shanties. The apartments gave way to bigger apartments, and the bigger apartments to high-rises. There was no rich foliage here to ameliorate the urban eyesore.

At Thane Station, the signalman waited on the platform, green flag raised, as we flashed through. Thane, once distinguished as the destination for India's first railway service, was now just one more station in a straggling network. Thirty-three kilometres remained. The business brigade were restless to be going. They checked their watches; their cellphone fingers went to work and the incoming calls grew in frequency. The Deccan Queen overtook commuter trains filled to bursting point; those passengers by the open doors clung on by the slenderest of threads. Even in the Ladies Only carriages there was something approaching a squeeze, and first-class ticket-holders fared little better.

Factories now rubbed shoulders with apartment blocks. Laundry hung limply from balconies. All about were stagnant pools, tree stumps, crows pecking among mounds of rubbish, pylons, cranes, breached walls, thickening streams of people, and men squatting to defecate among the litter. So this was the city the landless and hungry aspired to, the fabled abode of Bollywood stars, industrialists, bankers and entrepreneurs, the magnet for dream-seekers.

We entered the maze of tracks leading to Victoria Terminus. A maintenance gang moved crabwise beside the tracks clipping weeds with shears no bigger than table knives. On every red-brick wall were streaks of charcoal-coloured mildew. And when I stumbled out into the stifling embrace of the humidity I understood why. It clamped itself around me like an immense compress.

I wandered the sticky streets with a sheen of perspiration on my face. Even Bombay's office workers, I was reassured to observe, were forever dabbing their brows with handkerchiefs. (Manual workers, as though in conformity with some immutable caste rule, preferred to use a scarf-like length of cloth which they carried over their shoulders or draped loosely about their necks.)

Bombay's roads, at least in the central district where the British had erected their banks, brokerage houses and insurance companies, were remarkably civil. Motorists were restrained, almost subdued, in their use of the horn, and auto-rickshaws, carts and other lumbering road-going impediments were banned. Pedestrians could move about with relative ease. I gazed admiringly at the architectural transplants from another corner of the world, tatty relics now, yes, and occupied to a capacity well beyond their designers' wildest imaginings, but still something of a wonder beside their modern-day equivalents, so many of which were severely utilitarian, of indifferent construction and liable to look fifty years old when they were in fact five.

And the contrast was that much greater when Victoria Terminus hove into view.* It is probably the subcontinent's most exuberant example of High Victorian architecture. Formerly the terminus and headquarters of the Great Indian Peninsula Railway, it sprouts monkeys, gargoyles, lions and sculpted dripstones, along with loggias, domes, turrets, spires and stained-glass windows. Every surface, whether of stone, iron, timber, marble or tiling, is embellished with some florid decoration. And yet it is an incongruous structure within

---

* Previously known simply as VT, the station is now known as CST after being officially renamed Chhatrapati Shivaji Terminus in honour of a Maratha leader.

an even more incongruous creation – Bombay itself. For where else can a stately Victorian streetscape be found perched on the shores of the Arabian Sea?

Seeking some kind of architectural pigeonhole for what seemed to me to be far too grand an affair for a mere caravanserai, I consulted my Murray's *Handbook*. But it allotted just fifty-eight prosaic words to the wonder of VT, speaking of its Information Bureau, refreshment rooms, bedrooms, dressing rooms and bathrooms. An earlier edition rather more helpfully described it as 'Italian Gothic, with certain Oriental modifications in the domes' and concluded it was the world's finest railway station. It must also rank as one of the busiest; each day several million passengers pass beneath its gargoyles before disgorging like a river in spate into the streets of India's most 'happening' city.

❂

Anthony D'costa was manager of Gunbow Garment Cleaners on Rustom Sidhwa Marg. It was nominally a laundry agency. Shirts and pants, no doubt washed with tremendous vigour by dhobi-wallahs on the rocks of some distant ghat, hung freshly pressed at the back of the shop awaiting pick-up. Two staff took care of things there. The real money was in the two telephones for local calls, Mr D'costa's area of responsibility. A day-long string of 1-rupee callers gathered at them. And that's how I met Mr D'costa – after ringing from his long-distance booth, which was fitted with a fan that scarcely stirred the air but almost drowned out the voice down the line.

Mr D'costa was from Goa, the sleepy former Portuguese enclave further down the coast where coconut trees swayed before the sea breezes. Nevertheless, he loved the Bombay rat race.

'What about Goa?' I asked. 'You could have an easy life there.'

'No,' he said, lowering his voice as though making an admission of guilt, 'it is too quiet. I could not last there.'

His daily routine was gruelling. He set his alarm for 4.45 am, in time to catch a commuter train at 5.40 am. Two hours later he would arrive at the shop to open up for the day – a day during which he never sat down and seldom stopped for lunch. At 6 pm he would set off on the two-hour return journey (central Bombay housing prices were truly at international levels), eat dinner, have half an hour in front of the television and then bed. Six days a week, usually seven. No paid holidays, no superannuation, no long-service leave, no sick leave. There was nothing boastful, no search for sympathy, in this recitation. It was simply how it was. Indians, you had to admit, knew how to work.

The multinationals had cottoned on, too. India's biggest company, Reliance, he told me, had bought 20 hectares outside Bombay and built an enormous call centre in a collaboration with some American and European firms. 'Do you know what they pay operators there?' he said. 'For a twelve-hour day? Fifteen thousand rupees a month. That's about 300 American dollars. An American worker would expect that for two days' work, yes?'*

I looked at him, with his high unlined forehead, his thinning hair and eyes peering out from wide-framed glasses, and thought, What a happy outlook he has. And yet his long repetitive day was taken up with nickel-and-dime stuff: jotting down the price of each long-distance call in a ledger, calling out reminders and orders to the two employees behind him, taking bags of dirty linen, scribbling chits, taking money, handing out change and collecting the phone charge from local callers, a good many of whom tried to skive off without paying. 'Psst,' he would hiss to one customer after another, and they would walk back and slap down a coin without the least hint of shame. 'They think that because I am talking to you I won't notice.' And this happened so often – the high-flyers, the deal-makers and brokers who congregated in the street weren't immune to it either – that I said, 'I don't know how you smile through it all.' The answer that emerged – and it came out in a reluctant, roundabout way – was that he believed in God and that all the greed, all the acquisitiveness, all the pushing and shoving, the attempts, in a hundred minor ways

* About 350,000 call centre and back office staff are employed by foreign firms in India for a fifth of Western wages.

each day, to rip off others, in the end amounted to nothing.

'Once it was enough that we Indians had roof over our heads and food in our stomachs. Now we all want fridges and cars and mobile phones and a big home. And what are we going to do with it all? Do we believe we are going to live a thousand years? No, we'll make sixty or seventy if we're lucky. Does that mean I don't need money? Of course not. I need to make a living. But I don't need to rip off others to do it. I meet maybe three hundred people a day and 90 per cent are negative. They're stressed, they're uptight, rude, they try to skip paying, whatever. Ten per cent might have a smile, a thank you … that keeps me going.'

Mr D'costa might have been a Christian (he had even studied for the priesthood) but he was not the conventional, doctrinaire type. Far from it. His liberality would have shocked most congregational minds. 'I've read the Hindu scriptures,' he said, 'the Muslim texts and of course the Bible. And do you know what? They all have a baseline. Follow that baseline and you will know God. All the rest is extras: the rituals, the food requirements, the dress, the whole lot is top-ups. The Pope in far-off Rome, he signs something and makes it official doctrine. But does it matter? Not a bit. A sincere heart … that is all you need to know God. But you must do it on his terms. The ones who go to the temple or church and say, "Dear God, I want this, I want that and here's a donation" – they're not approaching God on his terms, they're just being selfish.'

Mr D'costa's religious inclinations, I was happy to discover, weren't without irreverence. He asked my name and when I told him he laughed and said, 'I'll tell you a joke about St Peter. He is, as you know, keeper of the gates of heaven. But St Peter is also blind and he has to have some way of recognising the good from the bad. You may not know this, but priests and people in religious orders used to shave the tops of their skulls. St Peter decided those who were bald were more likely to be good Christians than sinners. So as each person stepped up, he would frisk their heads. The bald ones he sent to heaven, the ones with lots of hair he sent to hell.

'Now one day there was a very long queue and at the end of it was a tall hippie. You know the sort, long hair, loose living, lots of ganga' (with that Mr D'costa clasped his palms together as though drawing deeply on a bong), 'and he wondered to himself, What's going on here? He figured it out soon enough, so when he got to the front of the queue he did this …' And Mr D'costa bent down and pretended to drop his trousers and back his bare bum towards St Peter's outstretched fingers.

This one-time trainee priest with a humdrum job and a cheerful, noble-minded outlook knew everything that went on in the congested streets of the commercial Fort district. He also knew all about the daba-wallahs and their complex system of delivering thousands upon thousands of freshly made lunches to office workers throughout the city. All packed in identical tiffin tins and plucked from the hands of dutiful wives about ten each morning, they were delivered faithfully and without mix-up six days a week to their flagging husbands.

There was no central depot, no uniformed employees, no standardised procedures, merely an informal network of runners, some of whom met mid-train to collect or swap dabas (tins). The fee was 60 rupees a month, a nominal amount but multiplied thousands of times over it added up to a lucrative business. And all so the babus, toiling away at their desks beneath banks of droning fans, could enjoy a freshly cooked, home-made lunch each day.

Mr D'costa also spoke with some pride of the Bombay Municipal Council taskforce whose job it was to catch rats – a carryover from the days of the British, who had been keen to suppress rats and the risk of plague outbreaks. Each night the ratcatchers set out among the lanes and alleyways of Bombay. And since they were paid according to the number of tails they returned with, they naturally enough became expert at their job. To kill the rats they used nothing more than a stick, but it was thrown with such force and accuracy they could strike dead their targets at some considerable distance.

'Such things you will find only in India,' Mr D'costa warned me. 'Here you must expect the unexpected.'

Extolling civic virtue, Indian style.

The Jnaneswari Express
to Calcutta

THE JNANESWARI EXPRESS may be the fastest train between Bombay and Calcutta, or Kolkata as it now is, but it still takes more than thirty-two hours to cross India's girth. Four times a week travellers depart without fanfare from the suburban station of Lokmanya Tilak, and 1,968 kilometres later they are standing in Howrah Station. I was in no particular hurry, but this sounded the train for me: an express service, few stops, a pantry car attached and a sensible departure time of 8.20 pm. I boarded one Friday and next morning I was yawning and peering out the window as the signboard 'DHAMANGAON' flashed by. I checked my map and saw we were deep in Maharashtra state. Nagpur, an important railway junction, was scarcely 100 kilometres off.

It hadn't been all plain sailing, though. I had barely slept, unable to shut out the excruciatingly laboured breathing of the old man in the bunk opposite. His wheezy rhythms were amplified by a hole in his throat, the result of recent surgery. A drip was taped to his nose and the attached tube, when not in use, trailed off into the folds of a shawl. His son, a silent dutiful youth, had lugged aboard three suitcases and immediately opened the largest, a mobile dispensary of lotions, creams, pills and plasters. With an aluminium pot, mixing bowls and a sieve, he had prepared a solution and poured it down a funnel into the drip, causing his father to splutter as he took some nourishment. Dinner over, the father hoisted himself into a kneeling position on the bunk for prayers. Between each half-prostration, he silently mouthed the prescribed verses of his faith, cupping his hands as though holding the Holy Koran itself. It was a praiseworthy effort for someone in his very frail condition and thus a doubly pious act.

Throughout the night the rasping inhalations and exhalations were punctuated by violent gasps and coughs. Each breath I could have sworn was about to be the old man's last. At frequent intervals he would flick on his reading light and use a hand mirror to inspect the weeping hole in his throat. He had a roll of toilet paper at his side and would tear off lengths and dab the hole. Satisfied, he would turn off the light and I would doze off, only to be woken by another fit of coughing or by the son as he got up to prepare a solution for the nasal drip. For variation, the fearsome *whoosh* of trains hurtling in the opposite direction also broke my sleep.

The weather in the morning did nothing to improve my mood. A drizzly grey sky hung low over the plains. Every stream was brown and swollen and seemed somehow fetid. A few tough low trees grew on the otherwise unmarked boundaries of fields in which most of the crops were shin-high and unrecognisable. No one was about except for the defecators, squatting along deserted pathways or behind walls, who faced the additional task of holding an umbrella overhead as they went about their business. The hamlets we passed, all sodden and grey-brown and sprouting sagging, improvised television aerials, looked dismal in the rain.

At Sevagram, where Mahatma Gandhi had set up an ashram, we paused long enough for a few passengers to rush aboard through the deluge. The street lights, at 9.15 am, were still on. In the compartment itself, it was also necessary to keep the lights on. Most passengers continued to sleep, stirring from their white cocoons only long enough to take breakfast. They were a subdued group, sitting or lying half-asleep, half-awake, in the gloom, the rain slapping on the carriage roof, as they stared into space. I had failed to extract more than the barest pleasantries from anyone, let alone a conversation. And it was odder still when one thought of the raucousness of crowds in India, surely the noisiest country on earth.

Finally, unable to bear the old man's death rattle any more, I fled to a vacant seat a few compartments along where I stared out sullenly at the narrow strip visible beside the track. Nagpur looked downcast, with everyone trapped indoors or under awnings by the rain, and I felt pleased to be aboard a long-distance train, content to pass through, to surrender to motion. During the ten-minute halt at Nagpur Junction I stretched my legs but found no vendors selling the famed local oranges. Nor did I see any of the aborigines known as Gonds who live in the surrounding districts. The Gonds have black skin, flat noses and thick lips and usually wear little more than a cloth around the waist. Their gods are smallpox, cholera and snakes.

Nagpur, capital of the former Central Provinces but today still within Maharashtra, is bounded on one side by the River Nag, hence its name. It is a vital junction for all long-distance trains, standing at the intersection of both east-west and north-south networks. In former days the Great Indian Peninsula Railway terminated here, the line on to Calcutta 1,140 kilometres to the north-east falling within the Bengal–Nagpur railway's jurisdiction. The British had provided Nagpur with all the amenities to be expected of a provincial capital: a secretariat, a legislative council chamber, a university and technical institute, churches, cathedrals, mission buildings and hospitals, a High Court, a Government House and not least of all a railway station with an imposing façade.

A pearly white, onion-domed building dominated the city skyline, but I could find no passenger who knew what it was, not even Mr N. K. Panda, who boarded at Nagpur and sat facing me. He looked like so many other men in the carriage: middle-aged, on business, travelling alone and carrying a single briefcase containing his work documents and personal effects. His loose, open-necked business shirt and polyester pants completed the picture of conformity.

Nagpur's city centre, he informed me, had been undergoing tremendous redevelopment, and I should not be misled by the slums around the railway station. They were built by squatters and would eventually be cleared. Since railway stations were noisy, generally undesirable places, the pleasant and well-arranged cantonments were as a rule built some distance away.

'As you move around India by train,' he said, a trace of admonishment in his voice, 'you may be imagining all our cities are ugly and full of slums. That is not so. That is simply where poor people are congregating.'

As the cloud cover lifted, and with it my spirits, the sun burst through briefly. Mr Panda, a coal-mine engineer, said changes were taking place in rural India, too. They were not immediately evident, but they were happening. Roads were improving, communications were improving.

I said, 'Compared with booming China, India looks slow-footed.'

'Yes, but India is a democracy and China is ruled by communists. Chinese rulers click their fingers and a million people must leave their homes so the Yangtze can be dammed. Such things we cannot do.' *

Mr Panda continued: 'Indian companies are also joining rush to invest in China – labour costs are same, but productivity is higher.'

'It's a shame,' I said, 'that Indian companies are not investing in their own country when so many are unemployed.'

'Government is to blame.'

I was a little incredulous. 'How is that?'

'Labour laws. Once you hire a worker, sacking him is almost impossible. He knows he can't be fired and he simply does not work.'

---

* Plans to dam the Narmada River in Maharashtra amply demonstrate the Indian government's difficulties. Continual resistance and legal battles by activists and villagers forced the World Bank in the early 1990s to withdraw from participation in the project, which, if fully completed, would sprinkle the Narmada and its tributaries with thirty large dams and 3,000 lesser ones, displacing hundreds of thousands of people.

This wasn't entirely a shock. India continued to be burdened by a plethora of state controls dating from Jawaharlal Nehru's socialist rule. Its public sector still ran according to Five-Year Economic Plans, mimicking its once closest ally, the Soviet Union.

Two hours after leaving Nagpur we pulled into Gondia beside lines of rusting goods wagons. The rain was still coming down. Mr Panda tried to get off to stretch his legs, but the conductor waved him back. In minutes we were again among paddy fields, grazing cows, herds of goats ... and more paddy fields, in fact a vast plain of rice in the making. Then without warning the train slowed as it curled up into thickly wooded hills. Hacked out of this lush jungle were clearings where roughly plastered cottages with sway-backed roofs stood in splendid isolation, their occupants presumably living out lives of the most primal obligations and pleasures.

Somewhere in those wild hills we crossed a state border, leaving behind Maharashtra and entering Chhatisgarh, a three-year-old creation carved out of the south-eastern corner of Madhya Pradesh. By the time we descended onto the plains again the sun was emerging from behind the clouds and women wearing brightly coloured saris and parasol-like hats were moving through the ripening rice in steady lines, like police troopers hunting an escapee, only their particular quarry was weeds.

Right about then the convalescent made the most horrific spluttering noise which drew a start from everyone within earshot. It was neither gasp, nor cough, nor gurgle, nor wheeze but an amalgam of the lot and it began to make me seriously wonder whether he would make it to Calcutta.

A whistle-stop at the steel town of Durg coincided with lunch, which was exactly the same as the previous night's dinner – and numerous other train meals before that. As we peeled back our tinfoil containers of rice, rotis, curd and vegetable curry, three Railway Protection Force guards with ancient Lee-Enfield rifles slung over their shoulders passed down the aisle, subjecting each of us to slow, deliberate scrutiny. Their presence brought back to me an incident from Victoria Terminus. There, two police officers had been escorting three arrested men to the cells. The trio had a rather downtrodden demeanour, hardly surprising in view of the fact that, innocent or guilty, they could not expect their fate to be decided swiftly so faced languishing in prison for an indeterminate period. But it was the way they were restrained that caught my eye. They walked in single file, linked together like a camel train by a heavy rope which was knotted around the leading prisoner's upper arm and then lashed to the second man's upper arm and then knotted around that of the third prisoner who carried in his hands, as inconspicuously as was possible with something so thick, the excess rope. As they were borne away through the crowds, this sad trio bunched themselves up in an attempt to hide the rope and disguise their status as arrested men.

The sun was now shining brightly and against the glistening ponds white egrets could be clearly seen, unmoving but alert as they awaited lunch themselves. In one of the ponds, water buffaloes wallowed blissfully, their heads alone above the water and cocked in a curiously human way. Behind them, a naked boy carrying a home-made bow and arrow tiptoed along an embankment with the light deliberate step of a tightrope acrobat. We sailed past the backyards of cottages where drying washing flashed in the sunlight, and tooted to a gang of trackmen who had stopped to rest, each man sheltering in any sliver of shade he could find.

I fancied a lie-down myself, but the only place where I could do that was next to the coughing old man. The antics of two Muslim men in the next compartment did, however, provide a temporary diversion. Each was heavily built and wore an immaculately pressed kurta, or long tunic, over pantaloons, a Nehru-style cap and a bushy beard shaved clear of the mouth in accordance with conservative religious sensibilities and dyed with henna to a rust-red to mask the grey streaks. From the moment of boarding the previous evening, the one in white (they were otherwise fairly indistinguishable) had been ceaselessly on his cellphone, when he wasn't yabbering in his companion's ear.

When we pulled into Raipur the pair got off, to be met by a large and boisterous welcoming party, each member of which rushed forward in turn with well-rehearsed spontaneity to place a garland of marigolds around the neck of the VIP. Some kissed his hand as well. The marigolds complemented the VIP's peachy-coloured kurta quite nicely, and as they grew in number his neck and then his chin became obscured. Before withdrawing, each supporter gave a ritual hug, moving his head first to one side of the marigold mountain, then to the other, then back again. At all this fawning and fussing the VIP expressed utter astonishment. When the supply of garlands was exhausted, a voice cried out a chant or slogan of some sort. (Mr Panda informed me later the group belonged to a Muslim political party.) This was answered by a cheer, then another, then a third, and the assembled crowd trooped off down the platform, apparently very happy with the way things had gone.

We pulled out of Raipur at exactly the same time.

Raipur, the chosen capital of Chhatisgarh, is built at the mouth of a vast amphitheatre formed by tiers of hills whose streams feed the Mahanadi River, which in turn irrigates the great grain-producing plains encircled within. Rice is the principal crop, but on this day it had no need of the Mahanadi's aid: the rain had renewed its onslaught. It was still raining when we reached Bilaspur and Mr Panda alighted. His home was to the north at Korba, from where a railway spur ran to an open-cast coal-mine, one of many dotting the region. I said goodbye with sadness; he was knowledgeable and companionable and a good deal more lively than anyone else on board. After that I sat alone staring glumly at the rain.

The sun broke through just as the Jnaneswari Express sped across the Hasdo River and into the town of Champa, turning the tops of the tallest buildings a buttery shade of yellow, before promptly disappearing for the day. A string of clouds like dollops of clotted cream sat on the peaks of the Mainpat Hills.

At 9 pm a bright glow from the giant steel town of Rourkela lit up the horizon. I could put off the inevitable no longer and returned to my compartment and the probability of another broken night.

Taxis queue at Howrah Station, Calcutta.

The Saraighat Express to Guwahati

IN THE CAVERNOUS MURK of Howrah Station majesty and melancholy assail the new arrival in equal measure. Here is a gloom where few shafts of light ever penetrate, where day and night seem scarcely distinguishable. The soaring stonework and wrought-iron roof spans, so intricately worked, are overlaid with a heavy and ancient patina of soot and grime, a reminder of better days and the certainty they will not return. Even at 5.30 in the morning, with the concourses deserted and the food stalls shut up, I sensed the unremitting strain placed upon this century-old red-brick edifice. The astonishing thing, of course, was that in a decade's time Howrah Station would, without upkeep or additions, be accommodating ever greater numbers of travellers.

With most of my fellow passengers having scuttled away, I stood bleary-eyed and alone, rubbing my stubbly chin and thinking of breakfast. I strolled passed the Office of the Platform Inspector – a makeshift booth in which a knot of uniformed officials sat about as a boy squatted under a desk running a rag over their boots – and came to the Refreshment Room (Veg) in whose canteen-like atmosphere I ordered breakfast.

One greasy omelette and one pot of weak tea later, I climbed the stairs to the Gents' First-Class Waiting Room where I shaved and showered away my weariness to the mounting refrain of train whistles. In the main hall of the waiting room, fans suspended from the ceiling on long canvas strops gave an almost sensuous quiver as they stirred up eddies of cool air. Seven elderly men had commandeered the planters' chairs and arranged them beneath the fans, flopping their legs on the extendable arms as they dozed contentedly, looking like pool-side sunbathers. One man snoozed on a luggage rack, his suitcase doubling as a pillow. Everywhere towels were hung out to dry before their owners departed. All in all, it had the convivial atmosphere of a private club or sanatorium, each individual maintaining a respectful distance from his neighbour.

Only once was my seclusion disturbed. A youth sauntered over and, indicating to a prisoner who had emerged under escort from the toilets, whispered in my ear, 'Australian.'

'Really? How do you know?' I replied.

'I am talking to the police. He is nearly sixty.'

I looked over. The shackled prisoner had a pepper-and-salt beard and wore a business shirt and trousers but no tie. He looked astonishingly composed as he picked up his overnight bag and was led away.

'What has he done wrong?'

'Terrorist.'

'I doubt it.'

'Yes, he was caught with stuff in brown bags.'

'Oh, you mean drug smuggler."

'Yes, drug smuggler. He was caught at Calcutta Airport. They are taking him to Delhi.'

'And if he is found guilty, what will he get?'

'Hanged to death, or twelve to fourteen years – minimum.'

'Will they hang him, a foreigner?'

'They might. It is the law.'

I thought a moment about a long stretch in an Indian prison – crowded, stinking hot, slops for food – and felt sorry for him, facing that prospect at his age.

The best thing about the waiting room was the balcony, a deep colonnaded rectangle protected from the rain, which was now fairly belting down, and equipped by a bank of ceiling fans. It had an aspect worthy of a five-star hotel. There was the first trickle of arriving and departing travellers at one's feet; then the humble tin sheds and ghats on the Hooghly River's eastern bank; then the Hooghly itself, its gunboat-grey waters undisturbed for now by boats big or small and advancing with stately deliberation; then more distantly the tenement sprawl of Calcutta's millions on the far bank, none of which, from this vantage point, gave any hint of the city's status as the former capital of British India; and of course linking the two sides and dominating all, Howrah Bridge, a colossal grey structure which somehow managed a certain grace despite its fretwork-like mesh of steel. It leapt across the Hooghly River in a single cantilever span and shuddered with the passing of claptrap buses, taxis and diesel-belching trucks and the footfall of uncountable numbers of pedestrians.

When the rain eased I walked across it. The soldiers at a guard box wagged their fingers at me: 'No *photo-graphee*!' The humidity was tremendous and that short walk left every stitch of clothing clinging to me, as though I'd jumped in the Hooghly itself. But the clamminess made no apparent difference to the coolies who cantered across the bridge at an impressive clip, bearing on their heads great baskets of bananas or bundles of sugar cane or misshapen gunny sacks bulging at the stitching. The Bengali who lived in Calcutta had routinely to endure great heat as well as great humidity – so hot could it become that the 27,000-tonne bridge was habitually more than a metre longer by day than by night.

On my way back three country boats were punting downstream, every available man pressed into baling out the bilges. The vehicles around me were on their last legs, too. At this time on a Sunday morning most were taxis bound for the station. It seemed to me, almost a decade after a previous visit here, that exactly the same fleet was out earning fares. These Hindustan Ambassadors belched smoke, sagged at the haunches and bore countless scars on their rusting yellow-and-black bodywork. But somehow, surviving monsoon flooding, rough roads and perpetual use, they were coaxed through another season's service.

Howrah, formerly so deserted, was throbbing with activity when I got back. Here and there on the platforms and concourses were bundles of belongings – bags and sacks knotted tightly with string, cardboard boxes and rolled-up sleeping mattresses, ringed protectively by the owners and slept on by their children – but otherwise it was all continuous movement: the rattle of parcel trolleys, the shudder of diesel engines, the incessant flashing of arrival-and-departure boards, the whirring of broad concourse fans, the impatient cries of porters clearing a path through the throngs, the ebb and flow of passengers, the drone of thousands of scuffing chappals.

All this thrusting and motion was presently drowned out by a downpour, which produced such a din on the tin roof, like a dozen jackhammers put to work simultaneously, that a riot would have passed off unnoticed. The stickiness dissipated rapidly, as if someone had thrown the switch on a giant air-cooler.

Eventually I resumed my place on the waiting room balcony. One corner was occupied by an outlet of the Eastern Railways Catering Service, a rather grand title for what was really just a grizzled man dispensing tea and biscuits at a counter. But from his urn, for a nominal 3 rupees, I could replenish my cup with a sweet milky concoction and pass the time. I was blissfully happy. And I had another train to board in the afternoon – to Guwahati in the north-eastern state of Assam. The next service was some days later and since my schedule would bring me back here I resolved to go immediately. For now it was sufficient to have dipped my toe in Calcutta.

❂

In a rather dramatic gesture, the skies chose the moment of our departure to open up. The cloudburst was accompanied by a string of tremendous thunderclaps. A constant film of water cascaded down my compartment window, all but obliterating any view. I could just make out the fronds of a few palm trees drooping beneath the force of the deluge. In twenty minutes or so I glanced up from my notebook and Calcutta had vanished. No dreary march through bustees and industrial estates (we'd immediately veered east rather than up Calcutta's straggling north–south spine), just beautiful palm tree-fringed ponds and tanks, glistening an egg-yolk yellow as the sun broke through the mass of clouds. Everywhere paddy fields sparkled like gold foil embroidered with a million emeralds.

This spectacle made no impression on my neighbour, who sat engrossed in his newspaper. On the fold-up table by the window he had placed his briefcase, his only item of luggage. After a time he put his paper aside, removed a pair of rubber thongs wrapped in old newspaper and placed them next to his shoes on the floor. Then he resumed his cross-legged position and his reading. When he had finished the newspaper he withdrew another and began to demolish that page by page, like a student chomping his way through a turgid textbook, methodically and without pleasure. The second newspaper gave way to a third.

'My God!' he huffed to no one in particular and put down the paper. He was already bored by this journey. He looked out the window but found no enjoyment there. The magazine and newspaper seller, the peanut seller, the soft drink seller with his bottles kept cool in a bucket of ice, the pen seller clutching a dozen ballpoints in each hand, the occasional beggar, the comb seller, the shoeshine boy – each had stopped to make his pitch, but he hadn't dignified their presence with the briefest of glances.

In appearance he was completely unremarkable: short, bald, thickly built, about fifty-five, in Western-style clothes, habitually removing his wire-rimmed spectacles to clean them. A government clerk, one might guess. He continued to sit cross-legged like a chubby Buddha, but without the Buddha's serenity. Since his demeanour discouraged questions I named him Mr Huffy.

The other two in my compartment were acquaintances of some kind. They munched through a packet of crisps each, never once pausing to close their mouths or to cease their breakneck chattering.

'Oh my God!' Mr Huffy said with a yawn, a world-weary yawn. Then a few minutes later: 'Oh my God!'

The sunlight grew a little stronger and the waterlogged paddy fields became a single enormous glittering lake of gold.

A quarter of an hour later Mr Huffy folded his arms on his stomach and issued his now familiar call-sign: 'Oh my God!' And two or three minutes later another. In between these punctuations there was only silence, but it was a silence laden with exasperation.

At 6.30 pm we halted at the pretty little station of Bolpur to allow a southbound train through. I strolled along the platform in the delightful still evening air. It was warm but not humid like Calcutta. Three old men sat on a concrete bench, their umbrellas laid at their feet. They did not look like travellers, being formally dressed in their best clothes, and they spoke to each other in a leisurely and considerate way, as though seated on a sofa in an upper-class parlour. It was a jolt after the way Indians usually bawled at one another. But then I remembered that the university town of Santiniketan founded by Bengali poet Rabindranath Tagore was only a little way off.

Further north we crossed a broad, almost treeless plain where rice grew uninterruptedly to a horizon denoted by a smudge of blue hills and above which brilliant-white clouds were theatrically massed in towering columns. In the setting sun, the whole scene was tinged a hue as vivid as turmeric powder. From the embankment on which we were travelling, the rice fields could be seen going on and on, swirling around a grove here, a cluster of mud-and-tin huts there, before sweeping ever on until darkness rendered their progress invisible.

❂

At 7 am the sun was shining out of a clear sky and cows were everywhere, munching along railway embankments, around ponds choked with pink-flowering water lilies, in grassy paddocks and at the margins of cultivation where the jungle growth was, with some difficulty, contained. Everything grew so exceedingly well here. Creepers had shot up the power poles and were now hastening along the lines themselves. A few farmers were out ploughing their muddy fields, but otherwise they had little to do except watch their rice, periodically weed their fields and wait for more rain. On this last score they were unlikely to be disappointed because the region's rainfall was tremendous. In the nearby Khasi-Jaintia Hills, close to the Indo-Bangladeshi border, is the wettest place in the world, Cherrapunji, which has an average rainfall of 10.82 metres a year. (In one year 22.98 metres fell, 9.29 of them in July alone.)

We were making good time as we moved eastwards through the bright morning air, clattering over scores of rivers intersecting our path. Every one brimmed with chocolate-brown water which frothed in angry whirlpools around the rail-bridge piles. Pouring down from the Himalayan foothills, these rivers would all join the Brahmaputra, which ran down the long wide Assam Valley, curved around the hilly Indian state of Meghalaya and crossed into Bangladesh. For now, though, the Brahmaputra would remain out of sight as the Saraighat Express maintained a course parallel to it, turning sharply to make a crossing only once directly opposite Guwahati.

Amid all the lushness of Assam, life was lived with surprising frugality. The humble train stations were unkempt and vandalised, their sidings roamed by goats and cows. The villagers waiting patiently on platforms wore plain threadbare clothes. I had yet to see a single metalled road, but there were plenty of dirt tracks weaving between bamboo thickets where farmers had built their tin-roofed huts. These pathways made ideal platforms for cyclists to get about their watery landscape, which they could do in perfect peace because motorbikes were scarce and four-wheeled vehicles scarcer still. The Assamese unquestionably lived simple lives – television aerials were non-existent and there was no rubbish: village pathways and backyards were as clean as a picked bone. Everything was used over and over again.

Mr Huffy, who had said nothing since rising, now gave a big yawn and his trademark exclamation, then repeated the process.

The pair opposite me, one exceedingly lanky, the other with heavily hennaed hair, had freshened up and were now ripping apart cold chapattis and scooping up the leftovers from last night's dinner, which was spread out between them like a picnic. The previous afternoon, soon after leaving Howrah Station, Mr Huffy had made it plain he was in no mood to field questions about himself, although he was happy enough to subject me to the usual interrogation about occupation, age, marital status, number of children, purpose of visit … The only piece of information he let slip was that he had left his birthplace of Sylhet in Bangladesh in 1949 (a casualty, I guessed, of Hindu–Muslim tensions in the wake of Partition in 1947).

When I had ventured to ask the purpose of his visit to Guwahati, he had declared airily, 'I am touring my country – just like you.'

I didn't believe him for a second. He was an intelligent man and an avid newspaper reader, a rarity among train travellers. I fancied him to be a government inspector who toured widely and incognito, rooting out inefficiency or corruption. Or perhaps a policeman or security official.

'You are a very mysterious man,' I had teased him and he found it hard to take the joke, though the other two laughed openly.

Later I had questioned Mr Huffy about how safe it was to travel beyond Guwahati and he had answered, 'It is not advisable. There are armed dacoits. At least twice a year they blow up the line when a train passes by – many are killed.'

The dacoits and numerous tribal groups fighting for autonomy or independence were, he intimated, one and the same: lawless types with only half-political grievances.

'What about here?' I had asked, pointing on my map to Silchar in Assam's south.

'That will be safe,' he said, 'but why don't you go here?' And his finger had landed on Shillong, capital of Meghalaya. 'Here there is a hill station with many temples nearby.'

'There's no train,' I said. 'If a train doesn't go there, I don't go there.'

Now, this morning, Mr Huffy and I resumed our tussle. When the lanky passenger asked me if Australians spoke English, Mr Huffy replied, impatiently, on my behalf, 'Yes, yes, it was a British colony.'

I said, 'At the very beginning it was a British prison.'

'Like the Andaman Islands,' he volunteered.

'You have been there?'

'No, but I will be going to Port Blair in a few months on … on my tour. I lived there once.'

After a time, and I knew he was building up to this, he said to me, 'What is the subject of your study?'

I knew all my note-taking had been silently bugging him.

'India,' I answered airily myself. 'What I can see out the window.'

I knew he didn't believe this for an instant.

'Why don't you bring one of those … those computer things?'

'Laptops?'

'Yes, laptops,' he acknowledged, grudgingly. This was the first time he had been lost for precisely the right word. (Earlier he had lectured me on the distinction between supper and dinner.)

'Because,' I said, holding up my pen, 'this is much lighter and won't break down.' Emboldened by all his questions, I asked him directly, 'What do you do for a job?'

'I don't have a job. I just tour around.'

'That must be nice, not having a job.'

He gave the slightest shrug of his shoulders and the other two smiled broadly.

'But you live in Calcutta?'

'I don't live anywhere.'

'Then you really are the mysterious man I said you were.'

He coughed and spluttered, and then, in his booming voice, said, 'Enough of this nonsense.' Later he gave an almighty yawn, uttered an 'Oh my God!' and stared distractedly out the window.

Then without forewarning we were crossing the Brahmaputra. It was not the breathtaking river of my imagination. At this narrow point opposite Guwahati, steep banks hemmed its passage, and its mud-red waters squeezed through uneasily, like a plump woman forcing herself into a corset. Despite appearances, it was a momentous river and it had already made a momentous journey. Rising as the Tsangpo in the snowy plateaus of western Tibet, it had covered 1,930 kilometres to this point, flowing east across the Tibetan highlands before pouring through a chink in the Himalayas' ramparts, a 5,075-

metre-deep gorge, and then breaking out into the Assam Valley on a reverse south-westerly course. It still had another 920 kilometres to go, crossing the watery lowlands of Bangladesh, themselves already shattered into a thousand fragments by other rivers, before merging with the Ganges and Meghna to empty into the Bay of Bengal.

'Brahmaputra means son of Brahma,' volunteered Mr Huffy in his booming voice as we clanked across the bridge. 'In India we have many gods, thirty-three crore* actually. Brahmaputra is one of them.'

This sudden instructiveness took me by surprise.

Guwahati, so full of palm trees, looked pretty and unhurried. In fact, it hardly looked like a city of 600,000 inhabitants at all, so concealed was it beneath dense foliage. But that was the outskirts. The city centre was to prove as chaotic and dusty as any other.

'India resides here,' he resumed, his hand indicating out the window to the shacks flanking the railway line. They were startlingly clean and ordered and their roofs were held down by lengths of bamboo arranged in neat rows, not the usual randomly tossed assortment of rubbish. 'The real India is found in its villages ... the villages along the railway line.'

And that hand, palm held stiff and indicating towards the window as though it were a blackboard scrawled with something whose significance I, the slow-witted student, was failing to grasp, remained where it was long after we had passed on.

I was revising my opinion. Perhaps he was a school teacher. The next day I learned the truth.

The pair in the compartment, who turned out to be Railway inspectors investigating some financial irregularity at the Guwahati offices, stood outside the concourse entrance. They had lost some of their previous reticence. 'What do you think that other fellow did?' I asked.

'CID,' said one, through paan-stained teeth.

'CID!' I exclaimed. 'How did you know?'

'We didn't. Different things ... we put it together.'

* One crore equals 10 million.

So, he was in the Criminal Investigation Department, India's elite police force.

❂

At the Departmental Catering Unit, a stand-up counter on the main platform, I ordered a breakfast of coffee and steamed rice cakes called idlis and surveyed Guwahati Station. With its rust-streaked tin roofs and the sight of swollen tropical clouds at every point of the compass, it could more easily have been a depot somewhere in South-East Asia. The passing faces added to that impression. Their fairer skin, more angular features and stocky build suggested ancestral homelands in Bhutan, Burma, Nepal or even Thailand (none of which were so very far away). But no, they were from India's tribal states, the hill areas splintered off from the once monolithic Assam Province and now known as Manipur, Tripura, Arunachal Pradesh, Mizoram, Nagaland and Maghalaya. The intermingling of races was real enough, however, and was evidenced in the linguistics of the region. In the Khasi-Jaintia Hills, for instance, live the Khasis, who speak a tongue of which the nearest similarity is in Cambodia.

This was indeed frontier territory. There was something indefinable yet unmistakable in the air, some hint of lawless ways, an indifference to central authority. An obvious clue was the Border Security Force troops, numerous and heavily armed, who patrolled the station. Many more were in transit to postings north and east; some of these stood shoulder to shoulder beside me, canvas kitbags dumped at their feet, as they joined the queue for breakfast. To anyone who hadn't sensed the tension, signs repeatedly reminded travellers: 'BEWARE AND WATCHFUL ABOUT UNATTENDED AND SUSPICIOUS LUGGAGE/OBJECTS.' The separatists or rebels, or whatever label one cared to give them, had not abandoned their terror plans.

There was no denying the soldiers' vigilance. When I stopped on the footbridge to watch the freight wagons rumbling by, one immediately blew his whistle and waved me on. It was clear loiterers were regarded as potential bombers reconnoitring their next target.

And what a highly combustible target presented itself beneath me. Here was one reason India held its eastern provinces so dear: Assamese oil. Long columns of tankers, their top hatches and sides streaked a dull black, rolled through the yards. Oil and tea: these were the reason for Guwahati's existence.

I found a hotel to sling my things and then made for the Brahmaputra. The heat, in combination with the humidity, was terrific. Sweat trickled from me with the least exertion. I adjusted my gait, shuffling my feet and flopping my arms at my side, picking my way with care through the footpath crowds, alert to any fragments of shade where I could stop, hands on hips, and refresh myself. The sun beat down between clouds massed in tall, tapering formations, and this heating and dispersing of moisture into the air created a gigantic open-air sauna. In my notebook I could manage just two words to describe the whole effect: 'Fantastically hot.'

I crested a hill and there beside a wild four-lane thoroughfare was the Brahmaputra, broad and turbid and thick as porridge, carrying off at a steady inexorable rate large boughs and clumps of vegetation wrenched from their footings somewhere upstream. The far bank was heavily wooded, the city side lightly so. In a conveniently shaded spot dhobi-wallahs were waging war on their customers' clothes, walloping them against flat slabs of stone at the water's edge.

Boats of every size were tied up, a few sitting proud in the water but most floating lopsided or sinking into the mud. The river's edge was in fact something of a boat-wrecker's yard, many vessels having been denuded of every salvageable object before being abandoned to the mud's embrace. A number of double-decker ferries belonging to the Inland Water Transport Department had shoved their noses into the bank. One had been converted into a Crew Training Centre under the supervision of the Office of the Training Superintendent. It did not look to have been untied from the shore for a very long time. At the stern there was a stack of firewood, bundles of wire coils and cables, a line of washing and a very permanent-looking gangway fixed to the lower deck whose planks were scarcely the length of a man's forearm above the water level. Figures shuffled about the semi-dark passageways with the familiarity of permanent residents rather than temporary trainees. Out in the main current, an occasional low, narrow-beamed passenger boat chugged towards a distant ghat, but otherwise the Brahmaputra was left unmolested by boatmen.

The coming of the railways, in conjunction with the siphoning off of water from some rivers for irrigation schemes, greatly diminished the importance of water transport throughout the subcontinent, including in Assam, which until the 1860s had been a forsaken corner of British India. The only means of communication with the outside world was by a government-owned steamer that departed from Calcutta every six weeks. But the Assam line, eventually to become one of the world's great inland water services, and the ancestor of the tattered Inland Water Transport Department ferries tied up before me, changed that. And it was a gamble based on a single commodity – tea. In those days tea was a luxury in Europe, and a very costly one too, coming mostly from China in fully rigged sailing ships. The river steamer service enabled the small tea gardens of Assam, where local wild tea was found in 1823 growing alongside bushes transplanted from China, to convert their cottage industry into a viable alternative source for the growing English habit of tea drinking.

The history of Assam is the history of tea. By the mid-1860s the Assam tea industry had begun to boom. With a rush of investment many more tea gardens were established. Sparsely populated Assam – it remains that way today – could not provide the labourers for these gardens so thousands were recruited from other parts of India, and they and their families and belongings were duly transported up the river. The steamers' captains entered the river through the labyrinthine jungles of the Sunderbans, felt their way northwards, passed the junction with the Ganges at Goalundo and entered the broad reaches of the river. Some smaller ferries reached beyond Dibrugarh where the river debouches into the Assam Valley.

The steamers were enlarged with upper decks to accommodate more passengers, a modification that persists on today's ferries, which are faithful copies of the original design: a long shallow hull, with engine and boilers amidships, a light superstructure covering the whole length and an upper deck with a roof against the monsoon rains and through which a funnel projects.

They must have made a stirring sight ploughing up a channel between high walls of jungle, a spray of foam at their bows. Not so today's paint-peeled ferries. Several of the more unseaworthy examples had been hived off as floating restaurants, although the word 'floating' has to be used reservedly. At the stern of one, water lapped at the planking. A few plastic chairs and tables were scattered about the lower deck where the curtains had been parted and knotted at the bottom in an attempt to admit some light and where a handful of customers sat in a comatose-like state among the empty plates and circling flies. It was hard to envisage a more unappealing place in which to dine.

In the ferry's shadow, naked boys, their skin brown and glistening and their teeth rows of white brilliance, frolicked in the water as only naked boys can, now and then remembering the point of why they were there and lathering themselves with soap before leaping joyously into the water again from one of the capsized wrecks.

An occasional cooling breeze came off the water although it was a mere tease, lasting at most a few seconds and serving only to remind me how hot it was. A little way upstream I stopped and bought a soft drink at a restaurant, chiefly to be able to sit by the river in peace and quiet. The Brahmaputra was a colossal and mesmerising thing. Hard against the south bank there was a long band of water that travelled upstream against the main current. It was easy to spot by the branches that drifted eastwards, as if on a conveyor belt, while the main body of water swept its accumulated detritus westwards. Directly in front of where I had stopped, I could see the inshore debris preparing to make an eventual U-turn as it rotated in ever tighter circles awaiting a turn to join the main current, rather like department store shoppers queuing at the foot of an escalator.

Set a little back from the river was a memorial attesting, quite unintentionally, to the tremendous forces of nature at work here in addition to the rain and heat – the regular and catastrophic earthquakes. The memorial, described on a plaque as the Gateway of Guwahati, was built in 1874 to 'welcome Lord Northbrook, the Governor-General of India, on the occasion of his visit by steamer to the province'. At that time Assam would have been in the full stride of its tea boom. As a footnote, the plaque observed that the memorial, a series of arches forming an open-roofed rectangle, was the only surviving brick-built architecture of the nineteenth century in the region, all the other British buildings having been destroyed by the earthquake of 1897. But it was not the only severe earthquake to have struck the district. There have been others, and some have altered the topography of the country. One, in 1950, raised the riverbed beyond Dibrugarh, impeding navigation in the upper courses.

I turned back towards the city, feeling somehow in sympathy with the restless, relentless movement of the Brahmaputra. My own schedule would allow me little time to linger in Guwahati. I passed the dhobi-wallahs again; they had finished a batch of garments, formerly spread out on an embankment to dry and now gathered into two titanic bundles like swags which a cyclist was attaching to his bike. One bundle he roped to his rear carrier, the other he balanced over the crossbar before tottering off into the traffic, presumably bound for the ironing-wallah. In the same faltering manner, wilting in the heat, I followed him along the road.

Sunset over rice plains, north-eastern India.

The Kamrup Express to Dibrugarh

IT WAS DUSK BUT STILL breathlessly hot as I descended onto the main platform. Passengers stood rooted to the spot inside the whirlpools of cool air spun by the overhead fans, as though trapped in a row of food processors. I climbed the footbridge ramp in search of a breeze, a movement in the air, but there was none so I went back and found a place beside some porters. They had luxuriant handlebar moustaches and sinewy limbs and they wore their brass authorisation badges clasped around the forearms. They, too, were awaiting the Kamrup Express, which was now almost two hours late. There seemed an awful lot of them for the few customers likely to call on their services. And when the powerful headlight of a diesel locomotive proclaimed the approach of the express, their easy camaraderie vanished. Off they dashed through the dimly lit confusion of luggage and travellers even as the train was rolling to a halt. The reward after that long wait? Maybe 25 rupees – and only for a few.

As I found my seat, a young Sikh bounded up and deposited

himself opposite me. He was dressed entirely in white, including his turban, which made a fine contrast to his thick black beard. He was very tall, handsome and athletically built. A smile perpetually lit up his face. Had I been to Amritsar, he asked. Yes, I told him, I had. It was the Sikh's spiritual capital. And the Golden Temple? Yes, that too, I replied.

'Ah, good. You liked?'

'Yes indeed.'

And I meant it. Sikhs were proud of their holiest shrine and often asked such questions. The iron bangle (kurta) around his wrist and the uncut hair (kesh) tucked into his turban satisfied two of the five kakkars that distinguish an orthodox Sikh. He was not carrying the third, an iron-handled knife (kirpan), he might have been wearing the fourth, a wooden comb (kanga) round which the hair is rolled, and I would never know whether he was wearing the fifth, short drawers (kachh), ridiculed by some as funny underpants. Sikh means disciple. The Sikhs are disciples of a tradition of ten gurus, beginning with the sixteenth-century Guru Nanak, who taught the worship of God as Truth. As a reformed sect of Hinduism it inveighs against, among other things, caste, suttee, idolatry, the seclusion of women and pilgrimages to the holy rivers and tanks of the Hindus. The war-like Guru Govind, the sixth leader, established the religion on a military and political basis, giving rise to the strong martial traditions of the Sikhs, of whom my uninvited friend was an example. He was an army captain en route to a posting in upper Assam.

The captain had enlisted twenty-two years ago. He was in signals and his last posting had been at the India–Pakistan border crossing of Wagah, a half-hour journey from his beloved home town of Amritsar. On this latest posting he was leaving his wife and child behind.

When I asked if he had seen fighting in Kargil, the remote spot in the mountains of Kashmir that had been the scene of India and Pakistan's most recent large-scale military clash, the captain affected not to understand me and couldn't be manoeuvred back to the subject. Then, in the same way he had bounded over to me, he abruptly rose and sprang off down the aisle.

We moved out, and dinner arrived in tinfoil trays from the pantry car (there are no restaurant cars on Indian trains and alcohol is forbidden). Later a blanket and bed linen were handed out to those who had just boarded. It was a comforting ritual. Across the aisle from me sat four men who looked like old-age pensioners (yes, I had broken my vow never to book an 'outside' berth again). The closest unfolded an envelope of old newspaper and offered me a sliver of fresh ginger as an after-dinner digestive.

The quartet were great chatters. The rest of the carriage had turned in by 9.30 but they were still at it after 11 pm. One, a Railways official called Kalidas Ghosh, leaned across the aisle to discuss books with me.

'Have you read Tolstoy's *War and Peace*?' Mr Ghosh asked.

'No.'

'I am reading that now. Tolstoy wrote maximum books. And Tagore?'

'No, not Tagore either.'

'Tagore also wrote maximum books. What about Bose? Buddhadeva Bose? Also a very important Bengali writer. You have read?'

'No,' I confessed, 'no Bose.'

'Maximum books also was Bose writing.'

And on he went, rattling off authors, Indian and non-Indian alike. I was left in the literary dust by this man.

'I could read twenty-four hours a day,' he said.

I believed him. And it turned out he was a collector, too.

'When I built my house – a small one, mind you – I put one room aside for books. Now I have more than ten thousand. They go from here to here,' he said, letting his hand rise higher and higher to indicate his floor-to-ceiling collection.

I said I was envious of his well-stocked library.

'The climate makes it difficult,' Mr Ghosh conceded, ruefully. 'Every month I spend one to two hundred rupees stopping the insects that eat them. There is also the problem of the rains.'

'You could try a dehumidifier,' I suggested and explained how it worked. He made me write down the word on a scrap of paper and examined it for a very long time. Then he looked up and declared solemnly: 'I will make investigations and see if I can source it in the markets.'

Mr Ghosh was a delightful man. He must have been nearing retirement because he said his forty-year obsession with books had begun at the age of eighteen. His eyesight had so deteriorated that his nose almost touched whatever he was reading; and that was with the help of thick-lensed glasses that gave his eyes the enlarged, unblinking appearance of a fish. The one difficulty in communicating with Mr Ghosh was his habit of chewing the digestive paan. It had no let-up, and his words, softly spoken anyway, became further muffled during the journey from his voice box to the outside world.

❂

During the night the line turned south away from the Brahmaputra, curving behind the Mikir and Rengma Hills, which stood like an ineffectual stockade on the main floor of the Assam Valley. By early morning we were beginning to swing back towards the river, cutting through a corridor between those hills and the ranges of Nagaland to the east, in whose remote valleys hid tribal Naga fighters opposed to inclusion in the Indian Union. Their head-hunter ancestors had been subdued only with great difficulty by the British. The Naga leaders had pressed for independence before the British departed, and when that fell on deaf ears in 1947 a rebellion soon followed, one of many revolts to splutter on in India's north-eastern states.

This section of track was in a bad way. During the night, as rain drummed on the roof, the carriages rocked wildly from side to side and rose and fell with heavy shudders, like a galleon heaving in a big swell. I hardly slept and drew my curtain at 5.30 am, though the rest of the carriage snored on contentedly. Outside, jungle flashed by for long, long stretches before parting to admit a sprinkling of paddy fields, huts and dirt tracks. Then, just as abruptly, jungle crowded against my window once more.

We reached the town of Dimapur at six and disgorged a party of tribal students, smiling flat-faced teenagers who talked high-spiritedly among themselves without distinction for gender or caste, and then we were off again, flanking the Mikir and Rengma Hills.

Steadily more and more paddy fields began to appear. At this early hour, only a few farmers were bent over, shin-deep in water, attending to their crops. Long shreds of mist hung in the valley, which was utterly still but for the odd egret flapping past with casual elegance, radiantly white against the deep-grey sky. Two boys with bamboo rods sat still as scarecrows beside a pond fishing for their breakfast.

In this remote corner of Assam the very air radiated cleanliness and vitality. The bigger townships might have contained the familiar Indian symbols – the tiny tea stalls improvised against a wall, the piles of rubbish, the countless stains of expectorated betel juice, the bicycle-rickshaw-wallahs dozing until the next fare passed by – but the villages exuded wholesomeness, vigour and self-reliance. Neatly arranged fences, admittedly of flimsy bamboo, screened off crops from encroaching farm animals; flocks of geese abounded; cows munched at the edges of ponds; women gathered the rice, which they tied in tufted bunches and carried off on their backs; the menfolk wielded mattocks through the air as they went about repairing the banks of fields or clearing flat ground of jungle for the growing of more rice; and fathers pedalled bicycles in long straggly lines as they ferried their uniformed daughters to school. Here the bicycle was king, motorised transport a peculiarity. When I caught a glimpse of a shiny silver motorcycle parked in a backyard, it stood out as an apparition, a piece of gimmickry in an otherwise almost ageless setting.

The tin-roofed houses intrigued me: they were more roof than wall, more height than width, like metal top-hats made habitable. So did the contrast between paddy fields, by now vast planes of emerald water, and the lonely groves of bamboo they encircled, which rose sheer out of the ground, some specimens as thick as telephone poles at their base, and tapered up and up into curled points as delicate as a quill. For magnificence the soaring bamboo was matched only by the graceful areca palm, 'an arrow shot from heaven' as one admirer was prompted to describe its straight slender trunk and delicate crown of fronds. They were common here: Guwahati itself means 'grove of areca palms'.

It was not all one long unblemished idyll, though. I had not yet seen a well-sealed road: if it wasn't a dirt track, it was potholed and neglected macadam. Was this a result of the region's rebelliousness? And there was real struggle, though even the barest thatch hut beside the track was neat and its yard swept and the despairing, filthy poverty so typical of urban India was nowhere to be seen.

I went and stood at the open door to get some fresh air. A cook from the pantry car was smoking a cheroot in the coupling booth. The train began to slow down, eventually to a crawl, and up ahead freight wagons lay overturned in a concertinaed line down the embankment. We craned out the door for a better look.

'Bomb blast,' said the cook in a surprisingly sanguine tone.

So Mr Huffy had been right about this far corner of Assam. We edged alongside the wreckage. The force of the blast had shredded the steel sheeting of some wagons and snapped lengths of rail. Wheel-and-axle units lay scattered in a field.

'When did this happen?' I asked a passenger who had joined us.

'Two days ago, the same day as the Mumbai blasts. About three o'clock morning time.'

'But it wasn't in the newspapers.'

'Local papers only,' he replied.

The blasts in Bombay's financial district had killed fifty and injured a hundred and fifty. Many speculated the explosions were retaliation by Muslims for communal clashes in Gujarat state to the north.

The sight of the bombed wagons didn't elicit much comment among passengers, but then the insurgents had been waging their campaign for a long time. Later, Mr Ghosh said the bomb had been aimed at a passenger train that had been held up. A goods train had gone through in its place; otherwise fatalities would have been inevitable.

I stayed at the door as the first smattering of tea gardens appeared, intermingled, rather peculiarly, among paddy fields. Then at a place called Mariani the squat tea bushes began to proliferate in earnest. Beside a pond dotted with geese, the dinosaur-like heads of three derricks bobbed up and down, pumping out the black treasure beneath. It was the old Assamese duo: tea and oil.

I said to the man beside me, 'People take care of their surroundings in this part of Assam.'

'Population levels are not so high here.'

'Even so, they could litter the place and they don't.'

'In India there are many castes,' he replied. 'Some are not so concerned about hygiene matters as others. They don't keep inside their houses clean, or the outsides.'

'Which castes are they?' I said, suspecting he wouldn't name names. One had only to look in the papers to discover the preference for faceless censure: it was always 'close sources said' or 'there is speculation that' or 'a spokesperson said'. True to form, he answered, 'It is different in different places. Here it is clean. In North India it is very dirty. There they don't care for such things.'

Back in my berth I studied my *Trains at a Glance*, the Ministry of Railways' 250-page almanac of main long-distance services. We were more than four hours behind schedule and still had some way to go. And as we slowed at one more out-of-the-way station, it dawned on me we had deteriorated into a Janata, or People, Express. No station, it seemed, was too insignificant to warrant a halt. Not surprisingly, the carriages were emptying out fast. But Mr Ghosh and his companions were still there, deep in discussion about whether British rule had been good for India. Rather like a college debate, two favoured the proposition ('they ruled for our prosperity') and two opposed it ('they ruled for their own purposes'). The intriguing thing was that they were still bothering about it, more than half a century after the Raj's demise. Finally, at Tinsukia, about 60 kilometres short of Dibrugarh, the four got down and I was on my own.

As we left town the road and rail line now ran so closely together that I felt momentarily bewildered: Was I on a train, or on a bus with its same elevated view of the road? Admittedly I was very tired, but I was close enough to reach out and touch the cyclists and motorists going in our direction. No barrier stood in the way, and any out-of-control vehicle, of which India's roads have plenty, would have been instantly crushed under the train's wheels. However, if one wanted to observe all the distractions of the Indian roadside without the attendant perils of the road, this stretch to Dibrugarh was ideal, although we progressed in a very staccato manner. Hardly had we got going than we stopped for a long stretch next to an unmanned checkpoint. We started again, only to stop a short way on. We started. And stopped. A string of lorries with immense loads thundered by, air horns ablaze with bullying self-importance, though their drivers turned meek at the sight of protected cows exercising their predilection for sitting in the middle of the road. Not even the most reckless driver would approach them with less than considerable caution – and the cows knew it. It was written all over their deadpan faces.

The tea estates kept on and on, but now a thin line of buildings spread itself between the road and the plantations: tyre repairers, dhabas where the truck drivers could rest and eat, television repairers, telephone kiosks, general merchants, hotels ('Foodings Only'), chemists, closed-up bamboo stalls, an almost limitless variety of one-man operations, humblest of all being the sellers of paan, cheroots and cigarettes – these last two items were for sale individually if finances couldn't stretch to an entire packet; and behind these rickety, dust-covered premises spread the tea bushes, a perfect green carpet, unvarying in height and thickness, each row flawlessly spaced from its neighbours.

Still we plodded on beside the road, by now a quilt-like collection of patches on which gangs were out in force adding further contributions. We could manage to overhaul only cyclists; all other traffic overtook us. By two o'clock it looked as though we really had left the tea gardens behind. Rice, briefly supplanted, was back, abutted by a thread of general engineering and fabrication shops, truck repair yards, marble wholesalers, Assam Oil filling stations, several schools where cows grazed on the playing-fields, auto-rickshaw stands, bicycle shops, an army barracks ... and then, six hours behind schedule, the edge of Dibrugarh came into view.

❂

But India can shatter every assumption, every illusion: our arrival was not quite the end of the journey. Inexplicably, the Kamrup Express stopped some distance short of the station and the much-reduced complement of passengers climbed down among the long grass and skittering goats and, dragging bags and suitcases, trudged towards the station, some veering left through a gap in a wall towards some houses, others marching straight on, and the remnants, myself included, turning right across the lines towards the station. This was indeed the end of the line.

Dibrugarh Town Station was in a bad state, its platform a mass of coarse rubble surviving from some long-abandoned resurfacing job, but what it lacked in services it made up for in service. Within minutes an assistant in the Chief Ticket Inspector's Office had processed all the paperwork and I was in a retiring room set partly below ground level, like a military pillbox, where the air-conditioning unit did nothing but produce a teasing hum. I could look out the front window and come face to face with the wheels of any waiting trains. The room was spartanly appointed with bits of worn-out furniture although an inventory fixed to a wall was exhaustive, right down to the smallest articles, listing, among other things, '1 stool Almirah, 1 tool, 3 window Purda & 1 door purda, 1 iron bucket, 2 palangs and 2 Matross'.

Showered and refreshed, I was bundled by the same helpful assistant into a waiting auto-rickshaw and dispatched to what turned out to be the town's flashest eating place where I was ushered into an elaborately decorated but empty dining hall. It was too late to back out. Staff hovered like flies, their attentiveness well meaning but excruciating. One waiter – there were four about at different times – spooned a little of each dish I had ordered on to my plate and used a tong to gently transport a naan to my side plate. As I neared the end of what was on my plate, he was at my shoulder ready to repeat the process. When I insisted on serving myself he retreated with a hurt look. I felt convinced that, if asked, he would have spoon-fed me. Thereafter, he and the others hovered about, resetting tables and polishing cutlery in the hope I might relent.

The bow-tie service was out of place in Dibrugarh, which was no more than a service town for outlying farming areas, its grid pattern of muddy streets well supplied with agricultural implement shops and tractor repair yards. The sight of a foreigner seemed to evoke more surliness than surprise. I was met by gazes that were at best quizzical or indifferent and at worst hostile.

Dibrugarh was spread along its southern bank, but the mighty Brahmaputra was nowhere in sight. It was screened off by a high embankment that acted as protection against the river's monsoon-fuelled ravages. And it needed to be high. During the rainy season, the Brahmaputra could rise by as much as 12 metres and spill out across a distance of up to 8 kilometres.

I took a walk along the embankment, which one resident assured me extended upstream and downstream of the town for a total of 6 kilometres. Judging by the steady stream of strollers, the rough track was unofficially Dibrugarh's main promenade. A lookout on a grassy promontory drew me off the main track. It was a pleasant and popular spot. People gathered to take in the views and catch the cooling breezes off the water. And it was there I met Sheema. Or rather, Sheema met me.

From afar, Sheema looked conventional enough. Like her companion, she wore the modest salwar kameez, but as they neared, I saw her hair was cut in a tight bob. Anywhere else in the world this would have been unremarkable, but in convention-bound India, where women wear their hair long, plaited and definitely uncut, it was almost heretical. The cut accentuated her long neck and delicate features, and as she drew nearer still, I could see just how exceedingly beautiful she was. She was young, slight and fair-skinned and her eyes were deep brown and luminous. Her friend peeled away and descended to the water's edge and was soon lost from sight. Sheema drifted, outwardly without intent, towards me, but it was clear she had singled me out. I was flattered, yet a little suspicious. Among male strangers, Indian woman are demure and retiring to the point of irritation. She had shown an unheard-of boldness in even approaching in my direction.

I succumbed and said hello. And with a smile she murmured hello back. Little by little we began to talk. She was an odd mix of coyness and self-assurance. She asked, out of what I took to be politeness, where I was born. To my response she replied that she had met another New Zealander in Dibrugarh, the only other foreigner she had ever seen in the town.

'He was big and tall like you,' she said in her quiet voice. 'I like New Zealanders – not like short Indian men.'

I gave a little start. It was hard to think of a tactful rejoinder to such a remark.

She said she wanted to leave India and travel.

'Where to?' I enquired. 'America, Europe?'

'I don't know, just leave.'

I began to guess her interest in me. She was a smart and unconventional woman – she had completed a Master of Science and was working towards a degree in pharmacology – and India offered her only constraints. To her I was a symbol of foreign opportunities.

'I suppose you could work hard and save your money,' I suggested, limply. 'Then you could travel.'

Her pretty face clouded. Looking straight ahead, she said, 'I will need my money for bribes.'

'To get a job with a chemist?'

But at that moment her English, deliberately or otherwise, failed her. Later, a pharmacist bluntly put me out of my ignorance. 'She will have to pay the examiners to pass her,' he said.

'If she passes with flying colours,' I resumed, 'surely there can be no question of her paying anything?'

'Top marks, yes,' said the pharmacist. 'But if her marks are in the middle … and with so many candidates … money will help …'

'Really?'

'Really. This is India.'

Sheema and I chatted a little longer atop our magnificent vantage point. Even as we did, separated by a respectable arm's length, I could feel the half-curious, half-disapproving glances of the men loitering about, especially those of two young Muslims nearby whose embroidered skull-caps indicated they had made the hadj to Mecca.

Sheema was striking, brave and trapped, a bird of paradise imprisoned in a cage that was far from richly gilded. Her friend returned and they prepared to leave.

'We have to be back at the hostel by 5.30,' she said.

'Or what?' I asked.

But there was only a tightly drawn smile that silenced any thought of further questions.

As she shrank from view I contented myself with the aspect before me, which was of quite surpassing beauty: a vast amphitheatre of hills, from which poured the Brahmaputra. It was a giant cul-de-sac: directly ahead of me lay the Indian state of Arunachal Pradesh, behind which loomed Tibet; to the north-east lay China; to the east and south Burma; and to the south-west Bangladesh. Filling everything in my view except the cloud-cloaked hills was the Brahmaputra and its dozens of islets, some of their sandy banks audibly collapsing before my eyes. With nowhere further east to go, this was indeed a majestic stop sign.

Daydreaming boy, West Bengal.

The Brahmaputra Mail
to Moghulsarai

DIBRUGARH THE PREVIOUS NIGHT had been sultry. Lumding this
morning sparkled in the clear air. The rains had drenched the
jungle and ponds and pathways and paddy fields, which shimmered
in the sunlight now that the mountainous columns of clouds had
moved off and the sun could beat down without hindrance. Out in
the fields, where the business of gathering in the rice was gaining
momentum or farmers were ploughing up their squares of muddy
water in preparation for planting again, almost everyone wore
parasol-like bamboo hats to a design straight out of South-East Asia.
The sight of their toiling under that broiling sun made me grateful
for my air-conditioned carriage.

The Brahmaputra Mail was a slowcoach. One by one the little
towns down the Assam Valley inched languidly into and out of view:
Lanka, Hojai, Majgaon, Patiagaon, each distinguishable only by its
name. The reason for the slow bumpy ride was the state of the track.
The Chief Station Manager at Dibrugarh blamed the region's high
rainfall for continually undermining the roadbed. But our unhurried
progress suited me fine.

Travelling with me were four cheerful ticket inspectors, wearing all white except for black jackets whose pockets sagged like udders from years of accommodating notepads, timetables, charts of various sorts, receipt books and other trappings of their profession. They had every reason to be jovial. Their workload was not a tenth of that of the bearers and pantry staff, whose tasks were seemingly never done. They were eminently practised at making themselves comfortable on the job. Each inspector was assigned a little snap-up seat in a vestibule, but this was inconveniently close to the toilets and doors where passengers congregated to smoke or get some fresh air and it was not air-conditioned. So the inspectors made a point of seeking out any empty berths in the air-conditioned carriages where they could carry on their banter and idle the time away. And if every seat was taken, someone could always be induced to move along and squeeze them in. If ever there was a ticket to ride a gravy train, it was the chromed TTE badge of the Travelling Ticket Examiner.

I breakfasted on the ubiquitous omelettes and vegetable cutlets with a Thermos of tea, and when we crossed the Kopili River I was able to fix us at about an hour from Guwahati. But then we stopped once more. The delay lengthened until an hour had gone by. I passed the time watching men slashing rushes beneath my window; when they had loaded their long skinny craft almost to submerging point they punted off through the marsh, balancing on a pin-head of space left at the finely tapered sterns.

Midday came and still we had not budged. This line, I concluded, was jinxed. But then came a ripple-like shunt as the carriages moved off. We gathered some momentum but about half a kilometre on we stopped at Jagiroad Station. Immediately the air-conditioning cut out, the clearest possible sign we would be stuck here for some time.

The shrewdest passengers dashed out to stake a place beneath the half-dozen platform fans. The air was an oppressive miasma of heat and stickiness. The smallest movement left a film of sweat on the skin. I could begin to understand Mr Ghosh's difficulties with his books, and a multitude of other household effects that would also smell fusty or spoil if not aired regularly or put in airtight trunks.

Tempers were affected, too, but somehow people adjusted themselves to the discomforts, knowing the clouds building in the sky would, like clockwork, empty themselves for several hours in the morning or afternoon and temporarily break the tension.

To cool off, some of the less bashful young men stripped down to dhotis and splashed themselves with water from a platform handpump. Everyone else milled about disconsolately as the long hours ticked by. The station was too small to have a waiting room or eating place; there was merely a handful of stalls selling soft drinks, snacks and coconuts. And before long I overheard complaints that prices had skyrocketed as the extent of the delay became apparent. A packet of ten cigarettes had shot up from 23 to 30 rupees, said one man who bottled me up in conversation. Mukesh Mehta was in a position to know because, as he readily admitted, smoking was one of his two vices. The other was rum.

'Less acidic than whisky,' he said. 'As for the cigarettes, my doctor says I must stop smoking. But look at me: no blood pressure, no heart problems. Why should I stop? When your time comes, it comes.'

Thereupon he lit himself another cigarette.

Mr Mehta was a tea planter from Margherita, a town to the east of Dibrugarh near the foothills of Nagaland. For a long train journey Indian men will change into more comfortable clothing, invariably cotton trousers or a lungi worn with a baggy shirt, but Mr Mehta had gone one step further, wearing a singlet and a pair of shorts so inconsiderable that even I would have shrunk from putting them on. They scarcely came halfway down his thighs.

Mr Mehta was a natural raconteur, and with so much time to kill he ranged across every imaginable subject about his country, but the recurring theme was corruption: it was the great handbrake holding back India's advancement.

'How big is corruption? I will tell you. It is in every drop of blood in our veins. Say a government department is allocated 10 crore rupees to build a bridge or tarmac some roads. Immediately the top man, the Minister for Roads, whoever he is, takes 8 crore for himself and begins to spend the 2 crore—'

'Hold on,' I interrupted. 'Don't you mean he pockets 2 and spends 8?'

'No, no, no. He takes 8 and spends 2.'

'I don't believe you.'

'It is true, isn't it?' he said, turning to Mr Konwar, a carriage engineer with Indian Railways, who was escorting his nephew to Allahabad for a job interview. Each nodded and smiled a small but slightly pained smile.

'It is all true,' resumed Mr Mehta. 'Sometimes projects are signed off as complete that have never even been started.'

'But fraud on such a scale, it must be found out eventually?'

'Who is going to find it out? Everyone is involved. The 8 crore dribbles down to keep everyone quiet. The big men keep the most, the little ones the crumbs. It is the way of things.'

'Okay, there must be auditors.'

'Auditors there are, but they are bought off. They come in and find, say, seven big deficiencies in a project. That is too much, too many embarrassments. So they are given some money and only two of the faults go into their report. And naturally the recommendations are never acted on.'

He saw the scepticism on my face.

'Look, I give you one more example. All primary school children were supposed to get a free lunch. But all they got were a few peanuts and some milk. The big shots kept nearly all the money. Even the peanuts were no good – they caused food poisoning. There was an inquiry. In the meantime even those puny meals were stopped. The inquiry was bought off and now there are no meals at all. I tell you, if they took five and spent five, India would start to progress. But eight–two, that is impossible. India could be a rich country but it cannot defeat such a burden.'

Mr Mehta paused to light himself another cigarette and then resumed. 'I give you one more example: the road outside our tea plantation. One day they came to tarmac it. They put down some aggregate and compacted dirt on top. Then they left and never came back. Actually, it had been a good road before that, but now in the monsoon months it is a deeply rutted dirt track – you can barely get through. But you can hardly blame the contractor. He won't do a proper job when he gets paid only 1 crore to complete a project that should take four. So he cuts corners – a lot of them – otherwise he cannot earn a living.'

I thought back to a report in the morning's paper about a bridge collapse in Daman, Gujarat. Twenty-three pedestrians and motorists had died when, for no apparent reason, the structure had suddenly disintegrated. Shoddy construction? There was no way to tell. One thing was for sure, Mr Mehta had made me more suspicious.

He was emphatic it was not just the big shots who were at it. Public employees everywhere were supplementing their salaries with scams of varying sophistication. One of the most bare-faced instances was in his home town of Bareilly, a city not far from Delhi, where there was an intersection manned round-the-clock by police – not out of vigilance or because it was a safety black spot, but because it was on a busy lorry route. Every truck driver was obliged to slow down and drop 5 rupees into the police post. Two officers at a time were on duty, just scooping up and counting all the money.

'What if someone just drives through, doesn't pay?'

'The police radio ahead, someone pulls him over and makes all sorts of difficulties ... "Driver, your papers are not in order", such things as that. If the fellow is lucky he will get away with having to pay only 500 rupees. Word spreads, and everyone pays.'

Indian Railways, the country's most efficient public organisation, was not immune either, it seemed. Mr Mehta put the ratio at what was a relatively efficient ratio of three–seven, that is, only 30 per cent of funds went astray and 70 per cent was spent as intended.

'Without the railways India would simply stop functioning,' he said. 'It is profitable – it makes a lot of money.'

But I later learned the passenger arm was a public service. The profits were in freight.

He was equally gloomy about politicians. 'Ninety per cent are corrupt. Their loyalties go to whoever will pay the most.'

He was right there. The papers ran stories about MPs moving as a bloc to an opposition party and later reverting to their former masters when financial inducements were dangled before them.

Mr Mehta ran through the principal players at the Centre, as the government in New Delhi was known. Prime Minister Atal Vajpayee was, in his estimation, honest. ('He is a bachelor and his family is wealthy so he has no real need for money.') Defence Minister George Fernandez was honest, too, because he led a life bordering on the austere. ('For the last forty years I swear I have seen him wearing the same pyjama and kurta.') External Affairs Minister Yashwant Sinha was also a good man. ('He lives in a very modest house when he could have a mansion with every room air-conditioned.') He rattled off a few other prominent figures, but the other five hundred and thirty-odd members of the Lokh Sabha, India's parliament, went unnamed and thus condemned.

For all the faults Mr Mehta could see in India, he remained intensely loyal to his country ('Some of the best brains at NASA are Indian.') and given half a chance believed it could do much better. A sense of national identity was one vital thing lacking. A Punjabi abroad, asked where he came from, said the Punjab, not India. So, too, the Bengali and the Tamil and all the others of their home states.

His pride in things Indian could have funny outlets. He was tickled to be able to say the beggar boys scavenging around the station could eat the muck off the ground and still survive, even thrive.

'You know, the black skin is stronger than the white skin. See how many died in that heat wave in Europe. Some 40-degree days. Pah! Nothing. And why? Because they have no air-conditioners. Tell that to the street dwellers of Calcutta!'

As the afternoon drew on Mr Mehta would duck away at intervals to his coach, and eventually I guessed, then smelled, the reason: rum. I could tell another way, too. Mr Mehta had a habit of touching me on the shoulder, a light touch with a finger, as he made a point (and he had many to make). 'Mr Peter,' he would begin, then the tap, 'you must understand that ....' This tap grew in strength as the rum took effect until I began to feel slightly irritated.

But he made good. 'You will have to excuse me, Mr Peter, but I have had a drink. Do you want one?'

I felt dehydrated and did not want to add a hangover to the discomfort. 'No thanks,' I said, 'I usually drink beer.'

'Shall I arrange?'

'No, you are too kind.'

With little prompting he told me about his life and his family. He was Cambridge educated and a member of the Rajput warrior caste, for whom chivalry and honour are much esteemed. His father, grandfather and great-grandfather had all been army men, as had his brother, who died in the 1965 Indo-Pakistan war. As the eldest son Mr Mehta had been forbidden by his mother to enlist so he had joined a big British-owned tea company and risen to the position of deputy manager of a plantation. Even so, I think he reviewed his life with a slight sense of regret; that as a Cambridge graduate he could have achieved more. There had been compensations: Assam was a clean, unspoilt place to raise a family, and the life of a tea plantation manager had the comforts of an air-conditioned office and car, a rambling bungalow, servants, the distractions of the planters' club.

But after thirty-three years he had quit his post. Now, with a slight paunch, thinning hair and no obvious prospects, he was pondering what to do next. In the meantime, there were his daughters to visit, one a journalist in Delhi, the other a student in Bareilly where his father, aged eighty, and mother, seventy-three, still lived in good health.

I was intrigued about why he should throw in such a good life. The answer, quite simply, was that he had had enough. Tea prices, he explained, were in a deep and prolonged slump. The Russian market, with its centralised purchasing by Moscow at inflated prices, had ended with the collapse of the Soviet Union. The former states of the Russian empire now bought independently and drove a hard bargain, too. The other factor depressing the market was the imposition of restrictions on trade with Pakistan, combined with tighter border security, as relationships between the two countries had deteriorated. A lot of tea had formerly been smuggled through Gujarat and the southern border areas to Pakistan. Gujarat had previously taken so much tea that it was commonly said Gujaratis had to be eating the stuff by the mouthful rather than brewing it.*

The downturn had had direct consequences for him. In better times he had enjoyed a household staff of fifteen. By the time he quit it was down to six. Labour disputes had grown in number, along with government red tape. The poor market had tipped the scale. One thing at least had remained unchanged: the tea planters' club with its swimming pool, tennis court and well-stocked bar.

'Left by the British of course, and a very good idea it is, too,' he said. 'Members only. And their wives and families. It was a place where you could really relax, let your guard down.'

I could readily imagine him, elbow on the bar, passing the long hot evenings with colleagues. And in fact it was after just such a night that he had his only encounter with the separatists who were setting off bombs, shooting people and extorting money. It was about two in the morning, he was under the weather and driving himself home, having dismissed his chauffeur earlier in the evening. He was on a lonely jungle road when, from out of nowhere, a motorcyclist shot up behind him at great speed, overtook his car and waved him to pull over. The rider asked him to give his pillion passenger a lift to his house. They were both tribal men from Nagaland and they both carried pistols. With no choice in the matter, he carried on his way with the unwanted passenger.

'He knew all about me, this stranger who sat next to me in the dark – where I lived, who I worked for, that I had two daughters. It was unsettling. He knew about all the other managers, too.'

When Mr Mehta reached his bungalow the man promptly vanished into the night and Mr Mehta went inside and poured himself a very large drink.

Conspicuous consumption in upper Assam was best avoided, he went on. Those tea planters who accumulated enough money through various sharp practices to build big houses and lead showy

* Pakistan is the world's third-largest tea market and imports 140 million kilograms a year, about three-quarters of it from Africa. Indian tea faces hefty import tariffs.

lives were frequently kidnapped by the rebels. Only a month ago there had been such a case. The police denied money had changed hands, but Mr Mehta was dubious. 'Without money they just kill you and dump your body.'

The rebels had severely arrested Assam's development, he said. Investment slumped after the insurgency began in earnest in 1979, nine years after he arrived. Nor did it help that little of the wealth generated by Assam's oil, which Mr Mehta said met 60 per cent of India's needs, found its way back to the state. But there were benefits in Assam's relative backwardness. It did not suffer from the pollution and overpopulation of other regions. His daughter in Delhi now appreciated all too well the space, clear air and jungles of Assam.

Mr Mehta was sanguine about India's population growth. 'Awareness is growing, people are having smaller families,' he said. 'Look at me: I am from a family of six children, but I am having only two myself.'

The problem was most pronounced among Muslims, he said, especially the poor and uneducated. He lowered his voice as he talked about Muslims, a touchy matter in overwhelmingly Hindu India. 'They say, "Each child is a gift from Allah," but Allah does not put food on the table for them, does he?'

Mr Konwar, who had rejoined us, gave an approving nod to this judgment.

Hindus were on the whole very tolerant, Mr Mehta said. Muslims were not. 'Look at Pakistan,' he whispered. 'There, Islam is the state religion. In India all religions are equal. Pakistan is a nation of troublemakers. This aggression is in the Muslims' blood. Look back at the Moghul conquests of India, the forced conversions' (a bitter edge entered his voice at the mention of this humiliation), 'each emperor killing all rivals. That was the fate of Mr Bhutto in Pakistan. Look at Saddam Hussein, he was the same. Nothing changes.'

He was not really the Muslim-hater he might have seemed. With some satisfaction he recounted two instances of Hindu–Muslim tolerance in his birthplace. One concerned a Muslim who made a hefty contribution towards the construction of a Hindu temple, an act for which he was ostracised by his family. The other concerned a Hindu who sold paan from a stall outside the entrance of a mosque. The paan-seller volunteered his services as the mosque's cleaner, explaining that because he earned a livelihood from the worshippers, the task was a repayment of sorts.

Mr Mehta broke away for another of his 'refreshments'. It was becoming a real trial, this standing about in the terrible heat, the fans whirring away beyond our reach, the labourers unloading a consignment of dried fish which grew more malodorous as each gunny sack was flung on the heap, the perspiration on everyone's brow, the numbing dullness of the minutes and hours ticking by … and always our departure time slipping from our grasp. Word rippled through the crowd: six o'clock this evening, it was definite. But six o'clock came and went. Word spread again: 7.30 pm. This continued until 11.30 was being whispered.

Mr Mehta returned, his glass refilled, and we drifted to the subject of arranged marriages ('With love matches, the couple feel lovey-dovey for a few years then the incompatibilities come through.') and dowries. He would take nothing from his bride's family though his own simple ceremony, attended by four hundred and fifty guests, had cost 20 lakh* rupees. Even the poorest villagers could ruinously spend the equivalent of years of income on a wedding. Mr Mehta's income must have been substantial because he had been able to send one daughter on an exchange to London in her final year of school. 'We said to her, "Enjoy yourself, but please do one thing: do not eat beef."' Then he added in explanation: 'Cow, she is our mother.'

Ten minutes before midnight, the long-awaited moment arrived. A warning bell sounded and everyone gathered themselves up and boarded. A signal light switched from red to amber, and almost on the stroke of midnight, a full twelve hours after our arrival, it turned green and we crept out of the station towards a bridge whose footings, we were told, had been washed out by the rains.

Mr Konwar and I leaned out the door, savouring the cooling rush

* One lakh equals 100,000.

of air. The countryside was silent and, without a light on anywhere, as dark as a cave. A kilometre on, I saw the glow of hurricane lamps and then we came upon labourers shouldering pickaxes and shovels as they made their way along the edge of the track towards the station. They looked weary and few returned the shouted greetings of passengers.

At last we came upon the cause of all our trouble: it was not a bridge at all but a culvert, and not a particularly big one at that.

'So small,' I said to Mr Konwar.

'Small yes, but dangerous.'

We crossed so slowly and the illumination from the lamps was sufficiently bright that I was able to make out the badge of a man who was overseeing operations. He reclined with a kind of courtly aloofness on what resembled a park bench. He was the Chief Engineer. But I had newfound respect for Indian Railways. Its engineers had been thorough and taken no risks, sending a freight train over first to test the work. Only when it had returned to the station had we got the okay to proceed.

Mr Konwar and I returned to our compartment and turned in.

'It was a good day, wasn't it?' Mr Konwar said.

Perverse as it sounded, it had been good, the camaraderie, the endless talking.

'Yes,' I agreed, 'it was good.'

❁

Waking up can be disorientating on an Indian train. You flick off the light and you are alone. But when you prise open an eyelid next morning, there in the formerly empty bunk not a metre from your nose is an utter stranger, and not always a pleasant one, snoring or scratching his head or simply staring shamelessly at you.

Guwahati had tossed up a family of five. All day long their crying and whining and bickering filled the compartment. But that could not detract from my pleasure at being on the move after yesterday's enforced idleness. It was good to feel the sinuous sensation of a train in motion, of making progress, of advancing across a landscape, even if in this case it was the endless sameness of rice plains. Crossing a river was a way to tick off the miles, to prove to oneself that the hours of rattling along the line were having some measurable result.

A sudden storm lashed us as we ran down through the Siliguri corridor, the 20-kilometre-wide neck between Nepal and Bangladesh that is India's only land link to its north-eastern states. The dark, soaked figures in the paddy fields, singlets clinging to their bodies and up to their knees in water, looked miserable. But then the rain passed and we were upon the rice plains of upper West Bengal. There, a recurring variation to rice was to be found: jute. Bengalis were busy gathering in what is still a useful cash crop. Harvesting jute is not as simple as taking to it with a machete. The tall green plants are first cut down, tied in bundles and submerged in ponds for several weeks to soften the outer skin so it can be stripped off as long continuous strong fibres. Ponds everywhere were dotted with these strange slumbering bundles. Then comes stripping, a laborious job. After washing, the fibre is dried in the sun – the plains here were dotted with teepee-like stacks – and twisted into big skeins for transporting to factories.

If the jute workers were industrious, so were the hawkers stalking the aisle. A succession of peddlers traipsed back and forth in search of business. In their numbers, tenacity and variety of stock they surpassed anything I had seen before. They flogged miniature travel irons, umbrellas, children's colouring-in books, cordless telephones, travel bags, watches, fluffy toys, assortments of peanuts, newspapers (one useful thing), cassettes, CDs, boiled eggs, a head massage service available in a choice of three oils (possibly useful but for the complete lack of space and privacy), lamps, batteries, nail clippers, pillowslips – in fact a pretty representative cross-section of a cheap bazaar, except it was mounted on a conveyor belt that went clunking past our seats. But it was fatal to look up, to show the smallest flicker of interest, to do more than incline the eyes a little their way. Only a poker-faced expression and perfect stillness could defeat them.

The family, so noisy and distracting that they drove even silently suffering Mr Konwar into his bunk to escape, now all slept. It was blissful. And of course it had to end. The family woke and spread tiffin across their seat. I went off and stood at a door, pressing my face into the breeze and smelling the reedy countryside and savouring the rhythmical clacking of wheels over rail joints. I stayed there a long time.

Towards dusk we made another halt at an obscure station, Kumedpur Junction. It was too small to appear on any map I carried. A convoy of cyclists, each weighed down by two sacks of potatoes apiece, struggled along a track towards the station. They were ultimately overtaken by a boy, sitting on a bullock, who led another by a rope. Behind the station grew rectangles of jute, three metres of stalk and a token tuft of leaves on top, which burst upwards and outwards, like chefs' hats. Near our coach, goats feasted in a rice field, while in the distance labourers were engaged in loading jute fibre on to bullock-carts. And lastly, at a tea stall sat a knot of old men, inert as temple deities, while boys kicked a ball about a stubbly field.

It was a singularly unchanged and, one was almost tempted to say, Arcadian existence (*almost* tempted, because the lot of the jute farmer has historically been one of extreme exploitation by landowner and jute factory owner). The pace of life was determined by the bullock-cart or, if one was the impatient type, by the bicycle, which was the only remotely modern contraption in the whole scene. There was, however, one giveaway: a hammer-and-sickle emblem of the state's communist party daubed in red on a wall. Once to be found everywhere in West Bengal during the party's heyday in the 1970s, the symbol was now a much less frequent sight. Bengalis are very alert and intelligent, but they are also capable of being intensely dogmatic and argumentative. Perhaps in politics at least, their intelligence has conquered their dogmatism.

❂

A low grey sky and the rice fields of Uttar Pradesh, India's most populous state, greeted me next morning. Masood, dapper as ever in his maroon jacket, knew our preference by now and, unasked, delivered tea and omelettes. Mr Konwar and I ate alone, the family having vanished in the night. Out on the fertile Gangetic plain, kilometre after kilometre of lush green rice shimmered before my eyes. The hugeness of the scene was daunting and scarcely changed all morning: some fields of sugar cane, a few boys fishing beside ponds who flicked their bamboo rods to and fro with all the expertise of fly-fishermen, a big Muslim burial ground with an imposing pale blue mausoleum in the shape of a mosque, six tractors – the first sign of farm mechanisation I'd seen – queuing at a rail crossing.

When a Rajdhani Express rocketed past us I rued aloud not having got down at Guwahati to catch the high-speed service, but Mr Konwar said bluntly, 'Rajdhani services are full of business types. This train is the real India.'

Even so, I was weary of the Brahmaputra Mail and when we pulled into Moghulsarai Station I decided on impulse to get off for Varanasi. Mr Konwar was disappointed. He hoped we might catch up in Allahabad where I had intended to stop. After a hurried farewell I watched the Brahmaputra Mail move off down the line.

Very conveniently, the Varanasi Shuttle was about to go in twenty minutes. It was a local train and since no one was going very far, there was only third class. I stowed my rucksack under a slatted wooden seat and before long we were on our way.

In forty minutes I could see Varanasi Station, its contours mimicking a Hindu temple with its elaborate curving towers. There was even a cow obstructing the reservations counter, these revered animals having learnt how to climb the building's steepest steps. All this was no coincidence: the station reflects the holy status of Varanasi, which is the religious capital of the country and one of the seven sacred cities of the Hindus. Every Hindu wishes to be cremated at the city's burning ghats beside the Ganges. And because of the belief that anyone, of whatever creed and no matter how great his or her misdeeds, who dies within its precincts will be transported straight to heaven, it has also become India's retirement capital.

But in India, it seems, sanctity goes hand in hand with filth. The holier the place, the dirtier, more bone-jarring and objectionable its streets. And Varanasi is a very old, cramped and twisting place, inhabited and condemned dwellings melding into a flawless continuum. It is claimed to be the oldest living city in the world; references to Benares and Kashi, as it is also known, occur in the ancient texts *Ramayana* and *Mahabharata*. The filthy sanctity extends to the holy Ganges itself, receptacle for a billion litres of raw sewage a day as well as any number of partially cremated bodies dumped into its waters.

A visit to the ghats where pilgrims ritually immerse themselves has long been an obligatory ritual for tourists. Dutifully I set off. The frequent sight of Muslim women enveloped in their black chadors brought home firmly to me that I was now in North India. One Muslim family on a bicycle-rickshaw especially caught my eye. The husband, hugely corpulent, immaculately attired and the soul of self-satisfaction, occupied four-fifths of the flimsy seat. His wife, a black shadow, occupied the balance, shoulders drawn in and eyes, when I happened to make contact with them, darting away. Their two young daughters sat on the floor of the rickshaw, twisted into whatever space they could find between their parents' feet.

Progress along the old quarter's crowded footpaths was so slow that I hailed a bicycle-rickshaw myself, but I soon vowed never to catch another. Perched precariously but commandingly on a bench seat, I watched the old man heave down with all his weight, first on one pedal then, shifting his weight, on the other pedal, his hands gripping the handlebars as he strained upwards to provide the necessary counter-balance to the downward thrust of his legs. Slowly and with sweat gathering on his brow and staining the back of his shirt, he gathered momentum, every bit of it hard earned, especially as the road surface was rough and potholed. Momentum achieved at such cost was not squandered. Like all the other bicycle-rickshaw riders, he was loath to apply his brakes, preferring to plough on through intersections and roundabouts. Somehow, and it was a miracle, everything went off smoothly; the rider, like other road users, gauging speed and distance accurately and achieving a collision-free merging of traffic. Overlaying everything was this tremendous jangling of bicycle bells and tooting of vehicle horns, a sort of mutual reassurance to all those participating in the mayhem. Even a hefty tip failed to assuage my guilt when I was deposited at the flight of stone steps descending to the Ganges.

One of Hinduism's charms is each believer's freedom to worship as he or she pleases, to pick and choose among the pantheon of gods and goddesses – who ultimately are mere manifestations of the eternal and uncreated Brahman – and to follow whatever path suits best, whether that of the wandering ascetic who has cast off all worldly ties, or the way of devotion to a personal god (bhakti-marga), or the way of knowledge: the practice of yoga and meditation (jnana-marga). Followers of all those paths to release from the cycle of reincarnation, what Hindus call moksa, could be seen about the ghats.

Up on a landing some yoga men stripped to loincloths were going vigorously about their postures like callisthenics champions. At the water's edge pilgrims disrobed for a ritual dunk. Among them was a group of elderly women, normally the height of modesty, who went under bare-breasted, fingers squeezing tight their nostrils to keep out that holy-but-oh-so-contaminated Ganges water. At another spot a priest squatted beneath a big tattered umbrella conducting a puja of great length and complexity. At intervals during his chanting he would pause to blow on a conch, which boomed out like a fog-horn over the water. At other times he would halt to read extracts from his collection of holy texts or to tinkle a little brass bell. The audience, all women, hung on his every utterance. But no matter what their path to moksa, all the out-of-towners took away with them a bottle or terracotta bowl of holy Ganga water.

No one took much notice of the tourists, Indian and foreign, who drifted by in hire boats clicking away with their cameras. A boat ride past the ghats was a more or less mandatory tourist trophy, like a gondola ride through Venice's canals, so I confined myself to walking. That did not stop the persistent ring in my ears of 'Boat, sir? Boat, sir? You take boat?' and 'Head massage? Postcard, sir?'

A devotee of Siva stomped determinedly past me, like a late commuter, only he was clutching an iron trident as long as a lance rather than a briefcase. He appeared anxious to be off. I wasn't far behind.

The Mahamagar Express was bound for Bombay, but I had no trouble getting a ticket on the spot to Allahabad, only three and a half hours down the line. The train rolled through the outer suburb of Kashi and onto a great iron bridge across the Ganges. From this vantage point, the city skyline with its temple spires, cupola-topped palaces, pagodas and minarets was a riot of pastels – duck-egg blue, yellow, pink, pale ochre – beside the chocolate-brown Ganges. As Varanasi shrank from sight I felt a deep sense of relief. The previous night had been long and sleepless. Varanasi is subject to frequent and prolonged power cuts, so most businesses have portable generators which growl away for hours on end during blackouts. The noise from so many petrol-powered engines going at once was shattering. The cacophony went on until almost dawn. And it had been hot as well as noisy: the wiring of my room's air cooler had been doctored to operate only on mains power so remained inoperative throughout the night.

The Varanasi Tourist Lodge where I stayed was the Indian public sector in microcosm; and that sector, even allowing for the deregulation and opening up of India's economy, remains huge. The employees of this Uttar Pradesh government undertaking, and there were many, lolled about drinking tea as the overhead fans, from which they seldom strayed far, fluttered the edges of hundreds of loose-leaf files that had piled up around them over the decades. The buildings were in a bad state, but with so many wages to meet, who had the money for refurbishment? Guests were an inconvenience. How I wished I had been able to recall Gandhi's thoughts on customer service and quote them to this indolent lot. The poster extolling those views had once been a common fixture in government offices. When I later sighted one it was, of course, much too late. 'A customer,' Gandhi had declared, 'is the most important person on the premises. He is not dependent on us. We are dependent on him. He is not an interruption to our work. He is the purpose of it. He is not an outsider on our business. He is part of it. We are not doing him a favour by serving him. He is doing us a favour by giving us an opportunity to do so.'

So much for the theory.

Because I had the flu I shrank readily into the air-conditioned refuge of my compartment. My throat and eyes stung from the dust, my head hurt from the noise. I drifted off and came to, shivering in the air-conditioning. The train rattled across the mighty Yamuna and we were at Allahabad Junction.

I walked north in search of a hotel through the city's Civil Lines, the spacious ordered district where the British chose to establish themselves away from what they regarded as the unsanitary chaos of the old quarter. Once synonymous with pleasant thoroughfares and municipal neatness, the area is now a less down-at-heel version of the old city. The broad verges have been appropriated for a hundred unintended uses: cows congregate there; bicycle-rickshaw riders doze there; hawkers flog everything from bananas to sunglasses there; mechanics repair scooters there. Everywhere are mounds of slimy rubbish, though the dappled shade of avenue trees is pleasant. The British bungalows, the picture theatres, the shops with their wood and frosted glass façades, the hotels and civic amenities wear a neglected face. They have weathered more than half a century of monsoons without a lick of paint or the attentions of a repairman. There is space, however, and that is the Civil Line's saving grace.

Hoisting her bag high on her shoulder Arjuna stepped aboard first and the boatman pushed off. A crowd of curious and bored onlookers and idle boatmen stood on the bank of the Yamuna watching us drift out into the current. Immediately we emerged out of the shadow of the massive stone-walled Moghul fort. A low grey haze ran from horizon to horizon, trapping all in a giant inverted basin of humidity. Both our faces were aglow with perspiration, though Arjuna, seated cross-legged at the bow, somehow remained immaculate in her teal salwar kameez.

She had seemed such an odd sight: petite, solitary, weighed down by her black overnight bag, standing at the muddy water's edge with her shoes in one hand, berating the assembled boatmen. But she could make no dent in their extortionate demands. Why not share the fare then?

Out to our left, a low grassy expanse on which water buffaloes grazed grew steadily nearer. This, the confluence of the Yamuna and Ganges, seemed to my non-believer's eyes an unremarkable spot. But to Hindus the junction, known as the Sangam, is a revered spot. At particularly auspicious times pilgrims in their millions crammed this sandy point. Today there were only a few hundred bathing beside a makeshift camp of corrugated sheeting and burlap. High overhead fluttered a dense thicket of pennants.

For his 200 rupees, the boatman, with scarcely a stroke of the oars, guided us towards this furthermost point. At the water's edge were the ritual bathers: the saffron-robed sadhus, the wild-eyed truth-seekers with their equally wild beards, the visitors from distant cities, the figures bent with age whose thoughts were more on the next life than on this one and the middle-aged husbands and wives engrossed in their prayers and submersions.

Anchored a little off from the camp were several dozen boats. Here other pilgrims were clambering into the water to erase their transgressions. Our boatman pulled up on the leeward side of this flotilla and Arjuna, an empty bottle at the ready, leaned over and filled it with brown murk.

'Here the *three* rivers are meeting,' she observed, feeling no need to explain the existence of the third river. Nor was any explanation needed. I knew of the mythical Saraswati, which is said to emerge from the earth to join the two visible flows and gives the Sangam its other name of Tribeni Ghat.

Arjuna unzipped her bag, stowed the bottle of precious water and withdrew five terracotta images of gods, one of which I made out as Ganesh. One at a time she let the statues slip from her hand into the water, moving her lips in silent prayer as each was swallowed up. I felt like a crass gatecrasher upon her private devotions. She made more offerings, dipped her fingers in the water and flicked droplets over herself. A few more prayers and it was over.

The boatman began the task of rowing us back. The boat was simple but very heavily built – I saw identical vessels carrying twenty or more passengers – and he made a course close to the shore where the current was weaker.

Arjuna now relaxed a little. She had come from Jabalpur in central Madhya Pradesh ('Famous for Marble Rocks. Have you been?') for a job interview with the Indian Administrative Service.

'The IAS?' I asked.

'Yes. Why are you asking?'

'Just a moment,' I said and flicked through my notebook for a line of graffiti I had copied down in Varanasi. The tone had been so restrained – and the words slapped so large over one of the ghat walls – that it was hard not to take notice.

'I saw this painted on a wall: *If IAS and IPS* [Indian Police Service] *do their duty selflessly only on their salary, the country will improve in a month.* Is that true?'

'It is true,' she answered without hesitation.

'How many are corrupt? Ten, twenty, fifty per cent?'

She shook her head and smiled at my foolishness. 'Ninety per cent.'

'That many. And you still want a job there?'

'Yes. Maybe the ten per cent can make a difference.'

I thought about that a moment. It didn't square with my experience.

'I suppose the honest ones don't get promotions so quickly?'

Arjuna nodded.

I asked if India's elite administrative cadre had job reservations for the scheduled castes, the untouchables and others who, from a constitutional point of view, were deemed to be downtrodden. The answer was yes, but Arjuna did not qualify. She would have to succeed on merit alone.

'Is that galling?'

'Of course. Everyone knows reservation system is not working. So many inexperienced staff must be given jobs because they have scheduled status. Efficiency is down. But it is getting votes.'

More and more, it seemed to me, Mr Mehta's grim picture of public morality was being borne out.

Soon the bow made a squelching sound in the mud; Akbar's fort loomed over us once more. The boatman demanded a tip which, feeling too hot to argue, I paid. Pious duty, like everything else, had its price.

Conductor, Himalayan Queen.

The Himalayan Queen
to Simla

THE PRAYAG RAJ EXPRESS left Allahabad that evening.* I turned in straightaway and woke as Ghaziabad slipped by, a motley assortment of jammed-together brick houses and sleeping forms on rooftop charpoys. Then it was across the Yamuna River, whose waters were so muddy – as brown and rich as cocoa – that they drew comment from passengers, and we began our entry into Delhi.

I pointed to a large onion-domed building and said to the man across from me, 'What is that?'

'That old fort?'

'Yes,'

'It is called Old Fort.'

He pointed to a modern-looking complex: 'That is where Asian

---

* The train's name honours the Aryans who inhabited an ancient city known as Prayag built on the site of present-day Allahabad, which Hindus call Prag, place of sacrifice. The merit attained by giving alms to Brahmans is said to be enhanced one thousand-fold if the gift is made there.

Games were held ... and over there is Supreme Court of India, highest court in the country, where the Chief Justice is sitting.'

More beautiful domes filled the skyline. Beneath us, broad tree-lined avenues, all empty at this early hour, criss-crossed our path.

'Here on business?' I enquired.

'No, I am Railways law officer. I am here to plead a case in Supreme Court.'

'Indian Railways is very efficient, I am told. In other government departments corruption is rife.'

'Indeed sir, we are very efficient. There is none of that hanky-panky with Railways. But you are right, corruption is everywhere. That is why the courts are so important – there is no corruption there. People have a place to go for redress. If courts were tainted by corruption there would be civil war.'

'Civil war? They are very strong words.'

But he said nothing, contenting himself with that endearingly Indian gesture, the sideways wobble of the head; he stuck by his assertion.

'And the case you're pleading now?'

'A contractor matter, many crores of rupees ... it has been going on for three years.'

So, I thought to myself, it was just getting going.

❋

The Madras Hotel in Connaught Place, New Delhi's circular-shaped downtown, is where South Indians can go to feel at home. The menu contains all their familiar fare: idlis (rice dumplings), wadas (deep-fried lentil rings), dosas (lentil and rice pancakes), uttapams (another freshly prepared snack like dosas), puris (fried puffed flour), upma (a pilaf-like dish of semolina) and thali (a medley of dishes served with rice on a round stainless steel tray). Everything is dunked in thin fiery sauces, then flung in the mouth. To finish off, there is frothy sweet coffee (or tea if you must), served in a glass.

The hotel opened its doors in 1935 and I doubt much has changed, certainly not since I first visited almost two decades ago.

There is still a mushy sameness about the food. It simmers in outsized aluminium pots; and in the gloom of that same smoke-blackened kitchen a scullery hand can invariably be observed before a mountain of spuds and red onions. The eating halls are as well scrubbed and crisply painted as ever; the marble-topped tables and bench seats are still there; the family room still operates in one corner ('Gents allowed along with ladies only'); and the round-shouldered cashier may well be the same man I last saw behind the desk, since Indians are job-for-lifers. It is devoid of furnishings, severe almost, but it is clean. It is, in fact, how all India could conceivably be – simple but clean. In Poona I had walked around the grounds of the National Institute of Naturopathy. They were a delight. There was no litter, only care and neatness and calm. Potted plants edged the pathways, and big trees shaded the lawns. At the doorway of the doctors' reception, visitors respectfully removed their shoes. I stopped a woman who was escorting her elderly mother to an appointment. 'This is beautiful,' I said. 'Why can't all India be like this?'

She laughed. 'It is population, sir. There are so many of us. Imagine if a billion people came to stay at your house. With the best of intentions it would still be a mess.'

'Yes,' I laughed back, 'I think you're right.'

But I kept rolling that idea around in my head. What did it really mean? That there are so many people that degradation was unavoidable? That individual responsibility was futile? That concern for the environment was a sentimental Western luxury because Indians were too preoccupied with merely surviving? Or that the physical world was an illusion and escape from reincarnation was the only meaningful goal? The noise of traffic down below in Connaught Place was tremendous: you almost had to shout your order to the waiters. That fantastic hubbub of tooting horns and screeching brakes and roaring engines was perhaps India's answer to all my silly introspections: The slumbering elephant had arisen and was now marching inexorably into the modern world.

✵

Dawn broke over the city as the Himalayan Queen pulled out of New Delhi Station. All along the line, the encampment dwellers were rousing themselves from their charpoys, stretching and scratching themselves and thinking about breakfast; a few had got fires going. It seemed a wretched existence, living among rubbish in dwellings made of rubble and rags. Within half an hour we were in something resembling suburbs: a factory here, a water treatment plant there. I looked up and quite suddenly it was all gone – there were only fields and trees half lost in mist.

My chair-car coach had seats arranged like those on a plane. The few occupants were mostly holidaymakers bound, like me, for Simla. Two guards detailed to security sat down opposite me and promptly fell asleep, their weapons cradled between their legs.

Panipat, on the plains of Haryana state, loomed out of the fog and it instantly struck me as a contender for the title of India's ugliest and filthiest city. My map labelled it, rather enticingly, as 'Historic Town, Mosque, Tombs', but my guidebooks informed me it was reputedly the most fly-infested place in the country.* At this unremarkable spot three battles took place that determined the history of northern India. One, in 1526 between Babur and Ibrahim Lodi, King of Delhi, established Moghul rule in the north of India; the second, in 1556, shattered the Pathan dynasty called the Sur, founded by Sher Shah; and the third, in 1761, crushed the strength of the Mahrattas (in present-day Maharashtra) and ended in terrible slaughter.

The rain was now falling continuously, making the mud tracks momentarily smooth and marble-like. The rivers, all in spate, were thick and red as sambar. With each kilometre northwards, the countryside became more thickly wooded until the expansive views were lost among rows of trees planted as windbreaks.

We made a lengthy halt at the important rail junction of Ambala,

---

* By tradition the flies are attributed to the saint Abu Ali Kalandar who is buried in Panipat. When the inhabitants complained he had not done a sufficiently thorough job in ridding the town of flies, he is supposed to have rewarded their ungratefulness by multiplying the flies a thousand-fold.

then we were off again, into the rain. The water was everywhere, turning the red earth of low-lying areas into enormous pools of tomato soup. At a truck depot men waded knee-deep in water around their vehicles.

The sun returned as we pulled into Chandigarh. It was still out when we left, speeding along the last stage to Kalka, where the familiar rhythm of the broad-gauge system would end and everyone would have to change to a narrow-gauge train for the climb up to Simla. Even so, the route soon began to climb imperceptibly through trees and scrub, the Himalayan foothills drawing closer until hills surrounded us on three sides. We crested a rise as the air-conditioning was turned off. My ears popped. On we climbed, my anticipation rising with the altitude.

At 11.30 am we pulled into Kalka Station. Goats nibbled tufts of grass along the tracks, oblivious to the pelting rain. Everyone filed around the corner to the waiting narrow-gauge train. The rain crashed violently on the tin-roofed platform shelters, like volleys of bullets. The din was so great I could barely hear the steady rumble of the locomotive's diesel engine even though I stood right beside it.

Kalka marks the transition from plains to mountains, and the carriages demonstrate that point unmistakably: the roomy chair-car from Delhi makes way for low, square carriages designed for about twenty or so passengers. I felt a stirring of excitement at the prospect of boarding the little blue carriages, glistening wet in the dull light. It might have looked like a plaything, but the Simla train had a real job to do. For five hours it would haul us up through the Shivalik Range to a height of 2,075 metres, a 95.5-kilometre journey through one hundred and two tunnels (not one hundred and three as the markings might indicate because tunnel forty-six does not exist). For such intricacies I could thank the overhead information board, which further informed me there were 845 bridges and 919 curves, that the longest tunnel, at Barog, was 1,143.6 metres and that the line was finished in 1903. It did not, however, mention that this mammoth three-year struggle by engineers and coolies against gravity and common sense had but a single prosaic purpose: to make British

India's rulers more comfortable on the annual journey to their hot-weather capital.

Darting from my shelter, I boarded a few minutes before the loco, with eight carriages in tow, pulled out into the full fury of the rain. Everyone immediately clamped the windows tight so that they fogged up and turned the compartment into a steam-bath before we'd gone 100 metres. I wiped my pane clear but there was only driving rain to see. In minutes, though, I could make out the roofs of Kalka Station well below us.

'So bland,' said a podgy English backpacker a few seats down, holding up his empty Railways tinfoil tray to no one in particular. He wiped his mouth with the back of his hand and turned to a French couple opposite him: 'Tailored to British taste, I think.' The pair smiled back politely.

We passed through several tunnels, each clearly numbered at the entrance and dripping condensation all the way through. The stickiness inside the carriage was considerable but I discovered that, since I was facing downhill, I could open the window without getting wet. And what a glorious view waited below. For all our zigzagging up the steeply inclined hills, and the reversing on switchbacks through thick woods, we seemed to have gained little altitude. But now I could see that this was not so. Sheer below us, a river curving through a valley had diminished to a loose braid of red streaks. Mist drifted down over the valley peaks. In a blink, that scene vanished, to be replaced by the snaking grey macadam of Old Cart Road, the motor route to Simla. And then that, too, was gone, lost as we entered a forest of bamboo in which monkeys screeched and leapt away or watched us unblinkingly. The mist sank round us and we were back in the obscurity of drizzle and trees.

But always there was the reassuring *clunk-a-clunk-a-clunk* as the wheels beat time over the joints, carrying us upwards at a steady 25 kilometres an hour. And whenever we entered a tunnel, there was the reverberating roar of the locomotive's engine and then its aftermath, a lungful of diesel fumes.

Round and round we curled, as though we must surely catch up with our own tail; and certainly the curve of the line was enough for me to see children in the rearmost carriages poking their heads out the window for a better view or simply to delight in the breeze buffeting their faces. This service, almost uniquely among Indian trains, had no window bars.

The English backpacker, who reminded me of a gaudy smiling porcelain Buddha, had a view on everything, and in such a small coach it was impossible not to hear about the advantages of old SLR cameras, purdah in Pakistan, working holidays in the south of France, FA Cup soccer … The poor Frenchwoman, nearest to him, had long since crossed her threshold for punishment and switched off. 'There's no comparison between French and English food,' I heard him resume. 'English food is what you eat at footy matches: sausages, drinks in plastic cups, that sort of thing.'

The Frenchwoman affected to show interest. Her boyfriend looked distractedly out the window. 'You have a favourite soccer team? You must support your home team, don't you think? You have a team in Montpelier?'

We lurched around a steep slope and onto a curving stone bridge. Two more gallery bridges were in sight beneath us, piled rows of masonry arches, each row successively a little longer than the one beneath so as to span the required distance. They were as gracious as the Roman aqueducts they resembled. That moment made me realise what a colossal undertaking this line was, to forge a rail route up into the foothills of the earth's mightiest mountain chain.

'When I was in Cambodia last month …' said the Buddha, breaking into my thoughts. I tried to tune him out but he came back. '… I was in Bangkok and had four hours to spare and I thought, "What will I do?" So I got on the Internet and ….Hey! Look, blue sky out there … and anyway, I got on the Internet and looked up the Manchester website. Sad really, but it used up four hours ….'

We came to a halt at a tiny station. 'I just can't bring myself to throw it away,' he said of the cold roti in his Railways lunch and shoved it in his mouth. Then, dabbing his perspiring face with his scarf, he got down and returned with two sandwiches.

The station was one of eighteen en route, each tempting enough to get off at – picturesque, small, tidy, a complicated verandah, a well-tended flowerbed, the forested hillside sloping away dramatically just beyond the line and rising just as marvellously behind the station buildings. But there were no retiring rooms and nothing to do beyond admire the view. This example had a long, low stone building with a steep-pitched roof. Three boys dashed off, at their father's instruction, to pee behind one of its walls. A group of soldiers detrained, lugging their big metal trunks, and we chugged on.

At 2.30 pm we emerged out of the dankness of the line's longest tunnel and made a refreshment halt at Barog Station. There was a rush on the vegetable cutlets. The Buddha couldn't help himself and bought three when a kiosk employee passed by his window with a tray of them. The climbing resumed. The Buddha reached into his pack, a cumbrous thing that blocked the aisle, and withdrew a tourist brochure on Ladakh which he began to read – aloud, of course. God help the Ladakhis, I thought.

When we slowed at Shogi Station at 4.30 pm I stood at the door, and it was there that I caught my first glimpse of Simla: the rusty tin roofs of the lower bazaar shops spilling down the slopes from the main ridge. The ridge's best-known landmarks – 'a Gothic church, a baronial castle and a Victorian country manor' – were sunk in cloud. Soon we, too, were swallowed by a shifting vaporous greyness. It swirled about the tracks as shafts of sunlight broke through intermittently. Then snippets of Simla flickered between the deodars, like a reel of failing cinema film: old bungalows with names like Forest View and Sevenoaks; the flights of steep concrete steps that act as the town's roads; strolling holidaymakers with their cravats and jumpers, delighting in the unaccustomed cold; and soft-soled Nepalese and Tibetan porters bent over with supplies and sacks of produce.

A signalman holding a staff-mounted lantern and blowing a whistle cleared us through pretty Summer Hill Station with its Parcel Godown and Retiring Rooms. We were nearing Simla's doorstep. A man with a consignment of soap bars was the first to the door, and the moment we stopped he scuttled into the dusk. I craned my neck to take in the view up the slopes. It did not look like a destination worthy of the train. I set off up a pathway towards The Mall, crunching on pine needles and giving a wide berth to the monkeys that cast hungry looks in the direction of my pockets.

✱

'There are only three questions you need to answer in this life,' declared Colonel Chopra. 'Where am I coming from? What am I doing here? And where am I going?'

He paused to size me up. I must have passed muster because he continued. 'We are all here on a search, you know. What have you come to India in search of?'

'Nothing. Believe me, nothing.'

He appeared unruffled: Indian logic would somehow demolish that minor roadblock. 'You are interested in Indology?'

'Indology?'

'Yes, study of Indian history and philosophy.'

'I've come to India, so yes, I suppose I am.'

'Good, good. Then back to my three questions. Do you have the answers to any of them?'

'No. Do you?'

'For many years, no. Where do I come from? Who knows. Your mother does not know. Her womb is but the instrument of your birth. Does she apply science or mathematics to your coming into the world? No. I am retired army, but for many years I have been searching. First one area but without satisfaction, so I move on, begin my search somewhere else. But always discarding. Since an early age – before the army – I was restless, searching.'

'And now?'

'And now,' said the colonel, his voice suffused with bliss and his arms stretched wide and high in a glorious release, like a soaring bird, 'now I have the answers to the first two. The third, the hardest one, is still before me.'

'Is that why you come to Simla? To this place?' (We had just been praising the quiet of the castle-like YMCA where we were both staying and on whose balcony we now stood, within view of The Mall and its promenading vacationers.)

'Yes and no. It is peaceful, I come here for a few days at a time.' He looked out towards the deodar-covered hills on the far side of the valley. 'I could go to my retirement place over there ....'

'You have your own place here in Simla?'

'No, a place for retired army people. I come here to make myself walk up and down all these steep steps in Shimla. It keeps this in shape' – his hands ran over his somewhat pear-shaped body – 'so I can continue my search for the answer to question number three. As I am sure you know, if you are not working your body it gets sick and you die. I do not want to die until I have that answer.'

He seemed in little danger of an early demise, for I had seen him walking about the town full of vigour and determination, his homespun shawl tossed about his shoulders.

'If I don't know where I am going I will come back and back and back until I do. So I must keep this instrument of mine fit long enough to find answer number three.'

'Colonel Chopra,' I said, 'it has been a pleasure meeting you.'

He took hold of my arm and locked his heavy-lidded eyes on me. 'But I have not told you everything. My guru, he helped me to see these answers. That was thirteen years ago. Now I am sixty-five. He showed me that I had been born in Shimla once before, but had died as a ten-year-old boy. I know just the spot. My sister pushed me. It was just a prank, you know, like this (and he gave me a playful push), but over the bank I went. My guru put a brain picture of the accident inside my head ...'

'You mean you had a visualisation? A mental recreation?'

'No, I am meaning a brain picture. I saw it all happen.' He sighed. 'But that is in the past. That is where I came from. I do not talk of such matters now. Where am I going? I must find out so I do not come back.'

'And what happens when you don't come back?'

'Then,' he said, his eyes lifting towards the sky (and it was just the right sort of sky for his purposes – the late-morning sun had burst through a gap in the clouds and mist lingered in long delicate wisps, like unravelled candyfloss around the rusty rooftops), 'then I shall achieve moksa, merging with Universal One.'

'And that would be good? An end to human existence?'

'Yes, to achieve nothingness.'

Colonel Chopra could have passed for anybody's favourite grandfather, a sweet old man in the twilight of his life. But it was an illusion. He was engaged in a dramatic, life-and-death struggle, but one with an ironic twist: failure meant life, success meant extinction.

❂

Simla's Indian Coffee House, with its lumpy vinyl couches and dark recesses, is every bit an old man's club. The fusty atmosphere suited me just fine, even if the menu didn't, and I took a leisurely breakfast before strolling along The Mall with all its variegated examples of High Victorian architecture – everything from cathedral to mansion to hotel to a government building described by Edwin Lutyens, co-designer of New Delhi, as 'beyond the beyond' for the vulgarity and jumble of forms employed – but all displaying the extravagance made possible by a limitless supply of cheap labour. This summer residence of the Viceroy of India and his army of administrators had its share of detractors. Kipling called it the abode of the little tin gods.

The train ride up had been so exhilarating that it was hard to envisage the destination outshining the journey. But Simla's charms soon exerted themselves on me: the wondrous views of the hills, banks and banks of them rising in pleats towards the sky and containing every gradation of blue and green, from viridian, emerald and greengage to cobalt blue, sky-blue and delicate pastels, according to where you cared to cast an eye; the crisp air scented with pine resin; the absence of hooting vehicles (traffic is banned on The Mall); the respite from the heat and crowds of the plains; the smell, drifting on the cold dusk air, of corn-cobs crisping on charcoal embers; and the almost genteel manners of the town's residents, who regarded those from the plains as somehow of doubtful moral temperament.

Colonel Singh was, I felt sure, a holder of such views. Correct form was second nature to him. He was president of Simla's Amateur Dramatic Club, which operated out of the Gaiety Theatre and was, so he informed me, the oldest of its type in the country. At first he affected a sniffling condescension to my questions.

'Yes, yes, ADS was established in 1886,' he said, twirling a pen on the his distractedly. 'Before that time, ADS members used to perform in hotels in town … all long demolished now, of course.'

A club volunteer entered with correspondence to sign, and she appeared almost to tremble in his presence. He dashed off a few signatures and resumed: 'Gaiety Theatre, it was five storeys originally, did you know? But the Britishers, they weren't terribly good engineers. The whole structure was so heavy that seven years later they had to demolish the top three floors. Drainage problems there are, too. Now ADS has procured funds for its restoration. One hundred and sixteen years old it is, you know. An exact replica of the Royal Albert Hall, in miniature, naturally. Come, I will show you around.'

He led me out of his office, down a corridor and onto the stage. I sniffed the air. 'You do have seepage problems. I can smell the mildew.'

'Yes, yes,' he said, the impatient mutter back as he strolled about the empty stage, his pen held in both hands behind his back, like a baton. 'You see, there are many rooms dug into the hillside – even a tunnel so the Viceroy could make a secret escape in the event of an attack on his personage.'

Whether the Gaiety Theatre was a faithful replica of the Royal Albert Hall I could not say. The gilding was now tatty and the pink muslin curtain of the Viceroy and Commander-in-Chief's box was long gone, yet there was a cosy feeling to this little hill station venue, where many a visitor from the plains had passed an evening in innocent pleasure.

❂

Few train stations can have as precarious a hold on the world as Simla's. It clasps the side of a wooded slope, a rusty tin prow projecting out among the firs. The narrow building curves around the hill like a sickle moon, and the arc is so severe that within a few dozen paces of strolling off along the platform the departure point is out of sight. But it is very quiet and deserted between arrivals and departures. It is remarkable in another way, too: there are no cows or encampments of squatters or ragged beggar children, just the clear air and bright hills. The outlook is captivating and not easy to leave.

But at mid-morning the Kalka train pulled out, and I was aboard. I had a carriage almost to myself. A cool wind blew through the windows and clouds drifted among the trees. The train rattled through mossy tunnels, past washing drying on embankments and through the same pretty stations, all scrubbed clean and empty except for the signalman who waved us through with his fluttering green flag. Even going downhill we never made much speed, and moths with gunny- brown wings fluttered in and out of the windows.

I dozed and woke as we curled through Solan Brewery, erected first by a British firm that discovered good spring water in the hills, so the line must cut between its buildings. Two card games were in progress on the platform, a dozen men in each circle. To nip in the bud any thought of pay rises or strikes, a sign by the brewery gates cautioned: 'It is not the employer who pays the workers' wages but the product that does'. I dozed between stops, then opened my eyes as we tottered around a series of corners that dropped away to Kalka Station. More sharp corners and we were on level ground again. And back in the heat.

Forty minutes later the Himalayan Queen was taking me south, but only as far as Chandigarh, 24 kilometres away. Chandigarh is the capital of Haryana and Punjab states and home to almost a million people, though you'd never guess it because it is so spread out. Conceived by Swiss architect Le Corbusier and built by Indian hands in the 1950s, this planned city could be small-town America: the long, tree-lined avenues, empty much of the time, perfect for cruising, one elbow out the window while holding the steering-wheel absent-mindedly with your free hand; the succession of roundabouts sweeping enough that the speedometer needle need never budge off

50 kilometres per hour; and the low, comfortable houses set back behind absurdly broad verges and obscured from prying eyes by trees and boundary walls. But instead of corner milk bars, there are chai stalls, the usual improvised medley of tarpaulin, stools and kerosene cooker teetering on bricks and wood cast-offs; and the customers are not pigtailed teenagers but wizened men smoking cheroots.

The sixty-one sectors, or super-blocks, of Chandigarh look indistinguishable from one another – I never saw so many Indian motorists asking directions of passers-by – and go on without apparent end. The city's rickshaw-wallahs must be the busiest in India because walking, and even cycling for that matter, are all but out of the question: the distances are too great.

Sector One, on the north-east perimeter, houses the Secretariat and Vidhan Sabha, or legislative assembly. These are grandly executed monstrosities of concrete and reinforced steel with curiously upswept roofs. Inside, I found room after room jammed with clerks seated at battered wooden desks, surrounded by filing cabinets and sheaves of yellowing files accumulating on every flat surface, like some slow-growing accretion on a seabed. As I walked along the corridors, the clanging of ancient typewriters forming an intermittent counterpoint to the chatter of voices, it seemed to me that the city's residents had done what they could to adapt to this high-minded experiment in town planning, but it was too premeditated, too inorganic ever to be made fully Indian.

One night in Chandigarh was enough. Next day I took a rickshaw to the railway station, which is in the countryside, 8 kilometres from the city centre, too far to attract the usual hordes of beggars and camp-followers. Crows squawked relentlessly in the heat. I took up a bench at the farthest end of a platform to catch a faint cross-breeze. At a drinking-water dispenser a man filled a bucket and took a shower, while three mendicants, skinny as rakes, scrubbed cooking pots – their only worldly possessions apart from a staff, shoulder bag and the rags they stood in.

I had two hours to kill so I bought a paper. It carried a prominent report on the granting of bail to former Punjab minister Sohan Singh

Thandal, who had been detained for nine months over a charge by the state's Orwellian-sounding Vigilance Bureau of 'having assets disproportionate to known sources of income'. Translation: corruption. It was a charge to be found over and over in the press; so much so that it seemed almost to be a rite of passage among parliamentarians and high officials. MPs at state level were among the most blatant self-servers. Many candidly admitted to changing their party allegiance according to who could provide the biggest inducement of bribes and privileges.

But what really caught my eye was a story about the conversion of some of India's tribal people to Christianity. The missionaries' work was upsetting some Hindus. Did a country of so many religions need the proselytising Christian, the paper asked? In answer it quoted C. F. Andrews, the missionary who became a devotee of Mahatma Gandhi. Andrews had this to say about his missionary experience in India: 'I have found Christ in the faces of those whom I have met: Hindus, Musalmans, Sikhs – and I have watched the Christ-like spirit of their lives. It has humbled me to the dust sometimes with shame to think that I came out to convert such people – "to make", as Christ has said, one proselyte. Religion must come from the heart and be shown in purity of life. A mere profession of a creed is of no value at all.'

❂

At 3.30 pm the Himalayan Queen whisked me down the line to Ambala and there the waiting resumed. Ambala Cantonment Station's main platform was jammed with luggage over which the owners sprawled to ward off thieves. The station buildings, some partly demolished, were the most squalid I'd stepped into. Rats scurried about the corners of the first-class waiting room chewing on food scraps, though a hard-faced matron still guarded the door checking tickets for right of admission.

At dusk starlings in their thousands descended to make the platform roofs their temporary home, and the racket drowned out the blaring arrival and departure announcements. Later, they all flew off as one body and I could enjoy the beautiful still evening, with its thin high cloud cover. An Amritsar–Delhi service passed through, leaving the platform momentarily clear of passengers. I stood on the platform's edge, brushing my teeth and thinking, more than a little fondly, about the routines and comforts of home.

Much later the Hemkunt Express collected me as it made its night march north and west towards Jammu, winter capital of Jammu and Kashmir state and the northernmost terminus in the Indian network. My two fellow passengers – like most of those aboard, they told me – were pilgrims returning from a ceremonial dip at Haridwar, a sacred spot where the Ganges emerges from the Himalayas. Kashmir cropped up soon enough. The younger one, with a thick mop of wavy hair, said Pakistan's hand was behind the trouble there, as it was in the Punjab during the separatist violence of the 1980s. Pakistan's army and the mullahs ran the country, he said, and its economy had fallen far behind India's.

'When they are not fighting us, they are fighting each other: Shia against Sunni, Mohajir against Sindhi … everyone is carrying arms – and using them too in disputes! You must be careful, sir, especially in Karachi. And Peshawar also.'

Our coach was just three from the front, and the engine driver had his finger on the horn all night long, the mournful repetitive tooting chasing off every approach of sleep.

Jammu Tawi Station at six o'clock was grey and muggy. I booked a retiring room and took a shower. Patrolling soldiers were everywhere, manning sandbagged emplacements on the platforms and standing at strategic places about the station.

The two employees at the station's tourist office were incredulous I was not venturing on to Kashmir, or at least to the summer capital Srinagar.

'Beautiful lake, beautiful houseboats, lovely treks – second Switzerland they are calling it,' said the older of the pair.

'I don't want to get blown up by a car bomb,' I replied. One had gone off only that week, killing seven and injuring thirty-seven.

'No problem, no problem. Militants are not after foreigners.'

Maybe not, I thought, but car bombs don't discriminate.

'Where do you want to go?' asked the other, a slim, angular young man with a fair complexion.

'To Kanyakumari.'

That was at the very southern tip of India, but neither raised an eyebrow.

'How long you stay in Jammu?'

'One day.'

'But there is so much to see: Raghunath Temple, Ranbireshwar Temple, Maha Maya Temple ... many temples ... Jammu is city of temples.'

But I had come to Jammu to catch a train, the longest in India, and because it left only weekly I could spare no more than a day. Nevertheless I went for a look around their city. New Jammu, on one side of the Tawi River, is the usual cantonment set-up. Old Jammu, on the other side, is the usual maze of congested narrow streets; a lot of noise and very hot. The patrolling soldiers were everywhere here, too; on every corner, roundabout and bus-stand, outside every public building and temple, whistling at any loitering person or stationary motorist to get a move along. Their presence created an atmosphere of unrelieved tension. Old Jammu's one distinguishing feature was its proliferation of arms and ammunition shops, almost all Sikh-owned enterprises.

I returned to the station where my train was scheduled to leave at 11.15 that evening. It teemed with soldiers barking orders at one another and hauling kitbags from trucks and buses. Next to all that purposefulness, my wanderings seemed an indulgence. I felt uncomfortable on another score, too: the trains were one of the Kashmiri militants' targets. A month later they detonated a bomb aboard an express leaving the station. Two months after that the station itself was attacked. When the smoke had settled, five soldiers and two terrorists lay dead and fifteen others were injured from gunshot and grenade wounds.

Fishermen's boats, Kanyakumari.

The Himsagar Express
to Kanyakumari

ONE NIGHT IN AN ORDINARY coach dispelled all doubt that air-conditioned class was somehow cheating. As the Himsagar Express had lumbered through the night every sound seemed to be amplified and transmitted to just beneath my pillow: the rattle of metal marauder-proof windows in their frames, the slamming of doors, the rattle and bump of rolling stock, the reverberating roar as we crossed a metal bridge, the heavy-footed passage of strangers along the corridor and the hiss of dusty wind through gaps in the windows. A guilty feeling had been niggling at me – maybe I was missing the 'real' India – so in Jammu I booked a non-air-conditioned ticket. It was first class but shabby and neglected because such coaches are being phased out; they are, in the view of Indian Railways' accountants, too spacious, accommodating just twenty-six passengers, and don't pay their way.

By the morning I had decided a good sleep was no luxury at all, though now some of the previous night's disadvantages became advantages: the noisy ceiling fans produced a pleasant swirl of fresh air and the windows admitted the smells and sounds of the outside world – the dull thump of a diesel pump out in a field and the smell of cow-dung smoke and spices.

But otherwise it was the usual coves aboard a train; in this morning's case a military inspector, a young Tamil whose nose was buried in newspapers and magazines from the moment of boarding and above him a tall, thin reclusive man who remained in his bunk and never uttered a word to anyone. While we gave our breakfast orders to the bearer, he sat stooped over, sniffing the air nervously like a mouse, as he consumed something brought from home. Eating was an especially furtive affair. He would reach into a plastic bag and his fingers would emerge wrapped around some wholly concealed morsel; the head would lower, the hand would come up and in the secret assignation between fingers and mouth the morsel would change places.

Inspector Vyavaharik, an officer of the Border Security Force, was himself rather self-contained. About all I could glean from him was that he was returning home on leave from his posting in Kashmir, his previous posting having been Shillong in Assam.

'You are not wasting your time,' he said at one point, observing me scribble in my notebook.

'Just jotting down some thoughts,' I replied, reluctant to inform him of my true subject matter.

Our tea and omelettes arrived as we pulled into Dhuri Junction, a beautiful little station with flowering creepers across its arches. A Sikh guard twirled his carefully cultivated moustache to peaks of perfection. Most of the men about the platform were wearing turbans, since we were in the Sikhs' home state of the Punjab. The place seemed to be bursting with fertility; growing on the surrounding plains were vegetables, pulses, rice, wheat, sugar cane, mustard and lots more besides. When we got going again, I spotted a cyclist advancing through this ocean of greenness: with his lower half obscured he appeared to coast along effortlessly, like a galleon before a following breeze. The domes of gurdwaras, Sikh temples, glinted in the sunlight, looking from afar as smooth as fine bone china.

The Punjab deserved its title of the granary of India. Its prosperity was partly explained by a degree of mechanisation I was to find nowhere else: modern harvesters rolled across the fields. Good irrigation also contributed: the Punjab's ancient name was Land of Five Rivers. But the main reason was the Sikhs' hard work and progressive thinking.

The company in my carriage was hardly thrilling so I went off in search of the conductor, working my way along the second-class compartments. These were jammed with people, four or five to a seat, playing cards or reading or dozing. Bony elbows and feet protruded from the fixed wooden bunks, and the aisles were blocked by the bedrolls and trunks of soldiers in transit to new postings. A beggar sang a plaintive tune as he played a country-made instrument resembling a violin. A string of cymbals along its neck clashed in a rough beat as he played, making the whole effect more Anatolian than Indian. In the vestibules, women clutching veils between their teeth and holding babies on their hips queued in the puddles outside the toilet doors.

The service's one air-conditioned coach was little more than one-third full. The inspector upgraded my ticket without any trouble and assigned me a berth, evicting a squatter as he did so.

The plains of North India rolled on and on as we crossed back into Haryana state. It was a familiar landscape: buffaloes around a shrinking pond; dusty brick houses three storeys high but each not taking up more than forty paces square of the earth's surface; a dozen old men seated beneath a banyan tree; some young men gathered admiringly around someone's gleaming new motorcycle; the boy on a dirt lane flicking a bicycle tyre along with a stick; a vendor pushing his cartload of bananas; a man having a shit behind a wall; the slow advance of a bullock-cart on disintegrating macadam; a handful of women bent over harvesting a crop; another group slapping cow-pats on a wall to dry ... and always the eternal plains and the grey clouds gathering overhead.

At three o'clock we struck Delhi's outskirts, a rather forbidding succession of shanty towns, polluted streams, lorry parks and laundry-festooned apartment blocks. The line wound through an old district. The brick walls abutting the line resembled the fruits of an archaeological excavation, each horizontal band slightly different from the one above and below it, as if corresponding to a distinct period in the city's fortunes.

At New Delhi Station we appeared to lose more passengers than we gained. And it was the same at south Delhi's Hazrat Nizamuddin Station, named in honour of the Muslim saint Nizam-ud-din, whose tomb was a stone's throw away. Mr M. Pitchai, the A/C mechanic, whose sole job was to monitor the dials of the air-conditioning unit in the vestibule, told me few more would board the rest of the way. He said he and the attendant, Mr G. Ayyappam, had been on the job for seven days straight. 'One hundred hours – *very, very* tired.'

In less than twenty minutes we had shaken off Delhi and were bowling along towards Agra. All that remained of the city were some water towers among the scrub and clusters of high-rise apartments under construction. Always in India, I noticed, there was construction, but seldom maintenance.

Intrigued at the half-empty carriages, I went to the adjacent compartment and sought an explanation from the attendant and mechanic.

'March to June and school holidays, then is very full,' said Mr Ayyappam through mouthfuls of lunch. 'Mothers, fathers, children, uncles, aunts – all are going to Kanyakumari.'

So it was another pilgrim train, in this instance ferrying Hindus to the sacred waters at Land's End. But I couldn't have been happier having almost the whole place to myself, and my two companions were also pleased: there was little work ahead, and the prospect of several nights' sleep in air-conditioned comfort, though Mr Pitchai assured me it was not against regulations to occupy vacant berths.

I looked out the window at the grey sky and ripening paddy fields. Late in the afternoon the unvarying landscape of rice was punctuated by a line of trucks queuing at a toll stop – we were crossing a state line into Uttar Pradesh. We skirted Vrindaban, 'Town of 1000 Temples', in minutes. Mathura, birthplace of Krishna and a sacred city to

Hindus, came and went without a pause. Agra, I calculated, might be reached by nightfall, in which case we might glimpse the Taj Mahal. But it would cause me no disappointment if we didn't. Merely to repeat the two words was generally sufficient to conjure up a vivid image, or what Colonel Gupta would call a brain picture, of Agra's tourist magnet.

Agra passed in darkness and the evening wore on. Gwalior twinkled out the window. We were in Madhya Pradesh state. As I lay awake I heard the slurred voices and roars of laughter of the A/C mechanic and attendant, who had clearly been drinking more of the whisky I'd seen on their lunch table. The ruckus went on a long time. I contemplated finding the inspector and asking for the Complaints Book (every public enterprise has one) but thought better of it. Now I could appreciate why alcohol was banned. In the morning I overheard Mr Pitchai lament, 'Manager does not understand me. Complaint! He is laying complaint!' When I went around the corner to tease him about the noise, he repeated his line: 'I am old man – nearly fifty – and very tired.'

Nagpur looked better in the bright sunlight. And this time round it was mild outside, and some of the famed oranges were for sale so I bought two big bags, at 20 rupees apiece. As the Himsagar Express pulled out at 9.15 am, twenty minutes ahead of schedule, I sprawled out and read my *Indian Express*, looking out the window from time to time to marvel at the vastness of central India, which grew increasingly untamed and unpopulated with each kilometre. There were no sharply defined fields and crops, no bare soil grown tired from overuse, no meticulous allotment of land, no huts, no goat-herders. Man's hand had scarcely scratched the surface here. Its immensity was a revelation: for hour after hour there was nothing but wildly unkempt, heavily wooded plains and hills, the grey sky and the *click-clack, click-clack* of the bogie wheels.

The paper carried an intriguing follow-up to the Pepsi contamination story, which was still making waves in the press. One of the paper's Delhi correspondents had been sent off to gather a selection of vegetables – carrots, beetroot, spinach and the like – from markets around the city. Laboratory testing of these samples showed massive contamination seeping into Delhi's soil, water and food. The vegetables contained extremely heavy doses of lead, along with *E. coli* and salmonella bacteria, which are usually found in faeces. The levels were scores of times higher than permitted limits in other countries. City authorities responded with vague promises of action, and there, I felt confident, the matter would rest.

I got out my map and ran a finger along our route to the next stop of any size, Warangal. We would not reach it until early evening. As I ran my finger on, I concluded this ghost train's schedule had something to do with its emptiness. From Delhi we had made a more or less direct plunge southwards, but now we were veering eastwards until eventually we would come out on the Coromandel Coast. Immediately we would change tack, striking off in a south-westerly direction to emerge on the other side of India, on the Malabar Coast, and only then advancing directly south again to Kanyakumari. All that zigzagging made a very long journey even longer still – 3,751 kilometres to be exact.

I nodded off, waking in the early afternoon as we pulled into the town of Ballharsah. Little by little the dense jungle was persuaded to admit some cultivated plots and small settlements. Roads were ribbons of red dirt overhung by trees; jeeps were the only thing to queue at level crossings. But then in what seemed the blink of an eye, the land flattened out and was transformed into paddy fields. Just as quickly the jungle returned. Then the paddy fields returned. Back and forth the landscape alternated until finally the paddy fields won out. But for all this rice from horizon to horizon, there was hardly a soul about: perhaps a solitary farmer standing admiringly among his crop, or half a dozen women returning single file from the fields, the soft late-afternoon sun making their iridescent saris glow with brilliance; or maybe a cyclist pedalling his black jalopy down a bumpy track, or a peasant leading his buffalo home. They were all scenes of great enchantment, provided one forgot the sheer, protracted effort required to turn rice seedlings into a meal on the table.

Warangal appeared about six o'clock, dotted with the peculiar rocky outcrops found around Hyderabad to the west. The sun sank and the sky was shot full of fiery orange brilliance.

❂

With one tug of the curtain, South India was revealed before me. It was an orderly green place of palm-fringed paddy fields, thatch-roof cottages surrounded by vegetable plots, fruit orchards and straggly banana trees – and every man in a lungi. There were none of the dusty, rubbish-strewn plots of North India. Villagers took pride in the dwellings, however modest. The South seemed a gentler, kinder, less crowded place. And for a change, the sun shone out of a clear sky. Not far off were abrupt granite outcrops, one of which looked for all the world like a giant extracted molar. They formed part of the Javadi Hills, many of which had steep, soft-coloured rock-faces, and in this sparkling morning light they looked exceedingly beautiful.

I knew for sure I had arrived in the South when breakfast arrived: it was the Tamil favourite uppma, served with a coconut chutney.

Mr Ayyappam and Mr Pitchai were sharing a masala dosa they'd bought at Jolarpet Station.

'You don't buy your food from the pantry car?' I asked.

'Pantry car food very bad,' replied Mr Pitchai. 'Many people complain, call for Complaints Book, but money changes hands and nothing happens. You are VIP person. You should call for Complaints Book. Then immediate suspension.'

'I'll think about it.'

'Cooling? Is cooling enough?' he enquired.

'Yes, perfect.'

Mr Pitchai was back to his old cheerful self. The drunken night and the manager's threatened complaint were in the past.

By now we were making a steady march across a dry, red-earth plain. The Shevaroy Hills (high point 1,649 metres) drew nearer, revealing themselves as colossal slabs of rock to which low scrub somehow clung. In the courtyards of village temples was an equally fantastic sight: giant representations of deities and their mounts painted in a grab-bag of gaudy colours.

Between Salem and Erode, an hour's journey, we glided along a high embankment with views of the surrounding plain. There was a welcome variety in the scene that unfolded: cotton crops, mango trees, coconut plantations, fields of deep purple brinjals, a spindly plant, widely grown, whose oil was extracted for hair and skin products, the ever-present and infinitely graceful areca palms and every now and then rocky hillocks, shaped like plum puddings, around which farmers were forced to plough and plant.

At Erode the Himsagar Express bifurcates, a small number of carriages, including the air-conditioned coach, peeling off for Madurai. So I went to the station canteen, bought a takeaway thali, which was wrapped in a banana leaf rather like a packet of fish and chips, and reboarded my original coach.

At 12.30 pm we pulled out. Tamil Nadu had looked hot from behind the tinted glass of my previous coach; now I got to feel it first-hand. Luck was with me, though. Compartment B was fitted with an emergency escape window which had no bars. That meant I had an unobstructed view and could lean out the window, even if a furnace-like wind was blowing on my face.

I sat alone but was soon joined by the ticket inspector, a small clean-shaven man who seemed intent on making my compartment his home for the duration. He took his personal comfort and grooming very seriously. First, he removed his black jacket with its prized TTE badge and placed it in his briefcase with all the reverence of a flag-lowering ceremony, each fold of the cloth a precise and delicately executed movement using straightened fingers. Then he went off to freshen up with soap and water. Then he slapped some perfumed water on his cheeks and neck. Then he removed his shiny black shoes and placed them at the foot of the seat. Then he laid a square of white material on the seat (the cursed dust) and lowered his backside onto it. And only then did he feel properly able to pick up his newspaper.

For the country's longest rail journey, this train seemed to stop at an awful lot of stations. Tiruppur was next, exactly forty minutes on. In the shanties at the foot of the rail embankment I came face to face with the daily routine of India's women. Their days seemed to pass slowly at home, staring vacantly out doorways; squatting in groups of three or four in the shade of a passageway, gossiping; sitting alone, looking forlornly into space; washing a child, one hand holding the reluctant infant, the other scooping water from a brass pitcher; fussing about in a courtyard; or killing time, idly watching the passing trains. It was not a life I envied.

Then we were back among the coconut plantations. We entered the outskirts of another city. The ceiling fans whirred away madly and ineffectually but I could still hear the clink-clink-clink of aggregate workers whacking rocks with their hammers at the side of the road. Lorries monstrously overloaded with bales of cotton trundled along a highway, somehow keeping pace with us; and tufts of cotton blew in flurries from cotton-ginning factories, spilling along the roads and onto common ground to join that blight of the South, plastic litter.

Beyond the industrial estates rose the distinctive shape of the Nilgiri Hills. Unlovely Coimbatore again! We approached the station, passing labourers hauling sacks from freight wagons into a string of warehouses. The sacks reached the rafters. The ticket inspector, seeing me peering, said, 'Godowns of Food Corporation of India.' He rose to leave, taking the opportunity to comb his hair before the compartment's mirror, then added, 'Rice, dahls and dried goods they are storing there for trucking all over Tamil Nadu.'

Whereupon he left.

He was replaced, rather as if in a fresh scene of a play, by another Railways official. Mr M. Viswanathan deposited himself opposite me and loosened his tie. He was a TTI, or Travelling Ticket Inspector. His job, he explained, was to check on the checkers, the TTEs. He would roam from train to train, getting off and on as he pleased, or, in his words, 'according to our programme'. But having checked my ticket and mine alone, and having encouraged the new TTE, as he passed, to do the same, he considered his duties at a close.

Mr Viswanathan unburdened himself of his domestic worries. He and his two brothers and their families lived in one extended household, with separate bedrooms, kitchens and bathrooms and shared living areas. He liked the arrangement. 'But now my brothers are wanting to leave,' he complained. 'They are wanting freedom to go out and see the world.' He regarded this restlessness with suspicion, especially in his two children, aged thirteen and sixteen, who harboured similar ideas.

He questioned me about my salary (a hastily calculated sum since it had been some years since anyone deposited a regular sum in my bank account). On the surface, it compared very favourably, though his, at 14,000 rupees a month 'including allowances', was certainly not to be sneezed at.

'India is very cheap for foreigners, I am thinking.'

'Yes, it is.'

I was better off, but not by the huge margin the inspector imagined. The haircut, for example, that cost him 15 rupees set me back the equivalent of 5,000 rupees. But my choice of illustration was not, perhaps, apt. He was as indifferent to his grooming as my previous companion had been particular about it; his grey bristles were unshaven, his hair tousled, his shoes unpolished and his shirt collar worn.

After a time staring out the window he said, quite unexpectedly, 'The problem, you see, is water.'

'Water?'

'Yes, water. There is not enough of it. See out there, soil is good, labour there is plenty. We could be growing many, many vegetables and other foods. But not enough water.'

He gave a little sigh and closed his eyes for a catnap.

As if to give the lie to Mr Viswanathan's statement, we presently entered a lush and heavily forested valley. Rice fields flashed among the palm trees. It was a Garden of Eden after the desiccated plains around Coimbatore. I couldn't quite believe my eyes and checked a map. The explanation was simple: we were wriggling through a breach in the Western Ghats, between the Nilgiri and Cardamom Hills, into which remnants of the south-westerly monsoons dumped their life-giving bounty.

Somewhere along that leafy corridor we crossed into Kerala state – and into a recognisably wealthier land. The prosperity was evident in the sturdy houses sandwiched against the track. Most conformed to a well-defined template: an all-encompassing verandah, a terracotta-tiled roof, pretty wooden windows, a sweep of steps to the front door where shoes were deposited in a neat row, the yards' coconut husks raked into piles, and at the gate children who waved and shouted themselves hoarse at our passing. But larger houses of modern concrete construction were also to be seen, invariably paid for by remittances from the Gulf to which so many well-educated Keralans flocked for work.

Palghat Station appeared. Mr Viswanathan, woken by the commotion on the platform, rubbed his eyes and departed for checking duties elsewhere. So I was on my own again as the Himsagar Express rolled through this idyllic backdrop, the air cool and refreshing, the jungle-clad hills a close and perpetual shadow. Flocks of ducks were feeding on a weed-choked jheel and their barrage of wheezy honking was audible over the engine's rumble.

Ottapalam had the prettiest little station yet, framed by luxuriant jungle and resounding to the clanging calls of ducks on the Aluva River, which flowed against a bank beneath us.

Trichur was another impeccably clean Keralan station surrounded by jungle. It marked a turning point, however. Having emerged on the Malabar Coast we now turned directly south on the homeward stretch. On my map, the way ahead resembled a loosely threaded string of pearls, each circle denoting a town of anywhere between 10,000 and 100,000 people. (Kerala's population density is among the world's highest.) But we steamed right through most of them, and at one, Chalakudy, we stopped so fleetingly – it was more of a rolling stop – that a heavy-set woman in a blue sari, the only waiting passenger, looked on in anguish as she realised she had been too slow. Her friend urged her to run and jump on, but she lacked the courage and I watched her disconsolate face fade from view.

For all our haste, however, this section had the homely feel of a hill station climb, intruding, as it did, into Keralans' backyards and private lives. Their dolls' houses were almost within touching distance if I cared to stretch out my arm, and every face was smiling and relaxed. Even a work gang toiling to stack sleepers could spare a grin and a wave when they saw me leaning out the window. In this miniature fairyland the Himsagar Express felt like a great diesel-powered Gulliver snorting and thumping its way through a realm of quietly behaved, tropics-dwelling Lilliputians. But the snaking red intruder did not have things entirely its own way: the hills that rose and fell in rapid succession forced it into an unending series of cuttings, their embankments almost pressing against the carriages.

In time we emerged onto the flatter reaches of central Kerala with its inland waterways and swathes of coconut trees, above which rose slender blue minarets and the crosses of whitewashed churches, a reminder that a multitude of people of a multitude of religious persuasions lived cheek by jowl here – and in surprising harmony.

Dusk descended as villagers began to light rubbish raked into piles among the trees. We drew into Cochin, 30 kilometres on, in darkness – and in silence. The absence of tooting horns and all the associated commotion of a city of almost two million seemed extraordinary, even to my India-adjusted ears.

At Ernakulam Town Station, I climbed down to get a fresh coffee, which South Indians prefer over tea, and the stall-holder 'aerated' it for me, pouring the milky concoction from a container held in one upraised arm into a second held in the other lowered arm, then reversing and repeating the process to produce a series of rather impressive frothing arcs. I made another discovery, courtesy of a fellow traveller: protruding slightly from the ceiling of one of the toilets was a plastic nozzle and valve-release handle: a cleverly disguised shower rose! If only I had known earlier; I had four days of grime to wash away.

We resumed our southwards roll, and as we did I could make out faint lights, not many, in the trees that crowded against the line. Mostly, though, it was darkness, except for the silvery glow of the moon, which was beginning to inch above the tips of the palm fronds; and silence, except for the croaking of frogs and chirruping of crickets, audible somehow above the train's own growl.

At a tiny station with a big name, Changanacherry, we halted to allow an up train through. As we slowed I heard a rushing sound, like water splashing against the sides of the carriages. But no, it was foliage, heavy leaves and creeper-entwined branches brushing the coachwork. It was so dense and close that some of the vegetation pressed through my window and slapped my face. The up train thundered through and once more we rattled off into the hot, jungle-filled darkness.

I finished my book. For weight's sake I had been tearing out the pages as I went; now very little was left to toss under the seat. I dozed. Quilon Junction Station, at 10.15 pm, was shut up. I turned out the light and dozed again.

Much later there was a knock at my door. 'Sir, wake up! Wake up!' called out the ticket inspector. 'In ten minutes we are in Kanyakumari.'

We were stationary.

'Are we in Nagercoil?'

'Yes. Ten minutes more.'

I rubbed my eyes and looked at my watch: 1.30 am. I propped myself up by the window, leaving the lights off. The high moon cast a beautiful pale light over our path which, freed of twisting jungle-clad Kerala, ran unimpeded across a final barren strip of Tamil Nadu towards the cape. Elongated rectangles of light from the other carriage windows rippled across the ground. Bright stars shone in the sky and a strong wind was shaking the trees. It was one of the most beautiful sights I had ever seen. Everything – the rocky hills, the trees, the fields – had been stripped of detail and texture and assigned varying shades of silvery-blue, rather like an artist's preliminary block sketch. And the whole thing was mine alone to enjoy. Finally at 2 am, and just one hour behind schedule, I made out a string of fluorescent lights ahead: Kanyakumari Station. I was a little curious about how many were still aboard and did a rough count of the silhouettes drifting towards the terminal. Fifty at most, out of a possible 1,300.

A very long journey was over. All I wished for was a bed wide enough to accommodate my frame comfortably, one that did not rattle and shake and sway from side to side, one in which I was not woken each morning with the inquiry: 'Coffee! Coffee! Coffee! … Coffee, sir?'

❁

Mr S. Subramanian, MA Policy Administration & Journalism, and Kanyakumari's tourist officer, was emphatic that no ferry ran to Sri Lanka. 'Only today, sir, Centre announced it was suspending proposed Tuticorin–Colombo service.'

'Because?'

'Because of security issues. LTTE [Liberation Tigers for Tamil Eelam, or Tamil Tigers] may be bringing in more noxious substances to—'

'Noxious substances? What do you mean?'

'Heroin, bhang and such things, sir. They pay for its terror campaign. A little thing like this (and he held up one hand as though clutching something the size of a cricket ball), such a thing in heroin may bring in two or three crore* of rupees. It is the same with terrorist organisations everywhere. They pay their way with nefarious activities.' Mr Subramanian was in full stride now. 'Mrs Jeyalaliltha is not liking Tigers. She is number one on their hit-list,' he chuckled.

A portrait of Tamil Nadu's well-nourished, rosy-cheeked Chief Minister hung on the wall behind him.

'She has turned down a plan to build a bridge linking our two countries. Engineering-wise, it is easy, but she wants to keep Sri Lanka and its problems at arm's length.'

He halted to send a boy off for tea. Mr Subramanian had cleared up one matter for me: there was no point in heading for Tuticorin. I would have to double back to Trivandrum to catch a plane.

We never really got a chance to talk again because a string of acquaintances passed through his office door for a chat. Their conversations, to my untutored ear, sounded like shouting matches. They flung words at each other like bursts of machine-gun fire, each

* A crore equals ten million.

directing long, clattering volleys over the voice of the other. The subject became apparent when Mr Subramanian said to me, 'I am closing now for half-day. We are all going to a big Muslim celebration at Thuckalay.'

'You are not a Muslim, though.'

'No, I am Hindu. But Christians, Hindus, Sikhs – all are invited. It is for social harmony.'

'Social harmony? You mean promoting goodwill between Muslims and Hindus.'

'Yes. There are many going from all over the district to Thuckalay – maybe one lakh of people. The District Commissioner has declared a public holiday.'

Peer Mohamed Oliyullah, he explained, was a famous poet, saint and journalist who wrote many poems in Tamil. The gathering at Thuckalay, 35 kilometres from Kanyakumari, would be a celebration of his life's work.

I waited as Mr Subramanian locked up, fitting three weighty padlocks to the front door, a rather excessive security measure, I thought, for a government building containing no more than mismatched sticks of furniture and a few sun-faded posters. Then he sped off out the gate on his moped, in high spirits at the break in routine.

I had plans, too. After days of enforced inactivity I was aching for some exercise. I set off around the fishermen's huts by the shore, down narrow stinking alleyways thronging with snotty-nosed kids and abuzz with flies, past the fishermen mending nets and preparing to take their canoes out in the evening. They all looked as poor as church mice. The one modern convenience or luxury I saw was television sets: Mr Subramanian had said cable television cost 100 rupees a month but everyone still had it.

A Roman Catholic church with a tall spire loomed over the tightly compacted hovels. I went in, followed by a gang of little girls chanting the heart-rending plea, 'School pen? School pen?' They eventually left me and sat on the marbled floor to eat their ice blocks. Half a dozen women lay in various alcoves and corners: the church offered a cool, quiet sanctuary for sleepers. One man sat cross-legged in prayer, while a woman in a gold-embroidered sari and with a countenance of great earnestness shuffled on her knees towards the altar. The interior, like a mosque, was without seating, and the various religious icons and figures had been embellished in the native manner with glittering cloth and garlands. A notice from the vice-rector warned that communion would be given only to those who had properly prepared themselves with confession. It was always a queer sensation to enter a church in India; its alien nature was pronounced and unshakeable.

I had come to Kanyakumari simply because it was the end of the line. That was plain enough at the station, a preposterously oversized building for so insignificant a terminus, and one with two tracks that came to a rather ignominious end before bumpers. Hindus travelled to this pilgrim town at the tip of the mainland to bathe at the ghat where the waters of the Bay of Bengal and the Arabian Sea mingle with the Indian Ocean. Mahatma Gandhi's ashes had been exhibited here before being immersed in the ocean. Pilgrims also visited the much venerated temple of Kumari, the goddess who protects India's shores and after whom Kanyakumari is named.

But many Indians also came to the town for a holiday break: to enjoy the ocean views and the cooling winds that sweep away the sticky heat of the plains and before whose unceasing blasts the coconut trees on this rocky promontory arch like bows poised to loosen off their arrows. Holiday homes for employees of public service organisations were as plentiful as potholes in the town's roads. What's more – and this must have been galling for residents – these houses were kept in immaculate condition, in eye-popping contrast to the government offices at which citizens must present themselves to plead for the delivery of essential services.

As I stood there, on the road leading up to the lighthouse, a couple emerged through the gates of one such lodge, the Holiday Home for Central Government Employees. They were well fed and smartly turned out, as were their two young children. I couldn't resist the temptation and walked over.

'Excuse me, sir, I couldn't help noticing you've come from one of those holiday homes. Are they subsidised?'

He blinked at me for a moment. 'Subsidised? Oh yes, tariffs are lower.'

'There must be fifty of those units in there.'

He sniffed trouble. 'I wouldn't know, sir.'

'Don't you think the government would be better spending people's money on things like fixing up the pavements?' I asked, pointing the flagstones at our feet. Every second or third one had cracked or collapsed, turning a casual stroll into an obstacle course across an open sewer.

He gave an embarrassed laugh: 'I couldn't say, sir. I really couldn't say.'

I continued up the hill, hopping from one unbroken flagstone to the next, and came upon a deliciously ironic find: a guesthouse, hidden from the casual eye behind a high perimeter wall and boasting glorious ocean views, for none other than employees of the Tamil Nadu Public Works Department.

❁

The Kanyakumari–Bangalore Express departed at 6.40 in the morning. And because I was up early anyway – loudspeakers mounted about the town's places of worship make sure of that – I had time to climb the station's specially built sunrise observation roof. This must be the only station in the world with such a facility. About twenty individuals stood about in various attitudes of prayer. The sun rose in a rather unspectacular fashion over the windswept triangle of rooftops below, and I left.

'Any seat in coach six,' said the clerk at the Same Day ticket counter. He was right: not one of the seventy-two seats was taken. It was a second-class-only service, but cheap: 62 rupees for the 80-kilometre ride.

The Western Ghats at dawn were a series of jagged blue rocks projecting upwards and outwards like the crowded, razor-sharp teeth of a shark. Between the ghats and the railway line were expanses of brown stubble where rice had been harvested. Without the silvery-blue moonlight, the landscape looked much less striking.

On we pushed through the steadily more numerous coconut and banana plantations, stopping at every station without exception, after which the diesel locomotive (this southernmost leg from Trivandrum was not electrified) chugged hard and blew clouds of smoke as it returned us to a modest canter. Before long there was not an empty seat to be had. Now I understood why it took two and a half hours to cover these 80 kilometres.

The sprinkling of thatch huts along the line thickened, then gave way to brick houses, which grew more profuse among the palms, and suddenly we were in Trivandrum.

Next day I bought another ticket, this one for a plane journey.

Housing within Galle's fort.

Train No. 50 to Galle

FORT STATION CUTS A FORLORN figure, surrounded by the grand colonial buildings and skyscrapers of downtown Colombo. Hardly more that a glorified whitewashed shed, it manages a few high-arched entrances, a few rows of ticket windows, then subsides into anonymity again. The first sight of it filled me with foreboding because it looked hardly more than a way station. Yet it is the hub, literally, of the network. Lines radiate out from here, and only here, like spokes on a bicycle wheel.

Train No. 50 (it had no other name, the ticket inspector informed me) set off along the southern coastal line at 7.15 am. For ten minutes it jiggled between the mouldy buildings of Slave Island before emerging beside the shore, almost within reach of the salt spray. On my left, rising among slapped-together lodgings, were swanky hotels, embassies and apartment towers; on my right, directly under my nose, the limpid surf of the Indian Ocean lapped onto the sand.

Until this point, the coaches had swayed languidly on the old track, like the hips of a belly dancer beginning her routine. Now, as we gathered momentum along the straight coastal line, languor gave way to excitable shaking and bouncing. Coaches snapped from side

165

to side in wrenching jolts. Over and over I was lifted clear of my seat. The ride was so wild my pen jerked across my page and my scribbling became spidery and illegible. The dancer was in full flight now, her act one long, barely contained spasm of gyrating. How, I wondered through all the violent shaking, could things have been allowed to deteriorate so far?

An unsteady walk through the second-class coaches revealed the extent of the neglect. Without exception every chair rocked on its hinges; every piece of upholstery was saggy and torn, every ceiling fan broken, every centimetre of floor like the bottom of a parrot's cage, every toilet unspeakable. I returned to my seat. Despite the heat and noise and wrenching ride, the four Sinhalese in my coach were already asleep. But the view of the glassy sea and curving coconut trees soon made me forgive the train its bronco ride.

At the first stop, Dehiwala, half an hour on, crowds of commuters waited in the oppressive humidity. The clamminess hung in the air like a great damp beach towel. Two suburban services trundled past, their open doors and windows a mélange of projecting arms and legs, and we edged out, shaking and rattling our way south again, past tumbledown huts three and four deep between the line and the lapping waves. The huts were fragile and small; some timber boards here, some tin sheets there, a packing case on top, a couple of plastic chairs in the shade of a doorway. The bare dirt ground was raked clear of litter, though, and some owners had attempted to brighten up their homes, adding potted palms or lattice fences, or planting hedge rows. To my delight, the schoolchildren emerging from these shacks wore immaculately white uniforms and bright smiles.

A flick through my newspaper – cursory because the words danced exasperatingly before my eyes – uncovered one reason why the railway was run down. Fares had not risen in almost a decade. According to the *Daily News* report, officials estimated 15 per cent of passengers were fare-dodgers. To lift revenue, the government was hiring extra ticket inspectors and, as an inducement to greater vigilance, planned to let them keep half of any unpaid fares they collected. Still, it was all small beer beside the huge drain on the

Treasury of twenty years of insurrection by the Tamils in the north – all those conscripts lolling about, now a ceasefire was in place, guarding intersections and government buildings.

Without the suicide bombings in the cities and the big battles in the jungles, the package tourists were starting to return. An hour on, we bounced past the first of the holiday resorts, and I saw the foreigners standing about aimlessly under an overcast sky. Flags of the world fluttered in long bright rows. Humbler, unseen accommodation with suggestive names like Green Shadows Holiday Inn and Sea Breeze Chalets was indicated by painted wooden arrows pointing off among the palm trees.

The bursting tropical beauty of this little island made the periodic sight of poverty seem alien and inexplicable, like prickly weeds in a bed of soft-textured blooms. And the idea of waging war here seemed equally unbelievable. The exquisiteness seized you at every glance. After crossing a river bobbing with blue-and-yellow fishing boats, we pulled into Panadura Station where frangipanis and hibiscus scented the air and the most fantastic-looking insects, like gargantuan bumblebees, darted noiselessly past my window. While we waited at another station, Kalutara North, langurs thrashed about in the trees. And as we bridged estuaries across our route, nature delivered a cooling rush of salty air through the windows. Papaya, mangoes and bananas grew within reach of the line. A little later the sun, emerging from castellated clouds building inland, shone brightly on the frothy white tops of the waves as they made their leisurely approach towards the sand.

At Kalutara Station, a decaying little stop like all the rest, a maintenance gang plucked weeds from the line, and my gaze fell on the sleepers at their feet. These old and cracked slabs of timber were, I guessed, the originals laid by the British a century or more ago. Ancient tracks and uneven roadbed – there was the reason for our bone-shaking ride. We rattled on, and still no one entered the carriage. Though we were never long out of sight of the ocean, we now re-emerged hard against the water's edge, so close that foam splattered the coaches and I could look down into the fishermen's outriggers pulled up on the sand.

As we neared the town of Beruwala, the backyard foliage thinned out, revealing everyday scenes previously hidden from me: a man tapping his toddy supply; a woman kneeling before a white stupa with a glass-encased Buddha at its base; an old couple at a spinning wheel turning coconut fibre into coir; a shop owner putting out his *Video Hire* sign; two fishermen pushing a cart along a dirt track with their morning's catch for sale, the heads sliced off to uncover thick blood-red fillets; emaciated pariah dogs sniffing at the edge of a stagnant canal; a housewife hanging out washing on a line strung between two palm trees; two women combing each other's hair; labourers in a sawmill cutting up coconut tree logs. The smell of smoke from rubbish fires wafted into the carriage.

For some reason we bypassed the centre of Beruwala and paused for five minutes south at Alutgama. Then it was across another estuary and among more coconut trees, these especially tall and elegant, like a slender woman's fingers, and arching seawards; then another waterway, another fleeting breeze, before the humidity clamped itself around me again and I returned to inspecting backyards through the curtain of exploding green foliage.

The dress code, I noticed, had crossed the Palk Strait – for the men at least: trousers and a shirt worn loose over the top for younger men. Among the older men the preference for the lungi persisted, as it did in India. Sinhalese women wore a blouse and a tight-fitting ankle-length skirt, sometimes pleated near the bottom to allow for a brisker step, a combination that showed off their tall, slim figures. Tamil women stuck with saris. What hadn't crossed the Palk Strait was the work ethic. Indians were forever building, fashioning, ploughing, harvesting, selling, manufacturing. The Sinhalese seemed to possess none of that drive or initiative. They were not idle or inactive, rather reposeful. In this land once known as Serendip, urgency and strenuous endeavour were perhaps unnecessary.

It began to rain and I thought of the holidaymakers, the Germans and French and Swiss standing about in their loud shirts and redundant sunhats, who had fled the grey skies of home. They prayed for sunshine. I was indifferent. I could watch the rain now belting against the window and feel no anxiety. My only concern was that the trains ran without interruption and preferably on time. For the rest, I didn't care.

And miraculously I got my wish that day. Galle appeared, almost on schedule, at 10.20 am. I trooped off in the drizzle, shaking my head in wonder. I was still on India time: there, three hours was barely getting going. But in this little teardrop of a country, three hours could get you a long way, even on a railway as clapped out as this one.

❁

Rauf (he preferred to be known by his first name only) was like few other gemstone dealers in Galle. He had no shopfront but contacts worldwide. He spoke nine languages: English, French, Italian, German, Korean, Japanese, Singhalese, Tamil and Arabic. His father had been a gem dealer and his grandfather, too. His father had traded in Vietnam before fleeing home at the start of the Second World War, hence the French. The German came via his grandmother who was German. The rest were picked up while acquiring his knowledge of gems. When most youngsters his age could think of nothing but cricket, he was immersing himself in gems. They were in his blood whether he liked it or not. They had made him wealthy, though he didn't care so much for that any more. Yes, he wore a Rolex watch, but his lungi was threadbare.

He was in a reflective mood the afternoon I met him. 'We are all, if we are lucky, allotted about seventy or eighty years,' he said. 'The beggar, he eats week-old, cast-off food. The surgeon with his specialist knowledge of the body's needs, the rich businessman who eats the very best – all are allotted the same amount of time here: seventy years, maybe eighty. The only thing we can determine is how we spend that time.

'The businessman, he leaves early for work, comes home late, worries about whether he can meet his commitments, cover his cheques. His mind is always on tomorrow. Such men are everywhere

– they have no time for family, they do not sleep well. I do not want to be like that. Such men are going behind the world.'

That phrase was a funny one, but he used it often and I came to know its meaning: it was to go against the natural order of things, and for a Muslim that was not such a hard concept to absorb.

Out to sea, a foaming wall of rain clouds was fast approaching the ramparts of Galle's fort. Now it hit Rauf's house with unexpected violence, so we lifted our cane chairs and carried them to the sheltered side of the verandah, within view of Flag Rock, the Portuguese-built bastion from where sailing ships were warned of dangerous rocks (Galle was for a long time the country's principal port).

'Money,' he resumed, 'yes, it is important, but it is better we spend our days well before it is time to leave.' He waved his arm to indicate the guesthouse. 'All this is really something to keep my wife occupied. Our only son will soon be leaving home and she is alone all day.'

When I asked if officials made life difficult for people setting up in business, he permitted himself a faint smile: corruption was getting as bad as in India. Every rule and regulation must be scrupulously observed. 'Be straight and be fearless – that is the only way.'

Patience, he omitted to mention, was the other vital ingredient, because the process of getting all the necessary approvals on an official document could be very tedious. 'A piece of paper goes from that desk to that desk to that desk. It can take five minutes or five weeks … or forever. How long depends on how much you pay.'

Officials and politicians had almost limitless opportunities to line their pockets, he explained. The luxury European and Japanese cars on the potholed roads were but the most visible expression of that ill-gotten wealth. One lucrative source was aid money. He recalled the case of the Korean tyre company that had committed funds to upgrading a trunk road outside Galle provided its tyres were the preferred choice for the government's car fleet for three years. The company handed over the money and the tender was called. But the relevant minister had the power to stipulate that the lowest tender would not necessarily be chosen. It wasn't. It went to another bidder. That company had to give the minister a handsome cut to get the job

– such a handsome cut, in fact, that the road contractor was forced to do a shoddy job to make a profit.

Now, however, more and more aid projects were being directly supervised by donor countries. Britain had sent out its own engineers, site supervisors and foremen when it funded construction of a dam near the central city of Kandy. The result was a structure built on time and to budget that wouldn't crack or subside. Luckily for corrupt politicians, such structural faults took years to appear.

Still, civic leaders and bureaucrats in Galle had a fresh source of bribe money courtesy of UNESCO's decision to make the fort precinct a World Heritage site. Property prices had skyrocketed. Things improved only when Colombo gave an undertaking to sell all government-owned buildings within the fort by 2010 as part of a plan to turn the precinct into a tourism zone. The frenzy of renovation work was impossible to miss as gangs of labourers went about restoring mouldy and broken masonry, replacing roof tiles, painting windows and doors and gutting interiors. The sound of saws and hammers and concrete mixers rose through the laneways of old Galle. Most of the made-over properties were destined to become boutique hotels, homestays or foreigners' holiday pads. The owner of the hotel where I was staying had already assured me Dutch-era villas of quite modest size were fetching $US350,000 and that prices had quadrupled in twelve months. Was I, he enquired, in the market for buying?

Rauf predicted the scramble to get hold of the government properties would be intense, citing the case of the circuit house sold off recently to a foreign hotel chain. The judge who lived there had been threatened by a disgruntled litigant and insisted on more secure premises outside the fort. The mayor's signature on the various approvals required for this transfer of ownership had cost the hotel chain $US200,000, plus a stake for the mayor in the hotel when the conversion was complete. Plus, the mayor would get a share of the profits from building the judge's new quarters because he put the work the way of a family-owned company. Quite a neat deal.

To Rauf, all this jockeying and scrambling, this pursuit of fast money, was no more than a source of mild amusement. It was, in his words, 'behind the world'. The rain went on and on, lashing the fort buildings and trapping a group of umbrella-less tourists beneath the verandah of the tea co-operative offices. In time, a coach driver came to their rescue.

Rauf's wife appeared with a tray of tea and retreated. She was as mild-mannered and self-effacing as her husband, who had a curious mannerism for someone so successful in the business world: he avoided all eye contact. But this chubby-cheeked gem dealer with liquid-brown eyes and a thick swirl of receding, slightly greying hair had a compensating quality – his voice. At the same time warm and lively and soft – so soft sometimes as to be almost inaudible over the rain beating on the roof – it was altogether a delight to the ear.

He was a man you instinctively could trust. That was fortunate because gem dealing was all about trust, on the part of the buyer and the seller. 'One without the other,' he said, 'is like trying to clap with one hand – impossible!'

His word was everything: that gems of the quality ordered would be delivered; that there would be no inferior or stolen stones, no slip-ups, no late deliveries. Trust was doubly important because transactions were in cash – American dollars, usually, and large amounts too. One mistake and a reputation was lost forever.

I asked whether he had ever been robbed. As a known gem wholesaler he must surely have been a prime target.

Only once, he said. An acquaintance had learnt he had $US49,000 in his house and put up three youths to seize the money while only his wife was at home. The robbery was bungled. Rauf was called home by his distraught wife to find neighbours holding one of the trio; the other two got away although police soon enough discovered their identities.

Normally in such cases, he explained, police would seize a family member of an 'absconding' suspect, in effect holding him hostage until the wanted man handed himself in. It had been a practice sanctioned by law. But parliament removed that draconian police power only four years earlier to comply with Sri Lanka's international human rights obligations.

I was astonished. 'Four years ago, I half-imagined you were going to say forty.'

'No. It is unbelievable, I know. The police chief here in Galle said to me, "I can do you a favour. We cannot seize someone from each of their families but we will harass their families ... go banging on their doors at all hours of the day and night."

'I agreed and that is just what they did. The family of one youth got so sick of it they made the fellow turn himself in. The other one was never caught. I wanted those two punished, oh, how I wanted that, but each time there was a hearing the case was delayed. For two years this went on, delay after delay.

'In Sri Lanka it is not like in the West where police prosecute the accused and you, the victim, do nothing. You must have a lawyer yourself, to grease the wheels of justice, so to speak. And eventually we realised that the lawyers, ours and theirs, were in cahoots ...'

'I suppose you got yourself a new lawyer then.'

'No, we still use him. They are all the same, lawyers. They must have a case to try every day or they do not make any money. We wanted the case ended. It wasn't just the money. My wife, she would get anxious each time she had to go to the police or the courts.'

'As a witness?'

'Yes, so I arranged for a court official to bring the file to my house for 1,000 rupees. Then I destroyed it. The case was over. It was the only time I have ever done such a thing.'

❂

The civil war had emptied old Galle's guesthouses of tourists, but I could still not take twenty paces without a tout whispering in my ear, 'Sir, you want gemstone? Very good gemstones at my uncle's shop. Please, you follow me.' I had no interest in buying gemstones, or anything else for that matter that would add weight to my rucksack; it already contained too many books.

Sri Lanka has 5,000 registered gemstone mines, although many are very small and primitive – just a hole in the jungle reinforced with planks to prevent collapse. The stones in Galle's window displays were nothing special. The cheap settings underlined that. An elderly Muslim beckoned me to enter his shop. His age softened my resolve and I agreed. After showing polite interest in his wares, I asked, 'Will the ceasefire hold?'

He stroked his Vandyke beard. 'No.' And when I asked why, he explained that there would never be peace because the Tamils 'will always fight'.

'But they must have some reason for being so angry in the first place.'

'No, they were imagining things.'

'Things? Like discrimination?'

'Discrimination is not there,' he answered. 'Tamils are in high places. The chief of police is a Tamil.'

'So all those thousands upon thousands of Tamils, they are all imagining things.'

'Yes,' he said flatly.

I left him to his unswerving convictions and carried on up Church Street, where I fell into conversation with the new owner of a Dutch villa undergoing transformation into a $US200-a-night hotel. For now, hidden behind the spruced-up façade, it was an enormous heap of bricks and rubble and half-poured concrete footings. Karl Steinberg had sold his Sydney pub and poured all his money into this new venture. He reckoned his $US1 million investment represented tremendous value: he would get a thirteen-room specialty hotel in a World Heritage site, huge profits (guests would pay in American dollars, but all his outgoings were in rupees), a tax-free status for anywhere up to twenty years and a very comfortable life in the East tossed in for good measure.

For extra cash Mr Steinberg acted as an agent to foreigners who hadn't yet bought a piece of this paradise. I told him I was just passing through.

'Take my card. If you're staying a few days you might change your mind.'

The locals, he let on, had made a pastime of enticing outsiders into buying at silly prices. So a little later I took his advice and peered speculatively at one place. A neighbour, an old man wearing a flaxen hat, leaned over the fence. 'Looking to buy?'

'Maybe. Are you selling?'

'I could be.'

'How much?

He rubbed his chin awhile. 'Five million rupees.'

I looked across at his dump. 'That's interesting,' I said, 'but I'm just holidaying.'

Mr Steinberg was telling the truth.

❁

Galle Station is a low, austere concrete box in the modern Indian tradition, the only concession to aesthetics a semi-circular entry hall. Booking staff, lacking computers, fall back on consulting well-thumbed registers, after which they annotate slips of paper and give them a good wallop with their rubber stamps before thumbing through stocks of cardboard tickets and scribbling illegible details on the selected chit – and there, for no more than a dollar, is your authorisation to travel.

The departure of the Galle–Colombo service was preceded by a stampede to get seats in the third-class unreserved coaches. During this unholy ruck women, children and the elderly were shown no quarter. In minutes third class was crammed to suffocation. I sauntered into second class, alone.

Promptly we were off on another round of railway rock 'n' roll. It was impossible to read or write and there was no one to talk to. I stared vacantly out the window. Darkness had fallen by the time we reached the beachside shanties on the edge of Colombo. Shorn of their ocean backdrop, they had lost all their quaintness. Bare light bulbs shone in unpainted rooms. Children tumbled everywhere, their parents out of sight. Fishermen drank bottles of beer, the nets they had been mending at their feet. The black, brooding shapes of tenement houses crowded against the line, like trees overhanging a forest pathway. Then the train stopped. For almost an hour we remained stationary in the hot, breathless darkness. Fed up, I clambered across tracks to a road and walked the rest of the way to town.

Coastal plain from Ella Gap.

The No. 9 and 8.45 am Local

COLOMBO FELT BESIEGED. Every downtown corner was marked by a sandbagged emplacement, out of whose shadows peered soldiers, their eyes unblinking, their fingers resting on the triggers of automatic weapons. It was disconcerting to stare down the barrels of so many guns, but it was obvious locals had long since ceased to notice the soldiers' presence. They rushed to work, jammed themselves onto buses, bartered at sidewalk stands and gave these motionless sentinels as much notice as lamp posts.

But the soldiers, like most Sri Lankans, could be induced to smile with just a cheery hello. And that must have been a feat after dull days under a hot corrugated roof guarding against attacks unlikely ever to come. The Tamil Tigers were giving peace talks a try and saw no value in striking at banks or the national airline or the offices of the District Commissioner for the Procurement of Water Supplies.

'How do you like Sri Lanka?' I was repeatedly asked and I found myself saying, 'The people are friendly.' I did like Sri Lanka, but something about it left me feeling faintly irritated. An apathy clung in the air, and a trace of anger. Perhaps the twenty-year civil war had left them spent and lethargic and resentful. Or perhaps nature was too bountiful for their own good: fruit fell from the trees and any seed tossed on the ground soon sprouted and flourished. Even the sentimental pop music squawking from car radios hinted at a dreamy unreality, an inclination to leave today's difficulties for another day.

One afternoon I asked a man if an Internet café up the street was still open. He shook his head. 'Closed, everything closed. Everybody always sleeping,' he said with a charming smile and made that universal gesture of slumber by pressing his palms together against a slightly cocked head. 'That's my people – always sleeping.'

'I've noticed things are very relaxed. What do you do?'

'Money-changer. My office is over there.'

He pointed across the street. He was lucky still to have a business in this part of town. Shop after shop was boarded up, strangled by the lack of pedestrians after all the roadblocks were erected in 1995 when a bomb blast killed hundreds and the government became obsessed with security.

The money-changer said: 'Office workers, they are supposed to start at eight o'clock but they turn up at ten …'

'What, all office workers?'

'No, government workers. They are bad people. They are supposed to work until four, but by three most are gone. One day a month they have poya. Then there are Christian holidays, Muslim holidays, Hindu holidays …. Ten days a month some are working. I am not joking. Yes, government people are very bad.'

Another man I met, a water-board engineer back home from London where he had lived for many years, was almost as gloomy about his country's prospects.

'Looking at all the new cars on the roads, you would think Sri Lanka was a developed country. And so many Range Rovers! Even in UK Range Rovers are expensive.'

I said, 'Someone told me the people driving such cars are all government connected, all paid for with bribery money.'

'Probably they are right. Twenty per cent of people are very well off. The other 80 per cent are dirt poor. The gulf is creating many difficulties. Sri Lanka's education system is also to blame. We have one of the highest literacy rates in Asia. Many are passing their O levels but there are no jobs. Smart unemployed people – now that is a recipe for trouble.'

❈

First-class train travel suggests sumptuous comfort, but in Sri Lanka it means no such thing. What it does mean is a seat of your own, upholstery that is not tattered, a passable toilet (in an emergency), a compartment that is not grubby and ceiling fans that work. But nothing more. No porters dancing at your attendance, no plush compartments, no catering service, just the rudiments of train travel, the absence of unpleasantness.

But the No. 9 train to Kandy did make one concession to creature comforts: the rearmost coach was a first-class observation car with a sweeping view out the back window. It was, after all, a tourist train. The morning's service had few foreigners, however: a British couple and toddler who pressed their noses against the giant viewing window the whole way; two Norwegian women shod in big hiking boots who lugged aboard colossal backpacks; a fat Indian woman in a floral sari who long and determinedly sang the praises of India's trains to her Chinese friend from Singapore. ('On Shatabdi Express it is taking just ten hours. Very fast! Breakfast they are bringing at seven, then morning tea at ten, lunch is at twelve … please, try one of these biscuits.') And in the far corner sat a Tamil businessman buried in his paper.

At seven, the German-made diesel hauled a dozen coaches out of Fort Station, past storage sheds overgrown with weeds, past rows of cannibalised carriages, past a handful of men walking along the tracks to the office, past boys flying their flimsy improvised kites, past an ocean of shanties whose corrugated iron roofs were softened by drooping velvety palm fronds, past stations whose platforms were jammed with commuters waiting in the moist tropical heat, until at last we cleared all vestige of Colombo.

Now, chugging at a stately 40 kilometres an hour, the loco hauled us towards the hilly interior. Crowding at our shoulder, and sometimes even overarching the line, was thick jungle, patched by grassy open spaces apparently put to no productive use. Certainly, there was the odd paddy field and rows of spindly coconut trees, but altogether there was land for the begging – unlike in India where there was a need, or perhaps it was a compulsion, to clear, demarcate and plant out every centimetre of cultivable land. Villagers seemed to move without purpose or industry. In fact, I'd seen no one really exerting themselves. The most industrious worker seemed to be nature itself, which was forever germinating and regenerating and leaping upwards and outwards.

In an hour and a half we had crossed the plain and reached the foothills. Up we went. A valley of paddy fields emerged on our left, rocky pinnacles rose up on our right. We entered a tunnel, then a second, which was especially long, and as our coach exited it a pall of diesel smoke drifted about the entrance, as though from the mouth of a smoker lazily exhaling his drag of nicotine. Facing backwards out the observation window revealed an odd thing: how much the track doubled as a foot-track for villagers. As we climbed, they would slip singly and in groups into our wake from the jungle shadows, a hoe or baby or bag in hand, and resume their morning's march.

The ascent was now steep, although the easy rumble of the locomotive's engine suggested the driver could have put on more speed. What held him back was the state of the line. The old timber sleepers and warped rails produced a generous quota of jolts and bumps. Signs repeatedly reminded downhill drivers: 'WARNING: SPEED DETECTORS' and, more ominously, 'MAX SPEED 10 KM/H. WEAK SLEEPERS'.

We went through Kaduganna Station without slowing. I caught sight of a sign informing travellers they were at 500 metres above sea level. We had reached the top of the pass. To our left, the Hill of Belungala, the Watcher's Rock, rose another 275 metres. It had once been used to observe the advance of any enemy across the plains. A quarter of an hour later, at 9.30, we made our first halt, at Peradeniya Junction Station. The Norwegians hauled down their backpacks from the overhead lockers and trudged off. The main line led south-east to the town of Badulla, the branch line to Kandy. In ten minutes we were entering Kandy's outskirts.

✪

I had arrived in town on the day people were gathering for a big protest, marching against a power-sharing deal Prime Minister Ranil Wickremesinghe looked likely to cut with the Tamils. In the protesters' view he was making far too many concessions and his deal for a federal Sri Lanka would only split the country. (They needn't have worried. The following year the President, Chandrika Kumaratunga, forced an election because she feared the same thing and Mr Wickremesinghe's party was defeated, putting an end to any serious peacemaking.) The three Sinhalese women I cornered among the crowd waiting for the protesters to pass were all of the same view: they wanted a single, undivided Sri Lanka.

'We don't want what might happen to the Palestinians and the Israelis,' one said.

'Don't the Tamils have some reason for feeling bitter in the first place?' I asked. 'Some discrimination or other?'

'Not at all,' said the youngest, a thin spectacled woman who clutched a briefcase to her chest. 'Poor people everywhere are treated badly. Also, many Tamils are doing well. The chief of police is a Tamil.'

'So I've heard,' I said. 'What's wrong with autonomy for the Tamils? Some sort of federal system? India has it. And the United States and Australia.'

But no, all three shook their heads. Give them autonomy and it would be the start of an unstoppable march to statehood.

Every idea I put to this trio was greeted with rejoinders about the pain Tamils had inflicted on Sinhalese.

'They talk peace, but they still hold the gun,' said the eldest, a greying woman in a pale-blue sari. 'Tamils can live in the south, but Sinhalese cannot live in the north. Did you know there is not one Sinhalese at the university in Jaffna—'

'Yes,' cut in the youngest one, riding the wave of resentment, 'they

181

even tried to blow up the Dalada Maligawa. A World Heritage site!'

The Dalada Maligawa, or Temple of the Tooth, stood across the road, circled by a protective ring of fences and armed soldiers. Five years earlier, in 1998, Tamil extremists had set off a bomb outside the temple, which is said to contain a tooth grabbed from the flames of the Buddha's funeral pyre. Since Sinhalese were Buddhist, an attack on the temple containing their most important Buddhist relic was an assault on Sinhalese themselves. It still hurt.

The noisy procession finally approached, led by robed Buddhist monks in single file and holding saffron-coloured umbrellas above their heads against the drizzle. They walked solemnly and silently, but the crowd behind them waved national flags and bleated into megaphones.

'Why do the monks lead the protest?' I asked one of the trio.

'Because when the country is in trouble the monks always lead the people.'

The shouts of the nationalists grew louder and louder as they passed our corner and the Temple of the Tooth. Onlookers watched from the pavements with a surprising nonchalance, hardly making a murmur in support of the protesters' chants.

I wandered off around Kandy, a pleasant jumble of shops and houses set in a bowl of hills, and then around the big artificial lake, which was pleasanter still. With its cool air and hilly walks, Kandy is a favourite resort for anyone seeking to escape sticky Colombo. As the last capital of the ancient kings of Ceylon, Kandy is also a stronghold of Sinhalese culture and nationalist sentiment.

The Tigers' violent methods could never be condoned – two decades of civil war had cost 65,000 lives and achieved next to nothing – but the Sinhalese seemed so unwilling to acknowledge that the Tamil problem was largely of their own making. The Tamils dominate the north and east of the country, but they constitute only a fifth of the population and have never posed a threat to the Sinhalese Buddhist majority. Yet just about the first thing that majority did after the country gained independence from the British in 1948 was to pass laws restricting Tamil civil rights. The most inflammatory measure was to make Sinhala the exclusive official language. In a stroke, Tamils' already limited access to higher education and government jobs shrank to almost zilch. Communal friction gave way to violence, terrorist attacks and anti-Tamil pogroms, and in 1983 Sri Lankans woke to full-scale civil war. Sri Lanka's Buddhist heritage should have made it a gentle, civilised country, but somehow things had gone off the rails in former Serendip. Why had it all gone so wrong? The answer eluded me.

❂

'The line to Badulla is a hundred and twenty-five years old,' Kandy's Chief Station Master said to me. 'And very good British engineering it is, too.'

He was a busy man, Mr Goonetilleke, even though Kandy was at the end of a branch line. He stood, in his pressed white trousers and shirt, at the apex of an intricate local bureaucracy. Earlier, I had noted with some satisfaction the offices of the station's various functionaries: the Station Master Operating, the Station Master Accounts, the Inspector, Signal and Communications, the Locomotive Foreman, the Railway Protection Force and so forth. He also had to keep an eye on the Rest Room for Clergy (the monks' waiting room) and the Cafeteria, although he must have borne his responsibility for the latter lightly: the upstairs dining hall was dark and filthy and served only gritty tepid coffee and plain buns.

The service to Badulla was not popular: there were just seven coaches, all unreserved second class except for the first-class observation car, which I boarded. The car's only occupants were a Sinhalese family, eating slices of mango for breakfast. Half an hour behind schedule we departed, retracing our steps to Peradeniya Junction, and swung south.

On our left was the road to Gampola, which was soon flanked by a river whose waters were a rich green. Now and then I glimpsed a paddy field, but otherwise we trundled through a narrow world of wooded slopes and, intermittently, villages. At one settlement, five men, all with the physiques of insects, sat trance-like at a tea stall.

The road returned, along with the river, just before the hamlet of Nawalapitiya, where the jungle was reclaiming a string of carriages abandoned at a siding. Then we wound round and round and in and out and up and up and by 10.30 we were among fir trees and grassy hillsides scattered with smooth russet rocks. It began to rain and I unlatched my window. Tea gardens appeared and before long they were all around us, planted out on hills in every direction. This legacy of colonial times was still one of the country's biggest exports. The grey sky sank lower and the rain became heavier but the tea pickers, mostly old Tamil women, worked on. Their existence must have been uneventful, for a few straightened their backs to stare at our passing. But excluding their shuffling forms, it was a surprisingly lifeless place, without people or animal life of any kind, not even birds.

We were getting high. Hatton Station, which we reached at noon, stood at 1,262 metres. The surrounding settlement was glum: a collection of damp tea pickers' huts and muddy lanes. Housewives in smocks stared warily at us from behind the half-open doors of their huts, which were simple in the extreme: a low rectangular box with a front door flanked by two windows – exactly as a child might draw a house. And the atmosphere of the station wasn't brightened by the crew of a maintenance train waiting for us to pass. A particularly wild-looking lot, they leaned out windows and slouched at doors, staring at us with less-than-benevolent intent.

We chugged on in the rain, passing through the longest tunnel on the line, through the township of St Clair, through a valley with a beautiful cataract-filled river, through tiny Talawakele Station whose turntable had been turned into a cabbage patch, and stopped at one o'clock at Watagoda Station, which was just a signboard and a boarded-up shed in the jungle. Two teenagers got down, dashed up the road and returned minutes later, each sheepishly, and rather miraculously, carrying a bottle of whisky under his jacket.

As we waited and waited, I read my newspaper until a tinkling sound like the urgent beating of a hundred triangles pulled my attention away. It was a Kandy-bound train going through. We were free to leave. Immediately we began to go higher, through tea gardens planted up sheer hillsides, before edging around a series of rock-faces punctuated by waterfalls and into the township of Nanu-Oya where mist licked against the station building walls. Then it was off into more tea gardens. Eventually these petered out and we were among clouds and trees and it got so cold I dug into my rucksack for another layer of clothing. We emerged into a giant market garden, with rows of cabbages and carrots and cauliflowers, potatoes, tomatoes and leaf greens, onto which farmers were tossing fistfuls of fertiliser.

At 1,900 metres we had climbed as far as we would go and dipped down a wooded hill and into a very long tunnel ('Collapsed in 1951'). Out the other side was a dry brown valley where smoke rose from half a dozen fires and behind which were lines of hills, softly contoured. On we curled through the trees and tunnels, maintaining our altitude and view of the valley with its huddles of tea pickers' huts and processing factories.

The town of Bandarawela came into sight, spread thinly down the valley. Schoolchildren flip-flopped past us through muddy puddles on their way home. The far hills had turned azure and the still air was full of the smell of smoke. We sauntered on, an hour and a half behind schedule, drifting down past banana and avocado trees and terraced vegetable plots, but much of the way it was still untouched jungle.

At five o'clock we stopped.

'This is Ella, get off!' called out the ticket inspector, who knew it was my destination.

I hadn't expected anything so small. Indeed, we appeared to have halted in the middle of the jungle.

'Quick, get off,' he again urged me.

For some unaccountable reason, trains in Sri Lanka did not dilly-dally at stations, pausing only long enough to provoke a mad push-and-shove contest between those disembarking and those hastening aboard. I gathered up my things and leapt from the moving coach.

Lifting up my rucksack I looked around. The station, small and delicate and ornate, could have been an English cottage. Behind it was a lane. I set off down the hill through the brooding jungle. Ella turned out to be a sleepy hamlet, a dozen shops grouped around a T-intersection and a few guesthouses scattered among the trees.

The light was fading so I rushed off to the Ella Gap to catch a sight of the coastal plains 1,000 metres below. Returning in the dark, I decided I had gone as far as I cared with Sri Lankan Railway.

Art College, Trivandrum.

The 10 am to Cochin

TRIVANDRUM IS, FOR INDIA, an oddity: an unspoilt capital city. 'This is the loveliest city in India,' I said to a young man, a dental surgeon, at Trivandrum Station.

'It is a quiet place,' he conceded. 'Good to retire to, but nothing much happens here.'

'So what do you miss?'

'Pubs, discos ...'

'You have a family?'

'Yes, one boy.'

'Then what do you need? It is very relaxed, very civilised. There is even a sign outside the station saying "Don't use air-horns".'

'But still they do.'

'Not very much. Not compared with other places.'

'It is unnatural for us, you know, not to make noise.'

He had hit it right on the nail, or on the horn, if you will – this need to be boisterous, part of a crowd: it was in their make-up. A quiet island getaway would be a prison sentence for most. I remembered the holidaymakers in Simla who didn't take themselves off on solitary walks through the hills but rubbed shoulders along The Mall.

The young dentist and I had been talking about Sri Mata Amritanandamyi Devi, the so-called hugging guru. Posters of her plump, smiling face were plastered around the station. She was about to turn fifty and four days of festivities were planned. The dentist said devotees had been flocking to her Kerala ashram for years for guidance and a simple hug, which was reputed to spiritually fortify the receiver.

I read later somewhere that she was reckoned to have embraced thirty million people in the past thirty years during the course of her daily darshans. As I left I took a promotional brochure to read. Her teaching was dead simple. The difficulty lay in its implementation. Amma, or 'Mother', as followers also called her, maintained that meditation and selfless hard work were the way to help alleviate human suffering and see the truth – that God was love and that the Divine existed in everything – in every person, plant and animal.

With a ticket in my hand for Cochin I had time to spare so I went for a walk up the main street, predictably enough called Mahatma Gandhi Road. With a population nudging one million, Trivandrum was, by Indian standards, just an overgrown town. I got up the hill as far as the public library, a Victorian-era building of grand proportions but with a paltry book collection. Next door was the city's College of Fine Arts. The head teacher gave me a tour. The quality of the work was surprisingly good; the choice of themes was broad, the execution modern.

'Would these sell in a gallery?' I asked.

'No. Quality is there and more and more Indians have money to buy original art. But no, people do not understand it, they do not have the training to appreciate it. They want traditional subjects – landscapes and such things.'

Students were at work on their canvases. They were enthusiastic but had no illusions about the difficulties ahead: the struggle to get recognition, to find a gallery to display them, to make sales.

'It's a brave choice, to become an artist in India,' I said to one group. They nodded in agreement. 'If it's any consolation, things are no better in the West.'

But that wasn't quite true. Artists there could get grants, artist-in-residence appointments, sponsorships, community funding and a dozen other disguises for handouts. In India artists sold or starved.

❂

Mr K. George John, Trivandrum Station Manager (Gazetted), evidently believed cleanliness was next to godliness. The station displayed ample evidence of both: its platforms were swept and clean and decorated with potted plants, and its walls displayed religiously uplifting quotations such as 'Right attitude is the first condition to make the life on earth smooth and profitable – Buddha' and 'Ahimsa is one of the world's great principles which no power on earth can wipe out – M. K. Gandhi.'

But the state of platform three, where I waited, would not have been entirely to Mr John's satisfaction. It was a disorderly assembly of lumpy sacks and tin boxes and porters hauling about big cartons in the last stages of disintegration on their journey to an unmarked destination; the obligatory handful of motorbikes packed in protective sacking; and tea chests stamped with the words 'THE NILGIRIS'. There were also catering supplies for the waiting pantry car, including boxes of potatoes and red onions and coffee and tea dispensers. When these were loaded aboard, the express service glided out of the city, although with such a dense covering of palms it was scarcely credible to use the word 'city'.

For an hour up the line I looked out the window thinking that this string of houses among the coconut trees must end. It did so only when we broke out into a series of lagoons and inland waterways, beautiful palm-fringed reaches running parallel to the coast. In and out of view they slipped, brought alive by the occasional Keralan getting about on his equivalent of a scooter or bicycle, a long, broad-beamed canoe; or by the district's equivalent of a bus, a square-rigged barge on its run to isolated villages.

To the north, clouds were building against a blue sky in fantastically tall formations. But it was still breathlessly hot outside. Everyone moved with calculated economy, whether the housewife walking home or the railway gang workers, stripped to the waist, hauling off old sleepers.

At Quilon, a handful of passengers boarded, but still no one entered my empty coach. Just beyond the sleepy canal town of Alleppey, the line crossed onto a thin peninsula that ran all the way to Cochin. On one side it was bounded by the Indian Ocean and on the other by the elongated Lake Vembanad. There was no water to see, though, just the modest palm-shaded houses of Kerala passing endlessly by. The one clue that we were on a peninsula was the greyish-white sand. It was a wonderful scene of fluttering washing and coir-making factories and men playing cards in the shade of swaying coconut trees. If you were fated to be born a poor Indian, this would be the spot to hope for.

❂

The streets of Cochin and its twin city Ernakulam were strangely subdued for a weekday. Many of the shops were shut. The manager of my hotel, Mr Chopra, put me in the picture. A by-election had been called to replace the district's MP in the Lok Sabha, who had died three months earlier. Voters were at the ballot boxes.

'How do you find India?' Mr Chopra enquired.

That was always a tricky question, so I said, 'It has its ups and downs.'

He reflected for a moment. 'Too much politics.'

'You mean too much corruption.'

He thought about that for a moment and laughed mirthlessly. 'Yes, politics *is* corruption.'

But no Indian city can be entirely still. And Cochin was readying itself for the hugging guru's birthday celebrations, scheduled to begin the following day. I saw few political posters about but plenty of the smiling Amma.

Next morning, as I stood outside my hotel wondering what to do for two days (my Rajdhani Express to Goa went only twice a week), I got talking to a man who introduced himself as Ravi Shankar. 'Yes, everyone asks me if I am related to the sitar player,' he said before I had even thought of the question.

Mr Shankar asked if I was going to the Jawarharlal Nehru Stadium for the birthday celebrations, and did I want to share an auto-rickshaw?

I said I had been toying with the idea of going along. Then I asked, 'Have you been a follower long?'

'I can tell you exactly – since 1997. In that year we had a vision we would have a baby and a year later we had our first child, Ravina. She was born on my birthday, April 10.'

'You say 'we'?'

'My wife and I. We both had the same vision: a short woman, all in white, dark skin, a beautiful smile … she was, how do you say, heavy …'

'Chubby?'

'Yes, and I remember she had a special fragrance. When I met Amma the first time I knew it was the same fragrance, the same woman in the vision. The fragrance, it just comes out of her skin.'

'You believed the vision then?' I guessed he was nearing fifty and that he and his wife had had fertility problems.

'Of course,' Mr Shankar said. 'We are brought up to believe in the mystical. We accept science cannot explain all things.'

As we stood outside the hotel foyer, Mr Shankar kept looking up to wave at his daughter, who peered from a first-floor window. He turned to me with a smile. 'We have another daughter too, now. Three months old.'

We set off for the stadium in a three-wheeler and I yelled to Mr Shankar over the din of traffic, 'I suppose you are too settled in America to return to India?' (He had worked as a management consultant in Virginia for the past seventeen years.)

'No, I might return. Mother has asked me to work at the Amrita Institute of Management. You know it?'

'Yes, I do.'

The brochure I picked up at the station declared that the institute's aim was 'to produce excellent managers with compassionate hearts'. That seemed to me an eminently worthy, if rarely found, combination of qualities.

'Mother wants me to oversee the technical aspects of the institute. I am thinking it over.'

The birthday celebrations, I knew from my morning's newspaper, had drawn some awfully big names, among them India's deputy prime minister, president and vice-president, plus a host of ministers and MPs. En route, Mr Shankar and I passed a cavalcade of such VVIPs. ('Yes,' laughed Mr Shankar, 'you must be VVIP today. VIP is nothing!') There were so many jeeps and cars, all crammed with gesticulating officials and soldiers, preceding and following the mystery visitor, who was hidden inside a tinted-glass Mercedes-Benz, that I had to laugh myself. There was even an ambulance and a police bus bringing up the rear. It occurred to me to count the number of vehicles in this mad procession of flashing headlights and wailing sirens, but by then too many had already roared through the bewildered traffic. I guessed twenty-five. There was a heavy theatricality about the whole business, a sort of state-funding big-noting, but it could equally have been a harking back to times when great fanfare attended the progress of maharajas and Moghul emperors through a city's thoroughfares.

The scene inside the stadium was just as I had expected: immense swirling crowds, a lot of tents selling booklets and tapes of Amma's words, canteens, a first aid post and a media 'cell' (or tent). ('We've got some big guns coming in,' said the Australian woman overseeing the foreign media section. 'There's the *Wall Street Journal*, the *Herald-Tribune*, *Time*....') There were speakers discussing inter-faith harmony and the protection of the planet. ('We cannot have spiritual harmony,' one speaker pronounced, 'without environmental purity.') There was even a special 'Western canteen' for the delicate stomachs of foreign devotees whose appearance exactly matched that of so many of the guests at my hotel: solemn, pious, robed entirely in white.

Intriguingly, one tent contained what could only be described as a shrine to Amma. Large framed portraits of 'Her Holiness' were draped with garlands, and candles burned at their base. That process of deification – which was, I suspected, proceeding with or without her approval – reminded me of my chat with Mr Francis down by the waterfront the previous evening. He was a Christian and was less charmed by the hugging guru.

'Do you believe in her?' I had asked.

'No, I am a Christian. I do not believe that she is a god. I believe in Jesus Christ.'

I said, 'I remember reading that, when questioned about her religion, she answered simply, "My religion is Love."'

'Yes, she does good things for poor people, sick people … that is true. But she is not a god, though people treat her as though she is one.'

Mr Francis was a slightly built man, sober-minded (he had worked for Cochin's Port Trust Authority for twenty-seven years) and very tentative in manner – something I put down to his minority status.

'Christians are very quiet, very peaceful,' he volunteered. And then he added, 'Muslims fight back when there are clashes with Hindus.'

'Why is that?'

His mouth moved noiselessly as he searched for the right words.

'Short wick, maybe?' I suggested. 'Like a short fuse on a bomb.'

'Bomb!' he exclaimed. 'Yes, bomb.'

'Why do you think that is so?' I asked.

'Because,' he said, lowering his voice, as so many did on the subject of communal relations, 'because Muslims side with Pakistan. Their hearts are with Pakistan.'

Hindu–Muslim enmity could not, I felt sure, be explained solely by divided loyalties and the hidden hand of Pakistan. There were many matches held to the powder-keg. But it was illuminating that a Christian was seeing deeper, hidden Muslim allegiances.

Whatever the causes, the consequences could be bloody. According to Mr Francis, a Hindu–Muslim clash in Cochin only a year ago had left thirty dead. There was no shortage of Hindu or Muslim hotheads. One such Hindu had just been given the death penalty for murdering a Christian missionary and his two sons in Orissa state in 1999. It was the top story in the news. The ringleader,

Dara Singh, and twelve others, who got life sentences, set alight the car in which Australian Graham Staines and his sons were sleeping because of resentment at Staines's activities in converting tribal groups and low-caste 'untouchables'. (Orissa already had a law on the statute books prohibiting conversion to another religion by use of force, inducement or fraudulent means.)

The judge, in handing down the death sentence, quoted Jonathan Swift. 'We have just enough religion,' he told Singh and his gang, 'to make us hate each other, and not enough to make us love each other.'

The judge, it seemed to me, had got to the nub of the matter.

❂

'The charm is all gone,' Mr Chopra declared when I said the old quarter of Cochin had gone to the dogs. 'I told the city authorities at a meeting last year, "You must stop putting up new buildings." But they don't listen. That Portuguese charm – all gone!'

He tut-tutted some more and said to me, 'Did you go to Mattancheri?'

'I walked to the synagogue in Jewtown, yes.'

'Council spent a lot of money last year cleaning up the canals and clearing the gutters. But now it is all back. Those people, they are never learning. Still they are dumping their shit in the street (it was the first time I'd heard an Indian use such a profanity). They live in a one-room house – father, mother, children, grandparents, goat, cow – and everything outside that one room is a rubbish tip.'

Mr Chopra was a stickler for cleanliness. His hotel was the most spotless I stayed in anywhere on the subcontinent, and it was far from the most expensive. This short, balding man saw neglect and incompetence everywhere. Cochin has an almost incomparable position as a natural meeting place for ocean-going vessels and inland craft, but Mr Chopra saw only the spread of the tenacious South American waterweed *Eichhornia*.

'It is clogging up all the canals! Even some of the smallest around Alleppey where all the tourist boats go are impassable. I said to these tourist operators, "Why don't you give a part of your profits to the panchayats to help remove it." But no, they have done nothing and tourist numbers are falling off. Everyone wants the money now; no one is looking to the future.'

The tourist officer at Willingdon Island took a different view. When I had finished griping about the mess around the Fort district, he said, 'Food, shelter and clothing – these take priority over everything. What comes first is that the farmer is growing enough rice. Beautification of tourist spots – that comes later.'

His office surveyed the impressive panorama of Cochin's busy port with merchant ships lying at anchor and ferries scurrying from the mainland to island jetties. He also had views across to the waterfront mansions and the cantilevered Chinese nets which creaked up and down like arthritic limbs, and the labyrinth of godowns where I had smelt air thick with the scent of cardamom, peppercorn, clove, turmeric and a score of other Malabar aromatics.

'But the farmer growing his rice has nothing to do with people dumping their rubbish,' I said.

'Slowly, slowly, sir. You must give India some time. We cannot afford European standards of cleanliness.'

'It takes no money at all to sweep up the litter – or not to drop it in the first place. And all those Indian tourists I saw looked to have plenty of food, shelter and clothing.'

He laughed nervously. 'Maybe we need a revolution, sir.'

Getting about, Cochin.

The Konkan Railway

THE BEARER, HASAM SINGH, woke me with tea as dawn broke and the Konkan Express thundered through the town of Ullal. We had exchanged the hard-worked Keralan landscape of coconut trees and rice fields for the dense jungle hills of Karnataka state. Every stream was a bottle-green collage of tree reflections, and my carriage, dimmed by this murky tangle of growth, was cool and shadow-filled like a crypt.

At 7.15 am we crossed the broad pale-blue reaches of the Netravati River. Three country boats drifted in the morning stillness, their lateen-rigged sails drooping like morose faces. The Netravati was just south of Mangalore, a port city of half a million on the Malabar Coast, but we skirted it and made a stop a few kilometres to the east at Kankanadi, a tiny halt in the jungle. A handful of passengers disembarked for Mangalore and we moved off, back into thickly wooded hills where a scattering of mildew-streaked rooftops offered the only proof of human habitation.

Hasam returned with the morning's paper. Kashmir as usual featured on the front page: Pakistan urging self-determination for Kashmiris, India urging an end to Pakistan backing of insurgents in its share of the mountainous region. Stalemate.

We entered a long tunnel, descended out of the hills into isolated pockets of paddy fields and made a rolling stop at Surathkal. There was no station building to be seen, and jungle grew to the base of the platform. Red-dirt tracks were hacked through the trees, and cows went where they wished, unattended by herders. Then we resumed our stroboscopic journey, through more tunnels, through more embankments and over more bridges – all testimony to the difficulty of building a railway line along the wild Konkan, India's tortuous western flank from Mangalore to Bombay.

The British, the world's most prolific railway builders, had rejected the idea of a coastal line: the region was simply too wild, too hilly, its soil too soft and too frequently broken by rivers to be conquered. What's more, declared the Controller of Railways, a Mr W. Hancock, in 1866, the region's inhabitants were 'semi-wild tribes, who live on jungle fruits, rats, roots … they would never travel by rail'. A long inland detour was devised, and it remained in use until 1998, when the Konkan line opened.

The task indeed proved formidable, taking seven years to finish at a cost of 76 lives. The engineering difficulties of the 76-kilometre route were compounded by the planners' determination to forge a route as straight as possible through the never-ending chain of foothills that descends from the Western Ghats to the Arabian Sea. That resolve necessitated the digging of ninety-two tunnels (six of them more than 3 kilometres long) and the building of 1,998 bridges; and every monsoon still threatens to wreck the whole hard-fought thing. Another complication was the colossal legal exercise of acquiring land from the 42,000 landholders along its route.

'Is coachman, is coachman,' squawked a cleaner who came by, mopping the floor around my feet with particular vigilance. (I was almost the only occupant of the coach.) His tools were a broom handle to which was fastened a length of cloth he periodically squirted with cleaning liquid. The effect of his labours was merely to moisten the floor. The grime was beyond his capabilities. The 'coachman' returned. He had grey stubble, a prison-issue haircut and standard-issue khakis. He held open a comments book before me: 'Good work' and 'Excellent' I read in one column. It was a prelude to a demand for baksheesh. I obliged and he moved on to more populated pastures.

The hills and the jungle enveloped us once more. We plunged into another very long tunnel. Hasam said this was nothing: north of Madgaon there was a 6-kilometre-long tunnel (it is in fact, at 6.5 kilometres, India's longest). All these Konkan Railway tunnels were preceded and followed by cuttings, and long periods passed in which I did nothing but stare at long deep gashes in the earth. But then we sailed high above the Sharavati River. It ballooned out upstream like an inland lake, and without any bridge structure visible beside or above us we appeared to be soaring unaided over the water – and for a minute or two on end, as this was the longest bridge on the route. Immediately we reached the other side and the town of Honovar we vanished into the darkness of one, then two, then three more tunnels; then out the other side among gentle hills and dirt roads.

About that time I had visitors, two fat jolly fellows who invited themselves into my compartment.

'You will take a hot drink with us?' asked one as he sat down.

'You mean tea or coffee?' I asked.

'No, hard liquor. You will join us?'

I looked at my watch. 'At eleven o'clock? No thanks.'

'Do you mind if we do?'

'Not at all.'

So the chubbier of the two, though it was a close call as to which really was the fatter, disappeared round the corner, reappearing with two glasses filled to the lip with a honey-coloured beverage.

He handed one to his friend and they clinked a 'Cheers!'

I said, 'My guess is whisky and water.'

'Close, sir. Brandy and water,' said the one sitting nearer me. 'Here, my card.' And he reached into his shorts pocket (they both wore shorts and thongs) and took a business card from his wallet. It read: P. P. Shameem, Director, Punathil Roller Flour Mills Ltd, Punathil Iron & Steels, Kannur (Cannore).

198

'Best brandy in the country,' Mr Shameem said after a long swallow. 'Ocean brand – his father's.' He pointed to his friend. 'Cannore Tata they call him.'

'All true,' his friend agreed. 'My father never smoke, drank or womanised. And I do all three. Ha!'

'So where are you off to?'

'Vadodara.'

'Business?'

'No, to see our girlfriends,' they said in a chorus of giggles.

That was not quite the answer I was expecting of two men in their thirties.

'Where did you meet these girlfriends of yours?' I enquired.

'On this train – going to Vadodara once. This is the third time we have been going there.'

'So you've met the parents? They approve?'

'My God, no,' said Mr Shameem, and this time he really threw back his head in a throaty laugh. 'I'm married. Here, I'll show you my daughter.'

And he brought up her image on his mobile phone screen: a six-year-old standing in the backyard making a funny face for her father.

The sight of a mobile phone prompted Mr Brandy to check his own mobile. His moustache twitched. 'A message,' he beamed. He called his girlfriend back. '… Karwar, … yes, Karwar, 11.40 …' and he rang off.

They made an odd pair, the adulterer and the womaniser, with their thin gangster moustaches and fleshy faces and bony calves, their brandies in hand before lunchtime and ready to play up.

'He can get married if he wants,' Mr Shameem said in an admonishing tone. 'He's only thirty-five – I'm thirty-two – it's not too late.'

'No,' his friend replied, momentarily subdued. 'I will always be a bachelor. We Hindus believe in astrology. Dates must be right for bride and groom. For Muslims, Christians, it is easy; if families agree and couple are right, then simple! It is done. But Hindus must consult astrologist. So many times the stars have ruined things for me ….'

I was curious. 'How many times have you called off a match?'

'Oh, too many times to count. My fate, I think, is to be a bachelor.' Whereupon he took a deep consoling slurp of his brandy.

'Do you want to get married?'

For the first and only time he lost his jovial drinking-buddy demeanour. 'Yes I would, I mean, if … but no, we have our girlfriends.'

And together they knocked off the last of their drinks.

As Mr Brandy went off to refresh their glasses I said to Mr Shameem, 'At this rate, you won't be able to get off the train at Baroda.' (It was due in at 1.30 the following morning.)

'Not to bother, we have our hotel booked.' He looked squarely at me and said, 'So tell me, my friend, are morals in your country like in America and Europe? Because here in India men are too attached to their families.'

I scrambled to think of some suitable reply. 'I think it is probably like India.'

'So only one woman?'

'Not before I married, no.'

'But when you married?'

'Yes, just one.'

He let the significance of that information sink in.

'Your marriage was arranged?' I asked.

'Of course. My father decided. Always I am answering to my father, no matter how old I am. He is my father and I do as he says. It is the Indian way. I know it is not like you in the West. You leave home and go your own way, yes?'

'That's true.'

Mr Shameem went on to describe the particular difficulties and complications of finding the right marriage partner. Throughout it all, the word 'caste' never arose. The codename was 'standing': how vital it was for Indian families that their standing not be diminished through marriage. 'If you marry a scavenger,' he explained, 'your standing will fall to that of a scavenger. So you must find someone like you. That way you don't slip down.'

His friend returned with two more drinks, filled to the rim, which they slurped at liberally while grilling me about my travels: why I travelled alone; whether I had been to America, where all cares and worries fall away.

'No,' I said, 'I haven't been there.'

'He has,' Mr Shameem said.

US visas were the hardest of all to obtain, he said, because American authorities feared Indians would overstay. His friend had got his only because he owned so much land, which consular officials figured he wouldn't lightly abandon to start a new, illegal life in the States.

'In Chennai,' his friend complained, 'the woman at the American consulate, she was so hard, she asks me so many questions; questions about this, questions about that! Why, some of them were ....' But his indignation petered out when it came to specifying the iniquities.

Mr Shameem took a deep breath, as though about to ask a delicate question, and then said to me, 'Indians, they think from seeing all those Western movies like James Bond that white men are always trying to have sex with a woman. Is that true?'

The naïveté took me aback. 'Perhaps I should answer your question with a question,' I said. 'Do you think masala movies are the real India? All those beautiful unspoilt places, endless music, ever-joyous people, fine clothes? Of course not. It's just pretend.'

'But in all masala movies there is singing, and song is very important in India, so in one way the movies do show the real India.'

'Possibly. It's stretching a point.'

Mr Shameem took a big slurp of his brandy and blurted out: 'White man does know how to do love, but *wagina* is dirty. To see blue movies where white man does with his tongue, what you call it?'

'Oral sex?'

'Yes, Indians think that is disgusting and white man is dirty. There is only one thing to put in *wagina* and that is penis.'

I was stumped for a reply.

The second round of brandies was gone. At this rate, trouble in one guise or another couldn't be far off. I was pleased to be getting down at Madgaon, which appeared soon enough. After expressions of undying friendship, I left them to their secret trysts and caught a bus to Goa's capital, Panjim, 35 kilometres away.

❁

Nand Kumar was a more sober-minded conversationalist, but a considerably more stimulating one as well. He was a book publisher from Bombay, and whether by effort or instinct he had developed a free-spirited outlook on life. He abhorred conformity, a fact that soon became apparent as we chatted in one of Panjim's restaurants.

'People all over the country are scrambling to get a toehold in Bombay,' he said, 'and I am trying to leave, to set up in Panjim. Everybody says to me, "You are mad. It is so quiet, the medical facilities are terrible. Don't go, you're crazy." But it has been my dream since I first came to Panjim in 1982.'

I told him it seemed a perfectly sensible plan. Panjim was slow-paced and civilised. Bombay was overcrowded, its weather atrocious and its house prices exorbitant.

'So true! My apartment is just two bedrooms, half an hour by train from the city centre and it's worth two-and-a-half million rupees.'

'That's good for you if you're heading south.'

'Yes, but things are starting to imitate Bombay here – the corruption, the pollution, the public works. Look at that road,' he said, pointing out the window. 'Do you think we Indians can't make roads? Of course we can. But contractors must pay such big cuts to officials to get the work that a shoddy job is all they can afford to do. It's partly deliberate, though. Then they get to repair their own work, and then re-repair it and then re-re-repair it. Another example. I went to the Rajiv Gandhi Teaching Hospital, and it is falling down. The state's best public hospital and it has damp creeping up the walls. The people who built that, the contractors, the architects, they should be shot – not with a bullet, but with cannonballs so that not one little bit of their flesh remains. A poor country like ours cannot afford such waste.'

Such strong, indeed almost violent, words seemed incongruous coming from someone so mild in manner and appearance. Among his few distinguishing features were a warty complexion, wavy grey hair and eyes that peered intently through square-framed glasses. His shirted stomach bulged over his beltless polyester pants.

Mr Kumar continued to offer other examples of what he called the same primitive state of affairs – the tangle of drooping wires of every power pole, the pollution from unserviced vehicles – and to decry the lack of official reaction. 'This country is without governance.'

I thought for a moment. 'Surely every public agency cannot be bad. What about the tax department? Governments the world over like to get every last penny they're entitled to.'

'Mr Peter, there you are wrong. My sister-in-law, she is working for Income Tax Department. She has hardly an hour's work a day. Overstaffed, underworked. The government employs not simply legions but whole armies of workers to do nothing. You cannot imagine. What's more, the tax burden falls on the middle class completely. The poor pay nothing. The rich pay nothing – they hire accountants and grease the palms of ministers and opposition MPs and customs people. That leaves only wage and salary earners.'

We ordered coffee and I said to Mr Kumar, 'You know, if no one will complain and push for change then you get, as we say, the government you deserve.'

He gave a slow, sad shake of his head. 'No, you can complain, make a noise, but it always comes to nothing. I myself have made complaints but these people at the top, they are ....' Mr Kumar was momentarily stuck for the right word and he ran a finger back and forth along the veins of his other wrist.

'You mean bloodless, without heart?'

'Yes. They say, "Here is Complaint Book. Have it if you must." And they look at you with eyes like fish. You write your complaint and then … nothing. The matter is always dropped. One thing you must also remember: many people are so busy working to feed themselves and their families they have no time to think about bigger things. The man rushing to get to work on time at eight o'clock –

otherwise he will be fired – does he have time to think about such questions? No.'

'Is there any reason to think India might change?' I asked.

'It appears hopeless, but there must be a way. Someone like Singapore's Mr Lee. A generation of a benevolent dictator might fix things.'

'But,' I countered, 'you'd only have to hand power back to the people who would still have to learn the lessons they appear to be failing to grasp right now.'

'Yes ... yes,' he mused. 'The other difficulty is that the politicians and the dons – the criminal bosses – are completely hand in glove. In places like Bihar state, the dons *are* the politicians. MPs are goons who carry guns and behave as though they are outside the law.'

It seemed an exceedingly grim estimate of the country's political stocks, but not one that conflicted with anything I had seen or heard.

Mr Kumar's scathing indictment of public life did not end there. He had no kind words for the press. The fourth estate was, in his view, dominated by Hindus who, to prove their liberal credentials, went out of their way to lambaste Hindus at the expense of Muslims. This approach was partly guided by self-preservation, however, for – in his view – the least criticism of Muslims was likely to bring down a torrent of abuse, and sometimes worse – physical harm. And when I thought about it, I realised he was probably right: the issue of Hindu–Muslim relations got very few column inches.

'The problem is,' Mr Kumar continued, 'that many Muslims, in their hearts, are not with India but with Pakistan. They are wanting shariah law for marriage, divorce, property matters and such things. They do not wish to be bound by Indian law, to join the community of India, if you will.'

'Why don't they go to Pakistan then?'

'A good question, Mr Peter. Only last month our deputy prime minister made a speech saying just that: Integrate or go to Pakistan.'

Mr Kumar asked about my plans. I told him I was off to Dwarka, which is at the end of the line in Gujarat's Kathiawar Peninsula. Founded by Krishna after his flight from northern India, Dwarka is a very sacred place to Hindus. In fact, it ranks as one of the Great Seven places of pilgrimage, along with Varanasi, Muttra, Hardwar, Ajudhia, Ujjain and Conjeeveram.

When I mentioned hearing of non-Hindus being prevented from entering the Dwarkanath Temple, Mr Kumar was emphatic that it was profane to deny non-Hindus entry. 'It is a house of God. All are welcome. You can even go in without any noble higher intentions. You can enter as a non-believer, as a curious tourist. All are acceptable. The person who says you cannot pray this way or that way, or that non-Hindus cannot enter a temple, is ignorant, completely ignorant.'

He himself seldom went to temples. He didn't like showy displays of piety. 'Religion is not about worship, it is about a personal quest to find God.'

I found myself in total agreement with his thoughts. Were there many like him, I asked. People who went only occasionally to temples to pray, but who were religious nevertheless?

'A small number, I think.'

'How small?' I pressed.

'Very small.'

Mr Kumar confided to me that he was an avid practitioner of Vipassna meditation, an ancient technique practised by Buddha. Initiation was through a ten-day course during which one meditated for a total of ten hours a day, and not a word was uttered – 'not even eye talk' – from rising at 4 am until lights out at 9.30 pm. 'It is without dogma, creed, rules, belief – the purest form of meditation.'

While observing the so-called Noble Silence, the meditator strove through self-examination to 'see things as they really are', to dissolve mental impurity and achieve a balanced mind full of love and compassion.

On the seventh day Mr Kumar got what he called 'the shivers'. He ran his fluttering hands up and down as though these sensations pulsed through his entire body.

'They should have grown on the eighth, ninth and tenth days, but they never returned. They did for others on the course. But it does not matter. It is the trying that is important.'

He strenuously urged me to make the four-hour train journey from Bombay to Nasik, the worldwide centre of Vipassna meditation. As gently as possible, I told him I could not spare a ten-day detour. I had trains to catch.

❁

Panjim felt damp to the bone. It was overcast when I arrived and it rained off and on for the entire three days I was there. (All the trains north were booked out by holidaymakers heading home to Bombay.) By the last day I was itching to be off. Still, it was a pleasant enough place in which to be stuck. In this former Portuguese enclave beside the Indian Ocean, villas drew themselves up in tightly packed lines, their frontages prettily faced with blue-and-white tiles, their interiors – if you were brazen enough to peer through the curly wrought-iron window bars – invariably adorned with framed images of Christ, his heart aflame.

A big whitewashed church overlooked the town square where the Bombay holidaymakers strolled about in what they regarded as fashionable Western dress; some of the young female visitors were daring enough to wear shorts and singlets. The middle-aged men among these out-of-towners had a fondness for an unflattering combination of walk-shorts and socks; their wives sensibly stuck to saris.

Life was relaxed here on the bank of the Mandovi River. Shops shut early in the evenings, and on Sundays they didn't open at all. Without the prohibition of some other states, there was an abundance of grog shops – wholesale outlets and dingy, one-room bars that must have been inviting to only the most hardened, cash-strapped drinker.

On the final day, against my better judgment, I took a sunset river cruise. A frenzy of drinking and manufactured jollity broke out the instant the jetty ropes were cast off, as if by the operation of some invisible switch. Revellers downed bottles of Kingfisher beer as fast as decency would permit, propelled on by the urgent beat of disco music. I retreated to the lower deck and watched Panjim glide by in the twilight: the Customs and Excise building on the quay, the Army signals HQ, the police central offices, the balconied old Mandovi Hotel and the boulevard by the wharf. Beyond a sweep of sand we came to the mouth of the Aguada Estuary and the overgrown remains of a fort. Eventually, in darkness and with the thumping of the sound system still overpowering the growl of the diesel engines, we tied up again. Another flick of the switch brought the party to an equally abrupt close.

Shore temple at dusk, Dwarka.

The Saurashtra Mail

THE SAURASHTRA MAIL SPED north for almost an hour before the lights of Bombay were extinguished and darkness enveloped us. Mr Thaker withdrew some fabric samples from his suitcase and passed them over.

'In New York and West Coast stores these are selling.'

I flicked through the richly coloured squares of cotton and handed them back. 'They're exquisite.'

'Only top end of market we are dealing in. Double-washing, best-quality dyes and manufacturing techniques.'

My companion – my only companion – was 'in the manufacshure and exshport of textiles'. The family business was doing well. One brother was in Miami handling marketing, another ran the Rajkot factory, while Mr Thaker himself went between Rajkot and Bombay expediting customs and export paperwork.

'We sell by the container load. Biggest problem for American market is timely deliveries. Labour strikes, poor rains, quality fluctuations in factory – all are causing difficulties.'

Mr Thaker did not appear unduly weighed down by these difficulties. Indeed, sitting opposite me, cross-legged in a white kurta and pyjamas, he looked the very picture of heath and youthfulness (he was thirty-seven) – a fact he put down to his vegetarian diet.

'Gujarat is most vegetarian state in India. Many non-veg people are having poor skin. Overweight they are too. And aggressive. This is because flesh of animals has uric acid. Eating meat causes build-up of this acid, and aggressive behaviour is result.'

'How do you know all these things?' I asked.

'My father is subscribing to homeopathic and ayurvedic journals, and these I am reading.'

'Your father is a strict vegetarian?'

'Very strict.'

'And in good health?'

'Oh yes, he is sixty-five and going strong. My mother, she is sixty-two and always very well. My father, he was going to Hong Kong and got sick last year. Chinese doctor looked at him and said, "You are vegetarian. You must eat meat to get strong." My father answered, "But are not the strongest animals in the world vegetarian? The elephant, the rhinoceros, the hippopotamus?" No, he would never eat meat.'

Mr Thaker believed in plenty of rest as well as plenty of vegetables and was soon tucked into bed for the night.

When I woke at seven next morning the train was streaking past the long deserted platforms of Viramgam Station. A blood-red sun was rising over the sandy plains. With few trees to obstruct the eye, I felt I could see for 20, 30 or 50 kilometres in whatever direction I cared to turn my head. And but for the metallic-grey sky that hung like a great inverted bowl over this scene, smudging the horizon, I might have been able to see back as far as Ahmadabad, which my *Trains at a Glance* informed me we had passed through about an hour earlier. Before that we had crossed a vast industrial strip stretching from Ahmadabad through Baroda, Bhroach and Surat back to Bombay, an assortment of belching factories and industrial plants without rival in India. I was glad to have slept through it all.

On this plain grew some stunted maize and, more importantly, groundnut, a low, inconspicuous-looking crop, scarcely knee height, which had been planted out in fields of long, evenly spaced rows. But wherever man had not hacked it down, there grew the babul, a tenacious weed with straggling branches that rapidly colonises barren soil. And on the bleak plains of the Kathiawar Peninsula, which also goes by the name of Saurashtra, farmers certainly had their work cut out. Mr Thaker said some farmers had bored to 600 metres without finding water. Average rainfall had halved in recent years – down from 60 centimetres a year to 30 – though this year's had been the highest in a decade. It looked to have made little impact.

The rawness of these weedy plains pleased me. I had as yet seen neither a farmer's hut nor any sign of permanent habitation. But then we came to Surendranagar. The station was quite a distance from the city, which was visible as a cluster of temple spires flying red flags, a water tower and some houses set amid trees. On the town's outskirts three youths herded flocks of goats along a dried-up riverbed, and in a field beside some kilns were stacked toilet bowls in their hundreds. Then, in minutes, I had my blessed bare plains back.

By mid-morning there were bare stony hills to the north. Mr Thaker lay on his bunk, still, a sheet drawn over his face like a cadaver in a morgue, intent upon sleep, while another passenger who joined us during the night lay in an upper berth in the same rigid position.

Wankaner, appearing soon afterwards, was hot, dusty and shadeless, its many brick-making kilns pouring plumes of smoke from cigar-shaped chimney stacks. The very air over the city was grey. We followed the road out of town. Traffic was slight – a bus, a motorbike converted to a trike to carry goods and passengers, a farmer on a creaking cart. The hills, all strewn with rocks and babul, grew in number.

Mr Thaker finally roused himself as the plains returned and another crop showed itself: cotton. All of it, he informed me, went to Coimbatore, in Tamil Nadu, for spinning before some of it was brought back to his family's factory.

We crossed a river, little more than a wide shallow stream flowing among rocks, and Mr Thaker said, 'For the first time in many years we are seeing water in the rivers.' Things had indeed been bad.

The Aji River through Rajkot, which we reached at 10.40 am, had a similarly modest flow of water. Mr Thaker departed. About half of the carriages were decoupled. They were not needed for the little-used final leg to Dwarka. An unappetising lunch was handed out: I gave mine to a beggar woman. She took it without a flicker of emotion or acknowledgment. It was my dharma to give, hers to receive.

An hour later, the Saurashtra Mail moved off, back onto the hot dusty plains, back among the patches of cotton, pulses and groundnut, back among the babul (now almost the size of trees), back beneath the unvarying metallic-grey sky.

It soon became clear that at Rajkot the service had metamorphosed from an express into a local. Every no-name station brought us to a halt. Not that I cared. I was trundling towards a place few cared to go to. There were only seven passengers in my coach, all of them asleep.

Jamnagar, the last town of any size before Dwarka, emerged out of what seemed to me the driest, least populated region of India I had yet passed through. At the station, a considerable delay ensued as the sacks flung from the luggage van with such abandon were now discovered to include some bound for Dwarka. The coolies huffed and shouted at one another as the mountain of sacks was searched, the miscreant items identified (they contained fresh betel levels for pan-wallahs) and then tossed back into the luggage van's hold. Throughout all this, a group of village women in black saris and brass anklets whose complexions were as leathery as their sandals sat watching in the full glare of the sun, apparently quite impervious to its ferocity.

Back on the vast plain, made more desolate by the yellow-brown clouds massing in all directions above the haze, we trundled along a course parallel to the Gulf of Kachchh. A series of rivers intersected our route on their way to empty into the gulf. Each was four-fifths bleached sandbanks, on which solitary figures were digging or erecting makeshift huts or just wandering about in the mid-afternoon sun. But that trickle of water was a much appreciated sight.

The inhabitants of Khanbaliya, the final outpost before Dwarka, seemed to have fallen into a collective slumber amid the town's plentiful rubbish and decaying buildings. I stood at the coupling door, diesel smoke, swirling dust and hot air blasting my face, and could discern only inert figures. One man lay dozing in the shade under a truck, a dog at his side; another was slumped over the front seat of a cannibalised car; pigs rolled about in refuse and stagnant ponds. Khanbaliya was plainly a place to pause at only by mistake or out of dire necessity. The return of Saurashtra's drab, endless plains made an inviting sight.

At four o'clock rain burst upon this scene even as the sun continued to beat down. It was difficult to believe rain could fall in this place, even though it was happening right before my eyes. And sure enough, it was short-lived. A quarter of an hour later the line edged around what looked like salt flats, which were rusty-pink and extraordinarily pretty. Flocks of birds swirled skywards at our approach. Any sign of man's imprint had become so rare that the most mundane manifestations – a dirt trail through the scrub, an abandoned shed, a broken chatty – caught my attention.

Now, as we began to swing northwards alongside the coast, the Arabian Sea flashed between tussock grass, the ever-present babul, and cacti with slender sage-green limbs, the only plant seemingly capable of contesting for space with the babul. Everything in this giant, wind-blasted scene had a muted tint – fawn, russet, salmon pink, silver grey, olive green – including the charcoal-grey tapering outline of Dwarkanath Temple, which soon reared up from the water's edge. It was all astonishingly beautiful.

Dwarka dented my conviction that the holier the pilgrimage place the more stinking its sanctity. In spite of the hordes who periodically besiege it, the place was clean, quiet and friendly, and the laneways were the preserve of cyclists and pedestrians. In short, it was more village than town.

'All visitors are noting how peaceful Dwarka is,' said the owner of a brassware shop I spoke to in the old quarter. (And Dwarka is old, somewhere between two thousand and four thousand years.) The town's main attraction, Dwarkanath Temple, was right next door, its exterior embellished with all the rich excess one would expect of an important Hindu place of worship.

Two plainclothes policemen told me the area around the temple was off-limits to vehicles because of the Hindu–Muslim riots in Ahmadabad a year earlier – in other words, fear of a retaliatory attack by Muslims. The unequal death toll from those riots – sixty Hindus, one thousand Muslims – spoke volumes about Muslim anger: that the Gujarati government had let the state's police force sit on its hands while Hindu extremists went on a rampage of slaughter and destruction. The Ahmadabad riots were a reaction to the torching by Muslims of a railway carriage carrying Hindu activists (fifty-eight died in the inferno) returning to the city from Ayodhya, a small dusty town in Uttar Pradesh that had been the site of the Babri Masjid mosque until it was torn down by a Hindu mob in 1992. Hindus regarded the mosque as a calculated insult, having been built by Moghul invaders over a temple that had marked the birthplace of their god Rama. So the deaths a year earlier had their origins in the fifteenth century.

That day, few out-of-town pilgrims were worshipping at Dwarkanath Temple. It was the locals who drifted about the marbled interior, most notably the hard-bitten farmers of the district who were easily distinguishable in their grubby white but fantastically eye-catching costumes, which consisted of pants like riding breeches of greatly exaggerated cut; a sort of shrunken frock-coat reaching no lower than the navel; shoes with curled-over, pointy toes; a heavy complicated knot of cloth for a turban – also of white cotton – and all topped off by thick earrings, a generously proportioned moustache and a gnarled and unshaven face.

Entry to the temple, a five-storey structure with seventy-two decorative pillars rising up around the main tapering tower, was no straightforward matter for foreigners. Besides depositing any bags and cameras in safekeeping (full particulars required before obtaining a chit, Rs. 2/-) and removing one's shoes (another chit) and passing through a metal detector (under the eye of armed police), and supplying one's name, passport and other details in a second ledger, there was also a declaration to be filled in, the gist of which was that the signer either believed in Hinduism, was a convert to Hinduism or, thirdly – and this was my choice – 'respected Hinduism'. All that done, I could enter.

Worshippers prayed as they wished, whether in quiet contemplation, group chanting, individual and unabashed reciting of prayers or, in the case of one old peasant clutching a staff, mumbled ravings. Only the ground floor was accessible that morning because, as a policeman informed me, 'Lord Krishna is having a bath.'

Even though his father worked for Indian Railways and despite fifteen years of pleading, Mr A. N. Arunachallam could not get a job with the world's biggest employer. He had had to content himself with a job in a photography shop in Dwarka. His wife was a nurse at the hospital. His hopes, he told me, were now pinned on his wife getting a job in America.

Had he any idea of what he must sacrifice? As I had seen at Trivandrum and Colombo airports where the future maids and labourers of the Gulf states queued anxiously in departure lounges, he would be exporting his labour but leaving behind his soul.

The Saurashtra Mail to take me back to Ahmadabad was still an hour away. Mr Arunachallam was waiting for the same train, which carried a friend from the port town of Okha, thirty minutes further along the line. Dwarka Station had one platform and three working fans. We stood under one, but it did no more than shuffle the hot air about. All around grew babul under a cloudless sky.

'Is it always this hot in October?' I asked.

'Yes, today it is 35 degrees.'

'Then what is it like in May and June?'

'Unbearable, sir. Gujarat is terrible then, especially Ahmadabad.'

No wonder communal tensions so often spilt over there: six million people living in squalid, polluted conditions surrounded by smokestacks and factories. A couple of months of 45 degrees, flies and fumes would melt the saintliest disposition.

But despite the morning's heat, which made the more distant track seemingly twist and float in the shimmering haze, time passed quickly as Mr Arunachallam sought to explain how slight differences in the dress of passers-by indicated the wearer's caste. 'She is from milkman caste,' he said at one point of a woman in a blue-black sari. Of another woman in a black sari, he said, 'She is Kutchchh woman of herder caste.' The subtleties, I had to admit, confounded me, and when the train wriggled slowly into view I was happy to give it up. At 12.10 pm, right on schedule, the Saurashtra Mail drew out and Dwarka shrank forever from sight.

Retracing our way past the bird-covered flats a little way to the east, I asked a passing passenger if it was indeed a salt plant. Yes, he said. I could not have asked a better person. Ganesh Iyer was an engineer with Tata Chemicals, which had a soda ash plant at Mithapur, a company town north of Dwarka. The plant took most of the salt product for the manufacture of detergents and soaps.

Mr Iyer now worked at the company's head office in Bombay, but he had been in Mithapur for six years and had enjoyed it. The company provided good markets, good water and good facilities, including tennis courts, football and hockey fields and snooker tables.

'Even in Bombay you cannot get tennis courts,' he said. 'They cost 2,000 rupees for three hours. That's nearly 40 American dollars. Who can afford that? Only Bombay big shots, the high-society types, and they book them out months in advance. In Bombay there are a small number of very wealthy people and a big number of very poor. Those in the middle like me are very small, too.'

I asked him if he liked living in Bombay.

'Very much. It is the best city in India. The people are very friendly and …'

'I found them in too much of a rush to be friendly.'

'You are right, they can be. But it is still a great city, very vibrant.'

Mr Iyer brought an engineer's perspective to the Kathiawar landscape. Nearing Khanbaliya he pointed out a power station, which he said was fuelled by coal shipped from Australia to the nearby port of Salaya. It supplied electricity to neighbouring industries, including those in Jamnagar where Reliance Industries had built a petro-chemical complex.

'Reliance has spread money around the politicians – that's how it overtook Tata about five years ago as India's biggest company. The Tata family are Parsees – very strict, very ethical. They have lost many government contracts because they will not pay bribes.'

Mr Iyer bristled with facts and figures about industrial and agricultural production in the region, including the growing of castor seeds (crudely processed before export to France and China for further refining); onions and garlic (shipped from Okha port to the Gulf in small freighters – small craft also used the coastline as a jumping-off point for people-smuggling to the Gulf states); and the babul, which he called 'mad babool' and which the Gujarati government was attempting to eradicate by means of an incentive scheme. This involved cutting down the babul and twice burning the wood to produce coke. Its spread in Gujarat – and parts of Rajasthan too, I was to discover – was so all-pervasive and so reduced every landscape to the same thorny, grey-green carpet that it sometimes wearied the eye to look out the window.

The plant's domination of the landscape was due, he said, to its ability to sink tap roots deep, deep down to water. Furthermore, it was self-seeding, very drought-tolerant, nothing would eat it and it was extremely difficult to destroy: cutting and burning alone had no ultimate effect. Not even acid could destroy it, he claimed. Its one small use, and this was limited to a particular variety, lay in the smallest branches, which, when stripped of their leaves, could double as a sort of country-made toothbrush.

With such a well-informed companion to pass the time, I regretted having chosen to break my journey at Jamnagar.

'Why are you going there?' he asked. 'There is nothing in Jamnagar.'

'An old walled city,' I answered, a little defensively.

'It is nearly all gone.'

'Oh well, it's done now,' I said, and got off.

Mr Iyer was, I soon discovered, telling the truth. The dust, traffic noise and disintegrating buildings were there in good measure. So were the jeering looks. I felt like the first white person to show his face in Jamnagar for a very long time. But Lake Ranmal, a rectangular body of water with a crumbling palace at its centre and subsiding chhatris around its perimeter, made an enchanting sight around which to promenade, provided you didn't cast your eyes down at the polystyrene and plastic detritus and old shoes lapping against the lake's embankments. I also visited the Bala Hanuman Temple, where the chanting of prayers has been going on without interruption since 1 August 1964, a feat of devotion that has earned it a place in the *Guinness Book of Records*.

On my way to the temple I met Ahmed, a Muslim, who wanted to practise his English on me.

'Hindus believe statue is a god,' he told me gravely.

When I suggested that the statues were representations of gods, he refused to budge from his opinion.

'No, and they have so many gods ...'

'They are all manifestations of a single god, Brahman,' I said.

Ahmed shook his head. 'They believe statue is god.'

Of course, representations of gods, and even of the human form, are abhorrent to Muslims. Koranic inscriptions are the only ornamentation permitted on mosques. Hindus, on the other hand, have granted themselves the freedom to pick and choose regarding God's ultimate form. *Indian Express* columnist Anurita Rathore, writing a few days later, said: 'I may be born a Hindu, in a family that believes in Shiv, Durga and Hauman. But, at times, I do feel that God has no form. He is all-pervading, a Supreme Power. There are also times I cannot imagine a God without some beautiful form. What's wrong if I want to believe that my God has a specific look? Neither is there any harm if I believe in a formless God. I can think of Christ as the ultimate saviour as much as I may know Brahma to be the Creator.'

❂

'I like to talk, I hope you don't mind,' said Shaikh Bhai, who sat opposite me on the Saurashtra Mail. 'Tell me if I'm interrupting you.'

'Not at all,' I said.

In the space between Jamnagar and Rajkot, where, because of some unfathomably complicated ticketing arrangement, he had to switch to another carriage, he ranged across every subject troubling the Muslim world. And a few others besides.

Mr Bhai was a gold and diamond dealer from Bombay. In appearance he resembled one of his diamonds – small, round and perfectly proportioned – his only flaw pock-marked cheeks. He was, as he quite rightly described himself, an educated Muslim. He was also tremendously positive in outlook.

'The Britishers,' he said at one point, 'we should thank them for everything they have done in India. They have built this train line we are on. We would never have organised ourselves to do it. We should be thankful, not angry. That is negative energy – it does us no good.'

What did disturb him was the state of Hindu–Muslim relations in the wake of the Ahmadabad riots. 'All this communal conflict, it is diverting us from so much important work. The politicians, they are mostly to blame – they stir up a frenzy to suit their own purposes.'

'People get the government they deserve,' I heard myself answering.

'You are right,' he said and wagged his finger in delight.

Mr Bhai said the Ahmadabad riots were a festering sore for Muslims, especially the lackadaisical hunt for the perpetrators. Those responsible for setting alight the Sabarmati Express carriage in February had been tracked down with great vigour. Seventy-three Muslims were eventually to be taken into custody. But no Hindus had been convicted for the killing of thousands of Muslims. The Muslim community felt a beleaguered minority, the punching-bag of a Hindu-revivalist state government.

'The Gujarati government wants to keep hidden the real number of dead,' said Mr Bhai, 'but we know it was fourteen thousand …'

'We? Who is this we? I thought one to two thousand died.'

'I cannot say who, but we have documentary proof, we know it was that many. And today the police cannot account for seven hundred Muslim boys. We know where they are: in Peshawar and Islamabad. They are training in camps to become fidayeens (suicide bombers). They will return to punish the guilty. The courts have let them off. They say, "We cannot convict, we don't enough proof." Chief Minister Narendra Modi is responsible for security in Gujarat, but he *is* the troublemaker. He had it in his power to halt the riots yet he did nothing. He has made many anti-Muslim comments, too. "Go to Pakistan if you do not like it here," and such things.

'All those boys, they have seen their families, whole families, burnt to death, hacked to death. They will return to India to avenge those deaths.'

The tone of his words, not to mention their substance, astonished me. 'Do you think they are right to do that?'

He opened his mouth and for a moment nothing came out. 'No,' he finally said, 'I do not. All that tit-for-tat will come to nothing.'

In that moment, though, he was swept up in the sweet taste of revenge. His hesitation was a surprise, too, because he had been unstinting in his opposition to Muslim fanatics elsewhere around the world – Afghanistan, Pakistan, Israel.

But he happily admitted to believing the United States was anti-Muslim and that all the security measures in the world would not halt terrorist attacks on home soil or on its interests abroad.

'Better they look at the causes of terrorism, at the climate of fear they have created for themselves. I have a very good example – my sister. She has lived in Los Angeles for the last seventeen years. When she came to Bombay last month she said to me, "Please, don't tell any of my friends that I'm here. If anyone finds out I'm an American passport holder they might kidnap me." My sister! In her home country! And me, her brother, here to protect her! When we went shopping it was in and out, just like that, before the bombs went off. What fear there must be in America. All their security, it will come to nothing. We must get to the cause of the discontent. Otherwise generation after generation will rise up to feed on the hate.'

The Israeli-Palestinian conflict cropped up, as I knew it would. It pained the Muslim world that the Palestinians were oppressed with the connivance of America, which appeared to have no qualms about condemning millions to dispossession and permanent exile.

When I asked why the Americans favoured Israel when they were supposed to be the arbitrators in the conflict, Mr Bhai told me it was because Jews controlled American business and politics.

'The strong Jewish lobby is only part of it,' I said. 'Americans have little sympathy for a Muslim world that embraces so few of their own values. How is it,' I asked, 'that of the forty-five Islamic countries in the world, almost all are run by autocrats?'

Mr Bhai readily acknowledged that Islam and democracy were almost total strangers. And he added, 'Pakistan will always be a threat to India as long as it is not democratic.'

'Why are so few Muslim countries democratic?' I asked. I had hesitated to raise that question because I feared he might take offence. But he didn't.

'The world is changing at a fantastic rate – technological changes like CNN and cable TV are bringing the world to the remotest villages. The mullahs and the kings, they are speaking out against change. They are refusing to bend. If you don't bend ...'

'You snap?'

'Yes, one day they will snap.'

'Are you saying Muslims are naturally resistant to change, conservative?'

'I suppose I am.'

That struck me as a very considerable admission.

We came to Rajkot and Mr Bhai had to switch carriages. I had lost another enjoyable companion from the Saurashtra Mail.

City skyline, Jaipur.

The Delhi Mail

FOR MANY YEARS Mahatma Gandhi made his home in Ahmadabad at an ashram he established on the city's outskirts in 1915. There he waged non-violent campaigns against his three enemies – poverty, untouchability and the British Raj – and continued his spiritual questing. Gandhi's association with the city has been sustained to this day. At Ahmadabad Junction Station, a cavernous concrete box in the no-frills style of modern India, I found the book stalls stocked with an exhaustive selection of his writings. And he had been no slouch as a writer. Letters, articles, newspapers, pamphlets, leaflets, books, declarations and ultimatums poured from his eloquent pen. I bought his autobiography, *The Story of My Experiments with Truth*, tucked it into my pocket and boarded my train.

The previous day I had battled my way up Ashram Road to his ashram on the banks of the Sabarmati, the river that splits Ahmadabad in two. A handful of the original buildings remained, reverently preserved along with a few of his very few possessions: a vegetable knife, kitchen containers, eating utensils, spectacles, his three monkeys. The simple bungalows, spaced among shady trees, represented a mode of living Gandhi believed would bring

221

contentment to India's citizens – not some sort of Ram Rajya, an allegedly mythical golden age of Hindu rule, but a simple self-sufficient life that encouraged spiritual development. He was suspicious of large cities, believing they would lead to moral depravity. He reasoned they were 'a snare and a useless encumbrance and that people would not be happy in them, that there would be gangs of thieves and robbers, prostitution and vice flourishing in them and that poor men would be robbed by rich men'.

If Gandhi had been looking for proof, he would have needed to look no further than Ahmadabad itself. The traditional centre of India's colossal textile business, it has always been a chaotic and dust-choked city, a place where capital has oppressed labour, Hindu has oppressed Muslim, Muslim has turned on Hindu, and now where the combustion engine assails everyone, spewing out fumes in crooked side street and broad thoroughfare alike.

Integral to Gandhi's vision of a peaceful and idyllic village life was spinning. It was a form of manual labour, and Gandhi believed every individual, for a balanced life, must devote a portion of his or her day to such activity. The coarse homespun cloth, or khadi, would reduce dependence on foreign cloth, and the spinning itself would occupy the hands of millions of underemployed villagers. Khadi was a vital step towards swadeshi, self-sufficiency. Progress towards this goal, like so many aspects of modern-day India, would have disappointed the father of the nation. Unsold khadi was piling up in godowns throughout India, especially in his home state of Gujarat, because of low demand: it was regarded as a dull and old-fashioned material. With this slump, khadi spinners' wages had halved, from 35 rupees a day to 17.

Two other sources of disappointment would have been Hindu–Muslim relations ('Do people become enemies because they change their religion?' he once asked. 'Is the God of the Mahomedan different from the God of the Hindu?') and the entrenchment of caste differences. I said to two elderly men visiting the ashram that Gandhi would be horrified at the way quotas for low castes to enter the public service, universities and even parliament itself were only entrenching the caste mentality. But they waved it off. In their benign view, caste was no more than a sort of trade union movement that had got out of hand. In ancient times, they said, the first obligation was always to family, and then to those of the same occupation, or caste. The evil had set in only when men began to rank one occupation above another.

If only it were that simple. Caste is generally regarded as an import of the ancient fair-skinned invaders from the north, the Aryans, who intended it as a sort of graduated apartheid system to ensure their racial purity, especially from the dark-skinned Dravidians of the South, ancient inhabitants of the subcontinent. The word for caste is *varna*, meaning colour. The four original varnas – priest, warrior, merchant and farmer, and labourer – evolved sub-castes that became increasingly specialised. This is one reason why the baffled sahib found he needed a score of servants to run his household because the cook would cook but not wash up and the cleaner would clean but not go near the toilet: that was an untouchable's job. The untouchables – the sweepers, washermen, slaughter-men and others – were too lowly to have a caste. The Indian constitution outlaws caste discrimination but that makes not a jot of difference. It is the pressures and practicalities of urban life that are dissolving caste rigidities, albeit with the qualification, applicable to all things Indian, that change is infinitely slow.

Gandhi was not opposed to caste per se, only untouchability, which he feared would eat out the vitals of Hinduism. This seemed to me a strange lack for an individual capable of so much idealism. Of home rule, for example, he said it was not enough merely to expel the English: 'We have to learn to teach others that we do not want the tyranny of either English rule or Indian rule .... Real home rule is self-rule or self-control.'

But sometimes he could overreach himself. He believed Western civilisation 'propagated immorality', while 'the tendency of Indian civilisation is to elevate the moral being'. This led him to remark: 'I feel in the innermost recesses of my heart that the world is sick unto death of blood-letting. The world is seeking a way out, and I flatter myself with the belief that perhaps it will be the privilege of the ancient land of India to show that way out to the hungering world.' Yet independent India, in its conflicts with its neighbours, had taken no moral high ground, conducted no demonstration of the superiority of non-violence. As in every other nation, *Realpolitik* has been its guiding principle.

❂

The Delhi Mail crawled across the Sabarmati and through the northern suburbs. Soon Ahmadabad, derisively called Gardabad, City of Dust, by one Moghul emperor, had reverted to dirt lanes, bustees freckled with round dark dung cakes, old men pedalling their sturdy black mounts and youths idling away a Sunday morning on their parked scooters.

After three-quarters of an hour we had rid ourselves of Ahmadabad altogether and gathered speed across a hot, flat landscape of drying-up ponds, goats, tamarisk trees and babul, which peppered ever stonier fields until cultivated land and encroaching desert became scarcely distinguishable. It seemed to me the most unpromising land I had yet laid eyes on. More and more fields of castor seed appeared – a sure sign of minimal rainfall and poor soil. (Mr Iyer said the return for farmers was only just better than planting nothing.) Patches of stunted maize grew alongside villagers' huts where bullocks stood in the shade of neem trees munching mechanically on feed.

For once I was pleased to have an aisle seat. The compartment opposite was occupied by a family of four and two foreigners, a long-limbed German who talked incessantly and a Frenchman with a hairless, almost waxy face who never spoke at all.

The husband, an English teacher from Kerala, enquired about the German's travels. It was a fatal error. He was a sculptor and painter and he launched into a protracted monologue about his artistic endeavours and his world travels. He produced a photo album of his works: sculptures in stone, swirling abstract shapes, and acrylic paintings, also abstract.

'What is this one about?' asked the teacher, pointing to a painting. 'You don't use words.'

'No,' the artist replied, placing a hand across his heart, 'I don't want to make a statement, I don't want to appeal to the intellect. I want to speak directly to the viewer's feelings. This work is about searching. There is tension down the bottom here. Can you see? A wrestling, a clash of forces. And here in the middle it is more peaceful. The colours are blending. And here at the top are the mountains – see them? – where you go to find more peace, serenity. Do you understand?'

'Yes ... yes, I think I do.' The teacher thought for a moment and asked, 'How much are your works?'

'This one, for example (he pointed to a Henry Moore-inspired sculpture), I sold for 7,000 euro. It was not so very expensive.'

'How much is a euro? How many rupees?'

'Forty-seven rupees to the euro, I think. So that is, what ... about 350,000 rupees.'

The teacher said nothing. I could see he was flabbergasted.

'Of course, if I worked in India I could not charge so much. I would like to do some artistic work here, not in the big cities – it is too much pollution – but in the villages where it is quiet. I have worked in France, in Italy, Japan, Australia, New Zealand ... I would like to work in India, too.'

The German's arms and legs were tremendously long and his fingers were no less elongated, like delicate antennae. The simple act of seating himself had necessitated an ungainly folding up of limbs, like some exotic soaring bird which, full of gracefulness in the sky, becomes unwieldy once earthbound.

His words were beginning to have a powerfully soporific effect on me so I dug into my rucksack for a book.

At one o'clock we made a five-minute halt in Sidphur. The charming little station was dome-roofed and painted a mottled ochre. Passengers promenaded along the uncovered platform, belching and smoking, grateful for the exercise. A man scoured the platform for cigarette butts: salvaged of their pinch of unburned tobacco, a dozen or two collectively represented a free smoke. Across the road, dirty-kneed boys flew improvised kites, several of which freed themselves from their owner's grip and floated up to join the circling eagles.

We rolled on across hot, dusty Gujarat, every riverbed across our path dry as parchment. There was the appearance of bountifulness and greenery until one looked closely: everything bar a sprinkling of trees was a weed of one sort or another.

A little later the southern tip of the Aravalli Range came into view, followed immediately afterwards by a Bagpiper whisky hoarding alongside the line: we had crossed out of alcohol-free Gujarat into Rajasthan state. Soon we were squeezing through the gap between the Aravalli Range and the Abu Hills.

By Abu Road Station, my earlier companions had gone and four middle-aged holidaymakers returning to Delhi swept into my coach and dumped their bags. Then the alpha male of the group, a stocky polo-shirted figure with cropped greying hair, cleared the compartment of rubbish tossed under the seats.

What I witnessed next said a lot about India's problems. With the tip of his shoes he pushed the litter out into the aisle, hard against an adjoining compartment. I noted the contents of the pile: a soiled hand-towel, a paper plate, a plastic spoon, two tinfoil containers with leftovers from lunch, a cardboard box and a plastic bag containing yoghurt, tied up airtight like a balloon. A passenger in the compartment next door, seeing the rubbish pile, considered it too close to his seat. Surreptitiously he pushed it away with the toe of his shoe, out towards the middle of the aisle. There it was kicked by a passing bedroll attendant whose arms were outstretched in a bear hug around a dozen pillows and who couldn't see his feet. This scattered the litter along the aisle. Passengers clipped or stepped over the mess but no one dreamed of picking it up. Nor would the attendants dream of touching it. And nor would I, because I wanted to see if anyone would stand on the yoghurt bag and splatter its contents all over the place.

Outside, all human habitation had given out – and it takes

something to halt the advance of land-hungry Indians. The Aravalli Range had drawn off, but much smaller rocky outcrops protruded nearby. Like the Aravalli they were flaky and fissured, and in profile might have been dashed off by Dr Seuss: improbable shapes and proportions, with drooping craggy peaks like witches' noses that threatened to collapse at any moment.

Now dry riverbeds intersected the railway line with increasing regularity, mustard-coloured lacerations through the camouflage-green sea of babul. Water had not descended from the Aravalli in years to moisten their sandy banks, which were criss-crossed by a skein of deeply worn foot-tracks.

So there it was, the babul and the rocks and the haze-shrouded hills and the empty rivers – barren and beautiful and uninterrupted all the way to Ajmer, where I got down. And left behind on the aisle floor, still primed to go off, was that yoghurt bomb.

✿

Pushkar, a half-hour bus ride from Ajmer, has drawn Hindu pilgrims since ancient times. Now the little lakeside town with its encirclement of brown, bony hills attracts pilgrims of another, quite unexpected sort. The pavement menu boards of eateries along the main street contain unambiguous clues: pizza, pancakes, muesli, 'special' lassis (translation: your yoghurt drink contains bhang), jam on toast ... yes, backpackers, but of a particular subset. They have dug themselves in for lengthy stays in India and have adopted indigenous markings – here dabbing a tilak on the forehead, there wearing a sacred Hindu thread around the wrist, or perhaps shaving the scalp but for a Hindu-lock, a tiny dark love curl on the top of the head. One or two had plucked up the courage to wear a sari or a dhoti. All sported a considerable assortment of bangles and beads with their cultivated air of ennui and their Ray-Ban sunglasses. They sat on hotel rooftops gazing out at the lake, glassy and entrancing under the blazing desert sun, or, when the languor had lifted, adjourned to restaurants where they could swap tales of the road and observe the passing parade of Indian pilgrims – everyone from ardent sadhus to well-off day-trippers.

Samir Savarkar ran one such café, just four or five tables at the end of a laneway. For seventeen of his forty-six years Samir had laboured under grey Irish skies, first managing an Indian restaurant, then running his own (and what other name than The Shalimar). No one could be in the hospitality business in Ireland without indulging in a drink or two. And as Samir freely admitted, he had once liked a drink or two.

'Our wine list was extensive – and I mean extensive. Who couldn't help sitting down after work and thinking, "Mm, tonight I think I'll have a French red, or maybe that Chianti"? One night I had this dream, it was silly really, that I would just die – you know, keel over without warning – if I didn't give it up. So I did. I sold up and came back home. It seemed right to come home ....' His gaze drifted away and then he added, almost in a whisper, 'I'm much happier here.'

When I asked if he missed all the Irish conviviality and drinking, he replied, 'No, I don't. Drinking is not really understood here in India, except by the very top segment of society – the really wealthy. Even the middle class are thinking it will lead to depravity: drunkenness, womanising, gambling.'

'Does it bother you then that you can't actually drink here in Pushkar?'

'I suppose you could sneak it in, but I have no interest in drinking. It's a different way of life here.'

Such is the holy status of Pushkar that consumption of alcohol or non-vegetarian food, including even eggs, is prohibited within its precincts. Indeed, one may not even come within 12 metres of the lake's ghats without first removing one's shoes. The lake is the holiest in India to Hindus and has at one end a Brahma temple, one of the few in the world dedicated to this deity. Over its gateway is the figure of a hans, or goose, of Brahma. The temple is very popular. The morning I passed by, many barefoot sadhus were congregated in an antechamber where one of their fellow truth-seekers had died the previous night. They were a striking-looking lot, with ash-smeared bodies, long matted hair wound around their heads in rope-like coils and fastened with pins, and a lot of cowrie shells and beads strung about their necks. They stood in contemplation around the body, which was covered by a rough blanket. Later, after elaborate obsequies, they would give their companion a send-off on a pyre.

Samir's return had reversed, in one case at least, the worldwide Indian diaspora in pursuit of a more prosperous life. Not that he had sailed into an easy life with his stash of Irish pounds in his pocket. For two years he did nothing ('With all that time on my hands I obsessed over the smallest things'), then bought his business and a plot of land on the edge of town where he planned to build a house, with a couple of extra rooms to let out to tourists. It was a sensible plan to ease into semi-retirement.

Living among the talkative Irish for so long had rubbed off on Samir, but he fell strangely silent after I asked him, 'What was the biggest adjustment in coming home?' He paused ... and paused ... and still he did not answer. Finally he said, 'Medical services. The thought that in an emergency the nearest good hospital is in Jaipur or Delhi.'

My curiosity was satisfied.

Samir was full of gossip about the town, especially the late-night partying and drug-taking of the travellers, many of them young Israelis whose aggressive manner made them unpopular with other backpackers. ('Their heads are stressed from compulsory military service.') More than a few travellers stayed for months on end in Pushkar.

'What do these people *do* all day?' (I had walked around the lake in an hour.)

'Nothing. They sit, relax, watch India go by.'

Later, I spoke to the tailor whose premises adjoined Samir's shop. He, too, was full of gossip, including about Samir himself.

'He is an outsider like me, from Dehra Dun. I am from Punjab. But he has so much money everyone is like cats and dogs to him. He has a superiority complex. He does not like it that I can speak English as well as him. He says I am a peeping Tom, that I stare at his customers, but I would not disrespect their privacy so. He says I am a crazy man. They all say I am a crazy man, to dirty my name …'

'They?'

'Sindhis. Pushkar is run by Sindhis. They did not like me selling cheaper than them so they tell all the tourists, "Don't go near his shop … he is a crazy man." Now I struggle but I must go on …. It is better than doing nothing. Everyone keeps saying, "He is crazy for starting up here".'

❁

The bus crawled back over Nag Pahar, the hills separating Pushkar from Ajmer, and I caught the Shatabdi Express to Jaipur, two and a half hours up the line. I sat among businessmen in chair class as the express slid smoothly across a pancake-flat plain. Outside, beneath a cloudless sky, women, shawled against the sun and wearing dazzlingly bright saris, were cutting maize. Igloo-like stacks marked their progress through the fields.

Next day I made a tour of the Pink City's principal tourist attractions, preyed upon remorselessly by every sort of tout. As one forthright man said to me, 'Here, everyone wants to get rich fast, from the politicians who rob the people of their money right down to the rickshaw drivers who want to rob travellers of their money. Only a few want to do business slowly, slowly.'

I became painfully aware I was just one more gawking tourist, jostling with package tours for a better view of miniature Moghul paintings and collections of Rajput daggers and swords and costumed models. ('Yes, we came from Agra. Wasn't the Taj Mahal *so* amazing! Tomorrow? Jodhpur. Just one night. Then back to Delhi for a day, then …') So I scuttled off to Jaipur Junction Station a good hour and a half early. It, too, is painted pink and topped by cupolas, like almost every building in the old walled city. There the Shatabdi Express carried me on from where I had left off twenty-four hours earlier.

We rolled north towards Delhi, and very soon it was dark. Sitting in my aircraft-style seat among subdued businessmen, I could have been on any inter-city service in the world. There was one diversion during an otherwise dull ride – my neighbour, Kaushik Dave, aged fifty. I knew his particulars because I had taken to checking the passenger list pasted by each coach door before departure.

Mr Dave was a fidget. He began the journey reading his paperback. The cover showed a man about to fire a pistol at another man whose face dripped with blood from a gash to the head and who had fang-like incisors. Behind these two men stood a woman with wild red hair who was screaming her lungs out. The book held his attention for a few minutes before he closed it and a series of nervous mannerisms took possession of him. First, he gave the knees of his trousers a tug – always right knee, then left knee. Next, he gave each shoulder of his long-sleeved shirt a pull (also right first, then left) so as to lift each cuff a couple of centimetres. Then a sort of fiddle near the crotch, a raising of each arm above the head (this time left, then right), a stroking of his hair to one side before he removed his wire-rimmed glasses, rubbed a hand over his face, stroked his moustache and put his glasses back on.

He resumed reading. But only for a few minutes. He wriggled in his seat, put his book down and repeated the whole sequence without variation: trouser knees, cuffs, crotch, arms, hair-stroking, glasses, face, moustache. Intermittently he would mutter to himself and wring his hands.

We spoke briefly. He was a policeman with the Criminal Bureau of Investigation in Delhi. He specialised in narcotics. But our conversation was cut short when he picked up his book again. Soon, of course, he tired of it and resumed the familiar routine: trousers, cuffs, crotch, arms …

Wagah border crossing, India–Pakistan.

To Lahore

TWO PIGEON-HOLES SET about navel height in an imposing brick perimeter wall constituted the frontage of the Pakistan high commission. There, on a pavement in New Delhi's diplomatic enclave, I found a horde of visa applicants stooped over, thrusting fistfuls of documents at the pigeon-holes and beseeching two consular officials who, like priests in confessional boxes, remained impassive blurs in the spherical gloom.

Visas had fallen prey to politics. Well, more than usual. India, accusing Pakistan of complicity in the terrorist attack on its Parliament in December 2001, had ordered most of its diplomatic staff out of Islamabad. Pakistan reciprocated with a tit-for-tat withdrawal. So to discourtesy could now be added a shortage of staff and reduced opening hours – just two hours a day.

Nevertheless, I queued for a form, rushed off to obtain a bank draft and letter of recommendation from my embassy and returned at 10.30 am, just in time to see the pigeon-hole shutters slam shut for the day. But the mob, deeply disgruntled by this treatment, stormed off to blockade the main gate, encircling any official who came or went, including, eventually, the high commissioner himself. With reluctance he gathered up enough applications, mine included, to placate the crowd and that afternoon I had my visa, though not before another bun-fight outside the pigeon-holes.

Next morning at 7.20 the Swarna Shatabdi Express left Delhi bound for the Sikh holy city of Amritsar. Not surprisingly, most passengers were Sikhs. The men were easily distinguishable in their turbans and beards, as were the boys for that matter, wearing a juvenile version of the turban to contain their uncut hair. And the reservation charts were full of Mr Singhs: the word means lion, a reference to the martial traditions of the Sikh religion.

The chair-car service shot up the same line I'd taken to Simla, but at Ambala it veered north-west for Ludhiana and Amritsar. For two hours a mist hung stubbornly over the plains. Finally the sun got up and a wind began to blow, revealing the mustard-coloured stubble of paddy fields harvested of their crop. Occasionally the dome of a gurdwara, snowy white in the bright sun, punctuated this flat, breezy landscape.

Towards lunchtime we broke down. The train slowed as we made our way across a bridge and once in the middle it simply came to a stop. The loco sighed and fell silent. For an hour or more we remained suspended above the river. A train came to tow us back to Ambala. Another delay. A replacement engine hooked itself up. At three o'clock we recrossed the bridge. I cursed. There was no way I would reach the border in time to cross today.

Ludhiana, reached an hour later, was a grimy, soulless city. Scrap metal stockpiled in mountainous heaps awaited the maw of roaring furnaces. Armies of scavengers sorted through the day's collection of cardboard and paper. A little west of the city we crossed a shrivelled Sutlej, one of the five principal rivers nourishing the state and giving the Punjab its ancient name. At 5.30 pm we clattered across the Beas, another of the five rivers, but this time there was water from bank to bank.

Dusk was beautiful, a blush of delicate tangerine that overlaid the evening stillness. We overtook three old men with ramrod-straight backs who were pedalling their jalopies at an impressive clip. Everyone else – the labourers drifting away from the fields, the herdsmen leaning on their sticks, the village women clutching their offspring – seemed as disinclined as ourselves to hasten to their destination. We had been at it for eleven hours, twice the scheduled journey time, and Amritsar was still some distance away.

❂

'I can speak English but I don't like to,' said the Pakistani border guard who was entering my passport details in a ledger.

'But you speak it so well,' I said.

'I know,' he snapped, 'but I don't care to. I prefer Pashto. Do *you* speak Pashto?'

'No I don't. But tell me, why don't you like to speak English?'

'Because English people hate us and …'

'But I'm not English. That's an Australian passport.'

He had no time for such hair-splitting. 'Why do you come to Pakistan?'

'To look around, catch some trains.'

He said nothing.

A walkie-talkie at his side squawked with chatter, the only sound for miles around. Out on the plain, nothing moved in the bright morning sunshine. Behind me, beyond the narrow stretch of no man's land, was another fence, another road block and the long, straight, tree-lined highway back to Amritsar. It took an effort of concentration to picture, here in this pastoral calm, the massacres that had taken place in the name of the subcontinent's division.

'Your passport, sir.'

'Thank you.'

I strolled along a corridor of trees to the immigration and customs sheds where the reception was almost as frosty. But it was no surprise really. The Wagah border post, the only land crossing between the two neighbours, was a highly attuned barometer of relations. Today it was deserted but for an Iranian (long delayed behind me), four

Muslim Indians (held up, too) and a lone blonde American in her fifties who wore a black salwar kameez, a headscarf, and a face erased of all emotion (she got ahead of me, was picked up by three Pakistani men in a beaten-up Datsun and vanished). The counters and waiting halls, big enough to accommodate hundreds at a time, were deserted. Relations were a gasp away from dead.

Searched, processed and stamped, I emerged into a lorry park, an expanse of ground stained with oil and spilt diesel. A handful of drivers sprawled on charpoys arranged outside a dhaba. There appeared to be no expectation of movement in their camp. Their long-distance trucks, lined up nearby, glittered like a row of Christmas trees. Every sort of gewgaw, bauble and tinselled embellishment was fastened to, or dangled from, the cabs and trays. But things did not end there. The paintwork was enlivened with brightly rendered patterns and various idyllic mountain scenes, complete with plump green hills and cool, gently flowing streams, perhaps in unconscious anticipation of the paradise awaiting good Muslims.

A local bus took me into Lahore. I kept expecting some convulsive change once across the border, but my eyes confirmed the very opposite: it was one and the same land, divided only by religious sensibilities. Where once a temple, mosque, gurdwara or church steeple might have pricked the skyline, now the dome and minaret were all-conquering. Babul, no respecter of lines drawn on a map, was everywhere. So, too, were the black scars where the rice stubble had been burnt off. And the same black water buffaloes cooled themselves in whatever shrinking ponds they could find. And the dusty, rubbish-strewn roadsides were there in good measure, too.

But what immediately struck me was the uniformity of Pakistanis' clothes. Most women wore a shapeless black garment like a maternity smock over their salwar kameez, and a chadar, or veil, invariably black, too. Others wore the all-enveloping burqqa, a garment shaped like a bell tent and, as it was intended to be, the least revealing costume ever devised for the female form, concealing even the feet. Usually black, it had just one opening, a latticework of embroidery over the face. The salwar kameez was a unisex garment. Males, right down to the youngest boys, dressed in what was fundamentally the same outfit as the women's: pantaloons worn beneath a loose long-sleeved shirt reaching below the knees. All of the men on the bus were dressed in a pale brown version (the women sat up front, out of sight, behind a mesh partition). Indeed, in their absolute sameness, my fellow passengers might have been members of some religious order, and in a very large sense they were: of the ummah, the worldwide community of Islam. In any event, it had the curious effect of eliminating, in a single sweep, the individuality of every male on board.

Conveniently, the bus ended its journey outside Lahore City Station. I got off and stood staring at it in wonder, rooted to the spot among the shouting touts and belching buses. It is more fortress than station, more mediaeval castle than stopping place. And this was precisely as its British builders had intended. After the Indian Mutiny in 1857 the authorities decreed that new stations in the north be more defendable in time of unrest, an instruction taken exuberantly to heart by William Brunton, the engineer responsible for its design. Even I, no military engineer, could see it possessed formidable defences. There were battlemented parapets, slit holes for sharpshooters and a long, massively built stone curtain-wall. And when I went to ask about a ticket I discovered the low, arched entrances through which trains come and go, and which can be sealed off with iron doors, converting the whole place into a giant bunker. The interior proved to be a succession of vaulted chambers, all exceedingly dark and echoing the slightest noise, like some enormous sepulchre through which, paradoxically, trains happened to pass from time to time.

The news on tickets was not good. It was too late to reserve a berth on the following day's service to Peshawar, and bookings were heavy for subsequent days. I would just have to turn up an hour early the following morning, at four o'clock, and take my chances.

That left little time to look about Lahore, a city steeped in history, much of it Moghul or Sikh but with a considerable stamp of the

British Raj, too. Indeed, it was reckoned by many Anglo-Indians to be the subcontinent's finest city. A walk along the main boulevard of the Civil Lines, naturally enough called The Mall, confirmed the gusto with which the British went about their empire-building here. There was the imperialist hauteur of the High Court; the Islamic-inspired General Post Office, then undergoing refurbishments; the Wonder House that was the Museum, containing everything from the second-century Fasting Buddha, which in spite of anatomical deficiencies must be the most powerfully haunting thing ever to emerge from beneath a sculptor's chisel, through to the massive statue of Queen Victoria, all jowls, bosom and ribbed gown, and ending with the Freedom Movement Gallery, more correctly a history of the Indian Muslim League and Jinnah, who, stylishly dressed in his pin-striped suits, bore a remarkable resemblance to the colonial overlords he was seeking to topple. There was Faletti's Hotel, where *absolutely* everyone once stayed; various tall-spired cathedrals; and, scattered further afield, any number of colleges, clubs, hospitals and municipal and secretariat buildings.

Under the Moghuls, Lahore had risen from semi-obscurity as a provincial centre into a capital city of the Moghul empire, sharing the imperial court with Agra and Delhi. The most visible reminder of the period was Shahi Qila, or Lahore Fort, standing astride the Grand Trunk Road en route from Calcutta to Peshawar and rebuilt in its present form by the far-sighted and tolerant emperor Akbar in 1566. The other gigantic example of Moghul architecture was the adjoining Badshahi Mosque, the last and largest of the Moghul mosques (it can accommodate 60,000 of the faithful), completed in 1676 under an emperor of an altogether different disposition. Aurangzeb had a murderous hatred of Muslim 'heretics' as well as adherents to other faiths. He abandoned the tolerance of his predecessors, reimposing the jizyah, the poll tax on non-Muslims, and doubling the taxes of the Hindu merchants. Worst of all, he ordered the destruction of Hindu temples throughout the empire. His successors abandoned his communalist policies, but the damage was done: the Hindu majority's bitter resentment towards the foreign Muslim rulers had taken root.

For centuries Lahore had been capital of a united Punjab. Now its vast Sikh population was gone and there was hardly a Sikh left. With Partition in 1947 the state had been cleaved in two, Muslims taking Lahore as their capital of the western portion of the fertile region, Sikhs and Hindus the eastern portion. Since the Sikhs could not have their spiritual capital of Amritsar taken from them, the boundary line was made to curl between the two cities, previously only an hour's journey apart before the border, with all its attendant formalities, was erected. Amritsar was briefly capital of Indian-controlled Punjab, but with relations between the two new neighbours so tense, it was soon thought prudent to build another capital at a safer distance. Chandigarh was the result.

My only irritation as I rushed about the sights, hastily absorbing all this history, was dodging the heaving, surging, relentless mass of traffic. Everything from camel- and hand-drawn carts to auto-rickshaws and grotesquely overloaded lorries congested the crooked streets and ring roads. The shrill whine of speeding two-strokes alternated with the impatient rumble of gridlock. Nor was there any immunity from the crush in the Old City, a honeycomb of a thousand lanes and alleyways which had long since outgrown the original walls. The effect upon this once elegant city was debilitating. Lahore now wore the drawn face of an actress too long on the stage and wishing to retire into seclusion. But with 5 million followers, how was she to shake them off?

At dusk, I found myself with a long trudge back to my hotel near the railway station. The light, refracted through the dust and exhaust fumes, briefly lent the chaos a grainy and undeservedly picturesque aspect. It was long after nightfall when I got back and I decided to eat in the hotel's dining room. Its sombre atmosphere, its stark décor, its smattering of customers with the moustaches of brigands and faces of undertakers, was a template for almost every eating-place I entered in Pakistan. It was exclusively male, quiet as the reserved room of a library, furnished with shabby tables and chairs, and offered a menu both limited and dull. Yet it was evidently as customers liked it.

Pakistani lorry crosses Khyber Pass from Afghanistan.

The Awami Express
to Peshawar

THEY WAITED IN SILENT KNOTS, barely discernible in the pitch-black, the women veiled, stock-still, protectively encircled. Pigeons cooed in the platform rafters.

'This train is greatly delayed,' Mohammad Izmit sighed and went off to perform fajr, the first prayers of the day, at a small mosque adjacent to the men's ablutions. Dawn began to creep over the city and still there was no sign of the train from Karachi.

Mr Izmit returned. He wore Western clothes and carried himself with military bearing, and it soon become apparent why. He was employed at Peshawar's Air Force Aeronautical Complex in some technical capacity about which he would reveal nothing.

'I will tell you this though,' he said, adjusting his spectacles by the curious means of placing a stiffened palm against each side of the frames, producing a sort of double salute effect, 'we are all nations of the subcontinent. We share many traditions. Many things there are in common. But the big difference is *religion*.'

That word was to hang heavily over so many discussions in

Pakistan. When it passed across someone's lips it had a way of stopping conversation in its tracks.

'This also I will tell you. The people of Pakistan, they are hospitable, they welcome foreign peoples as their guests. But in the international sphere some Western governments are pursuing policies many Pakistanis hate, you understand?'

His forehead screwed itself up into a knot of intense distaste. I sensed he didn't quite know whether to say Pakistanis were hospitable or hostile to Westerners. I think he was saying: expect both.

Out of politeness I asked Mr Izmit if he had children. Yes, he had one boy and four girls. The eldest was ten, the second eldest eight, the middle child six, the fourth four and the youngest two.

'They attend school?'

'Yes, many girls are not going to schools – there are no jobs – but mine are going. English medium, very good Air Force schools.'

'Five must be a handful,' I remarked.

'No, I have the means. Among rural people of Pakistan, five is not so very many. Six, eight, ten – that is not so uncommon. These people are not practising population control. Islam does not prohibit it, but still they do not practise it. For myself, I am practising in a very scientific manner.'

I dared not enquire about the precise details of his technique, though I was tempted. Judging by the meticulous spacing between each child, he had attained some considerable proficiency. Anyway, with sufficient daylight now to read by, Mr Izmit excused himself and went off to study his Koran. He was still at it when the Awami Express drew in at seven.

Half the carriages were decoupled, as porters in red jackets with brass authorisation badges fastened around one arm (in that instant of recognition I was transported back to India) made a restrained, almost apologetic advance on the air-conditioned carriages where the likely pickings were. Passengers boarded and detrained with the same self-restraint. There was none of the yelling and jostling and exuberance of an Indian train about to depart. It was rather like being bodily transported into a silent movie: everyone knew his place, his role to play, and went soberly and mutely about it.

I boarded a 'lower A/C' coach. It was simpler in appointment than the Indian equivalent but still much the same design: four berths to a compartment (no curtain) and a single continuous row of berths on the other side of the aisle. An elderly couple occupied the lower berth opposite me, and the woman drew a veil across her face as soon as I sat down. I tried not to feel snubbed: I was simply a male stranger. The train stayed put for half an hour, long enough to breakfast on a greasy omelette, bread and jam and a pot of tea.

Finally we pulled out. It felt long overdue. Soon we were among the fertile plains of the Punjab – Pakistan's Punjab – and in the process crossed the Ravi, another of the five rivers, whose course to the north marks for some distance the Indo-Pakistan border. Rice grew from horizon to horizon. But even on this rolling plain farmers valued their privacy, their houses solitary windowless boxes of unplastered brick intended to deflect strangers' gazes and enclose a courtyard for their womenfolk and animals.

A third passenger resumed his seat in our compartment. Dr Ashraf Mumtaz was on his way to Rawalpindi to sit an oral examination before his final registration. He had spent the past seven years studying in Moscow. The first year was taken up learning Russian. He had studied alongside Hindus and Sikhs and understood they had no enmity towards Pakistan. 'But the people in the country do not think so. That is why we need the armed forces so much. They are here to defend us …'

'From what exactly?'

'India, of course.'

'You think India would invade Pakistan?'

'Why not?'

'What if I told you India has its hands full with many, many problems of its own and would have more to lose than gain from invading your country?'

'I don't know. Maybe … maybe.'

'Take Kashmir out of the equation. Would it have any reason to bother you?'

'We have fought three wars since Partition, but it goes back a long way, hundreds of years.'

'You mean Hindus and Muslims?'

'Yes. You do one thing for me. You are a journalist. When you go back home write about how hospitable people are and how Pakistanis are not all terrorists.'

'Of course they're not. But Pakistan has two big image problems. One is its help for fighters in Indian-held Kashmir – no one believes it is giving only moral support. The second is General Musharraf – he has rubbed out democracy like so many military rulers before him.'

'You have a point about our leader, but the truth is we have got used to him.'

When I asked Dr Mumtaz what he considered the country's biggest health problem, he laughed derisively.

'We have many problems. The biggest? Diarrhoea and dehydration in children. Fifty per cent of hospital admissions are children under five. The cause is bad water.'

I suggested that perhaps it would be better to spend money on water than on weapons.

'Yes, but the West is partly to blame for all this,' Dr Mumtaz said, defensively. 'It is building these hi-tech weapons …'

'Pakistan doesn't *have* to buy them.'

'But it does. It must keep up with India. Also, the West, America and Britain, they are not stepping in to help resolve Kashmiri problem. Look what they did in Iraq. Immediate military action. For fifty years they have not been enforcing United Nations resolutions on Kashmir.'

Dr Mumtaz was not alone in believing Pakistan must have military parity with its giant neighbour, the economic elephant now stirring from decades-long slumber. General Musharraf himself had just finished thumping the table and vowing India would never gain a military edge, ignoring the fact this rivalry plainly was beggaring his country. It was a lopsided contest, but Pakistan was persisting nevertheless. Its puny economy had been stagnant for years, its people were dirt-poor, yet its missiles were nuclear-tipped. It seemed an odd set of priorities. However, there was a precedent for the country's military spending. Pakistan's first budget, prepared by Jinnah in 1948, allocated three-quarters of all spending to the military, a pattern that has endured to the present day.

We lapsed into silence as the Awami Express chugged northwards, the Grand Trunk Road our continuous companion. North of Wazirabad we crossed the Chenab, the fourth of the Punjab's five main rivers. Then, beyond the town of Kharian, we left the Punjab plains, so fertile that they can produce four crops a year, and climbed into rough scrubby hills resembling mine tailings.

Then the city of Jhelum was upon us, all minarets and flapping rooftop washing, and then the river of the same name, the last of the Punjab's big five. Out to the east rose the foothills of Kashmir, blue and alluring against the bleak moonscape of the Potwar Plateau, which we were now penetrating. Bounded to the south by the Salt Range and to the west by the Indus River, it is a no man's land of rocky soil, fractured gullies and eroded hills. The few men about – there were, as usual, no women – wore white spade-shaped beards, white skullcaps and white salwar kameez which fluttered like jibs in the stiff breeze. At the highest point on the plateau, burnt-red ranges could be seen unfolding all the way to the horizon. It was a desiccated wasteland but beautiful nonetheless.

Later, a conductor-guard deposited himself next to us. Riaz Ahmed was clean-shaven and wore a white uniform of distinctly Maoist inspiration. It consisted of baggy trousers and collarless jacket with oversized epaulettes and metal buttons and, fastened with the aid of a safety-pin, a red arm band with a crest of leaves surrounding the letters PR, for Pakistan Railway. Top and bottom of the crest were the words 'conductor' and 'guard'. He looked on quietly as the elderly couple took turns to pray on the bench seat, their foreheads touching the vinyl with each prostration. Others did the same, satisfying the requirement of their faith to pray five times a day, but I was surprised how few observed this regular piety. On we trundled, coming at the middle of the day to Gujar Khan, a town of low, nondescript dwellings. But glinting like gold among the gravelly vestiges of a prospector's pan was a liberal scattering of large gaudy homes, which Dr Mumtaz said were built with remittances from the Gulf where many townspeople worked. Soon another outlandishly modern construction appeared in this landscape where everything else belonged to the primitive past: the M2, a four-lane toll motorway running from Lahore to the twin cities of Islamabad and Rawalpindi (or Pindi as the military garrison town was commonly called) and destined ultimately to reach Peshawar.

Excavation pits and smoking brick kilns spread like a mottled red rash across the countryside. Rawalpindi was close. We crawled through a featureless expanse of low brick houses and motorways and deposited most passengers at Rawalpindi Station. I had half expected a waiting throng at the capital's main station, but it was a whisper-quiet shell like all the others along the line. Here the railway was an unwanted or at best half-forgotten inheritance.

We crawled on. Clusters of high-rise apartments were visible in the distance. It was Islamabad, Pakistan's version of Chandigarh, begun from scratch in 1961 and yearly drawing nearer the unruly bazaars of Pindi. The capital city's one truly dramatic landmark was Shah Faisal mosque, a modern construction capable of holding 74,000 worshippers. Even viewed from afar, it was apparent that its sharply angular lines lacked any of the gentle refinement of a traditional domed mosque. That sprawl of brick and macadam and bureaucrats' housing made me breathe a sigh of relief to be heading straight through.

At 3.30 we reached Attock City Junction, a pretty station of white plaster buildings and broad-canopied trees, before clattering across a big steel bridge. Far below, hemmed in by precipitous slopes, flowed the Indus, the Lion River, the lifeblood of Pakistan, which would spill into the Arabian Sea but not before it had been drained off at innumerable places by barrages and canals to irrigate the Punjab and sandy expanses of Sindh. At this point, however, its silt-laden waters were still full of force; in flood this reach rose as high as 30 metres.

Once on the other side, we were in the North-West Frontier Province and the Peshawar Valley. For a time it was a grassy oasis.

Long avenues of trees curved away into the distance. But the ground eventually turned to gravel and weeds, and bare hills reared up in our path, requiring many long cuttings and tunnels to force a passage.

At the township of Jahangira the elderly couple in my compartment departed without a word and once more I was almost alone at the end of the line. In the entire carriage there was just the conductor, Mr Ahmed, and a grey-haired woman who had boarded at Attock with a dozen floral-patterned duvets and who had promptly unwrapped one from its plastic wrapping and snuggled under it, falling asleep.

The city of Nowshera, which we reached at 4.30, was just a jumble of squat, mostly windowless brick huts like so many others scattered on hilltops beside the main road. Mr Ahmed chose this moment to perform masher, the fourth daily devotion, using the long aisle bench seat next to me. He faced directly into my ear, hands cupped as he silently mouthed his prayers of submission to Allah's will, while we whistled along the last 40 kilometres to Quetta.

The sun was now starting to sink before us, and poplars cast long tapering shadows across our path. Every kilometre took us deeper into a russet-coloured land where dust and rocks were rapidly prevailing over patches of rough grass and tamarisk trees. A few ploughed fields provided evidence that crops could be grown, but exactly what I could not imagine. Soon there was not a blade of glass anywhere. The Peshawar Valley was now as austere as the grey slopes of the Suleiman Mountains enclosing it. And everywhere minarets pointed skywards like stone fingers, invariably with a loudspeaker to amplify the muezzin's calls. There were so many minarets, in fact, that I scarcely noticed them any more.

Just on five o'clock the silhouette of Peshawar came into view, a Central Asian city outlined against the mountains. The duvet woman rose from her improvised bed and sat alongside me.

'You have a hotel to stay in?' she asked.

'No, I haven't,' I answered, quite taken aback by her question. On the few occasions I had sought directions from women in Pakistan they had turned away or stared straight through me. 'I was going to try somewhere in the old city.'

'That is good, there are many hotels there.'

We were now moving at walking speed between low mud hovels.

'This is backside of city,' she said.

'I see.'

'And this,' she continued, 'is cheapest market.'

Directly beneath us, in the narrow space between the track and backyard walls, was a bazaar selling second-hand goods, principally electrical items: radios, tape recorders, cassette players, cumbrous stereo systems (one seller carried a large hi-fi speaker on each shoulder); but also electrical components: circuit-boards, jumbles of wiring, partially disassembled innards tossed onto heaps as high as a man's shoulder. There were also bicycles in varying degrees of going order, used clothes, displays of perfume (only the extent of adulteration was in question), worn-out hand tools of every description ... the list was almost beyond enumeration.

'And this,' my guide resumed, pointing towards a fenced open space, 'is Jinnah Park. You know who Jinnah is?'

'Yes, Pakistan's founder.'

She smiled appreciatively.

We inched forward, deeper into the city.

'This is Bala Hisar,' she said, gesturing towards a huge, squat hilltop fortress brooding over the old quarter. The citadel was built by the Moghul emperor Babur, who gave the city its present name Pesh Awar, Frontier Town.

'Backside of this is Lady Reading Hospital,' she resumed. 'This is where you should look for hotels.'

We reached Peshawar Cantonment Station, as spruce and lifeless as every other, and I walked back to the old city to find a room. As I half suspected, that inconsequential conversation was to be almost my only interaction in Pakistan with the opposite sex.

❂

Peshawar is dusty beyond imagining. The chalky powder coats your clothes and shoes and skin and hair and eyelashes and even your watch face. It makes your mouth dry. It makes the cantonment trees droop. It turns every building a buff colour. It drifts like desert sand across the roads where traffic churns it up into your face once more. Yet it suits the town, a wild frontier place of faces dark, pale, brown, freckled, Mongoloid, blue-eyed; a place of beards clipped, straggly, spade-shaped, hennaed and carrot-coloured; a place of Afghan, Pathan, Kalasha, Gujar, Uzbek – to mention but a few – for each of whom a headdress communicates his native place as exactly as do his passport particulars.

The men are wild-looking, the driving is wild, the decoration of the buses that race one another for passengers is wild. On this last-mentioned point, 'wild' may actually be a grievous understatement. The buses flutter with pennants and flags, whirl with plastic propellers and jingle with chains and what-nots across every inch of panel work and glass. That includes the hubcaps, too, which flash with dagger-like projections and resemble the wheels of fighting chariots. The windows are low and unglazed, making passengers' clothes flap madly in the breeze and adding to the impression that these machines just might, with a little more speed, become airborne and never touch the ground again.

These colourful behemoths can be avoided in the old quarter, but its lanes still abound with traps for the timid, the disorientated, anyone not doggedly set upon a course. A compressed stream of cargo-laden cyclists, scooterists, pony carts, hand-pushed trolleys, absurdly optimistic motorists, three-wheelers (Pakistan's auto-rickshaws have side doors to hide passengers who keep purdah) and last but not least foot traffic; these lanes are ripe for gridlock and conflict. Scuffles and flaring tempers are regular events in Peshawar.

'There are many dangerous people here,' a bystander whispered to me as we watched two men shout at each other, then tug violently at one another's collar. A crowd appeared in seconds, drawn by the prospect of fisticuffs. The two Pashtuns wrestled with the reins of a horse while a third man stood on the cart, a helpless onlooker; the poor animal's head was yanked first this way, then that, while the big wooden cart wheels jerked backwards and forwards. Had the beast been less gentle-natured or not fitted with blinkers, it would, I felt sure, have given each an indignant kick.

Another time I saw two tribesmen sloppily swathed in black turbans tumble off a bus, a raging argument already in full progress. Friends pulled them apart. And a handful of times I saw reprimanded motorists and traffic police almost come to blows. The laws promulgated in far-off Islamabad were a hazy concern to the fiercely independent men who trod the streets of Peshawar. The women were of no account. The few on the streets glided by in their head-to-toe burqqas as though on invisible travelators.

Western faces were, I discovered, a rarity, and to stop on the pavement was to invite a circle of gawking faces. Few foreigners ever used to come, said a man at the Tourist Office in the cantonment, and after the events of September 11 things only got worse.

'You are the second today and that makes it a good day,' he said. It was after two o'clock. He was cheerful despite the absence of any real reason to unlock the door each day. 'September 11 hurt every Muslim country. Now we're all branded terrorists. It will take years to recover.'

One person undeterred by Pakistan's 'terrorist haven' tag was Zubic, a Canadian carpet buyer. He dressed in a salwar kameez to remain inconspicuous. 'You've had any negative reaction here? Yes? Then you should wear one of these. They're really comfortable. And if you're going to Quetta you'll definitely need one – it's very conservative there.'

But even though some hooligans had tried to run me down that day as I walked along the roadside I wasn't planning to disguise myself.

Zubic, who could not have been much under 2 metres, made a formidable sight bounding through the crowds in the old city, arms arcing high, like Roald Dahl's Big Friendly Giant. He even stood comparison with the swaggering craggy-faced Afghans who had washed up in their hundreds of thousands around Peshawar and were in no rush to return to their war-ravaged homeland. Zubic loved the Afghans. 'An Afghan I would trust with my life and all my money,' he said emphatically, though he said almost everything emphatically. 'I never trust a Pakistani – I won't do business with them. And I would never trust an Indian, and I've met thousands of them.'

He had been making regular visits to Peshawar for twelve years. It was a Mecca for old tribal rugs. Or at least, it used to be. They had became rare, and prices had gone mad. 'What I could have bought even three or four years ago if I'd had the money!' he lamented. 'Ten years ago I bought a really nice pair of saddle-bags – woollen, beautiful, really beautiful things – for 100 dollars. Last year I bought a similar piece – 5,000 dollars!'

The difficulty of finding good-quality examples did not deter him. Quite the reverse. He saw in it an opportunity. 'As soon as I get home to Calgary, I'm raising all my prices 30 per cent. Sure, some haven't been selling, but as I keep telling my customers, "There ain't no more where these come from."'

Zubic was self-taught. On his first buying trip he stumbled through, more by good luck than anything else. He read books, lots of books, about carpets. But books, he said, could get you only so far. 'You've got to *touch and see, touch and see.* With your own fingers and eyes. All up, I reckon I've looked at a million and a half rugs. This trip, I've looked at 200,000 and bought two hundred. Yesterday I looked at three hundred and fifty and bought five.'

In certain streets of the old city, men carried rolled-up carpets across their shoulders, hoping to catch the eye of passers-by. One whole block of hotels and offices had been converted into a labyrinthine maze of small overstuffed carpet shops. Big, small, gaudy, subtly coloured, patterned, plain: their stock lay in corridors, across every centimetre of floor space, jammed up high out of reach. Laid end to end, there were enough rugs in this town to reach halfway back to Lahore. Down on the streets, meanwhile, boys rushed glasses of green tea to prospective buyers, while other boys dashed past with handfuls of freshly baked naans destined for use as sops by diners squatting on pavement stools.

If anyone should fail to notice Peshawar's unruly instincts, one thing unmistakably gives it away: firearms. Sawn-off shotguns,

AK-47 assault rifles, elderly single-shot rifles with barrels as long and elegant as a gentleman's walking stick, pistols of every description – all were abundantly represented in the hands of security guards, policemen, private bodyguards, soldiers and, outside town, ordinary civilians themselves. Indian commentators assert that Pakistan's gun culture symbolises the breakdown of the rule of law. However, in the North-West Frontier Province, of which Peshawar is the capital, weapons are no mere instrument of crime. Here, men have a love affair with the gun. It is the arbiter of disputes, the settler of scores, the rescuer of honour, the defender of tribal territory. A youthful tribesman will reach for a rifle as instinctively as a young Scandinavian might clip on skis and, without tutoring, vanish down a slope.

In the hills around the Khyber Pass, the quarrelsome tribesmen shoulder their weapons casually and naturally. They live in fortified villages, clusters of small forts, each housing a single joint family and preferably built on an inaccessible and commanding crag, with mud walls 5 metres high, two or three loopholed firing-towers protected by sheets of iron in the corners, and entry only through a massive wooden gate. For the Pathan, his home is quite literally his castle.

Outsiders travelling up the pass have always been well advised not to venture off the bitumen and into tribal territory. An armed escort, formerly only advisable, is now obligatory. So, equipped with my authorisation from the Khyber Political Agent, I hired a taxi and set off past a big Afghan refugee camp – a dispiriting-looking sprawl of mud huts, canvas canopies and smoke – through Smugglers' Bazaar. We skirted the turreted mud fortress of Jamrud, built in 1823 by Ranjit Singh, the Sikh king of Lahore, to keep the mountain Pathans out of Lahore, and even today full of lifeless menace.

Beyond the fort lay a row of harsh, sharp-toothed peaks. One of those serrations in the Suleiman Range marked the Khyber Pass.

For long sections we followed an empty riverbed before the gradient changed and lorries shuddered up the zigzagging inclines. The driver flicked past them, paying no heed to blind corners and downhill traffic. The most extraordinary thing was the texture of the landscape: the shaly mountainsides, the braided stony watercourse, the fortified dwellings, the rubble slopes above the road – all were like the coarsest sandpaper. There was not a single spot anywhere to lay a finger and feel softness. Even the few stunted bushes were defended by long stabbing thorns, and children along the way threw stones.

Forts and depots marked where the Khyber Rifles patrolled the road, but their presence was really only a flag-showing exercise by the central government, which had always dealt gingerly with the restive local tribes. There was hardly 100 metres of the road that was not commanded by some crag or spur from where Pathan tribesmen could have picked off troops or terrorised passing traffic. Despite a terrain favouring the defender, countless invaders have swept down this pass and onto the plains of India, and for a few decades before the Soviet invasion of Afghanistan in 1979 it had been the overload route for a peculiar and previously unseen trespasser – the Western hippie, lured by the hallucinogenic delights of India and Nepal.

At Landi Kotal, the terminal for the disused railway line, the taxi crawled through a bazaar; a raucous, filthy place whose only memorable feature was the scores of caged chickens awaiting their final moment. Landi Kotal had owed its existence on this bleak ridge to the smugglers who operated over the mountains from Kabul and who were tolerated by the Pakistani authorities as part of the price to be paid for Pathan goodwill. Merchants reputedly stocked an exotic range of contraband, everything from Swiss watches and Japanese electronics to Russian assault rifles and opium. Even so, it was not the sort of place to go casually window-shopping.

A short way on we stopped at the roadside to look out over Afghanistan. There was not much to see. Brown hills, gaunt and ribbed like decomposing carcasses, stretched off into the haze. Intermittently, minibuses screeched around the corner, the Afghans aboard whooping and shouting as they neared home.

To the north I could see the railway line descending towards Landi Khana and the border itself, though this section down from Landi Kotal, the high point at almost 1,100 metres, was in disrepair and segments drooped in mid-air like rope bridges. We turned back, through Landi Kotal and down the zigzags. The railway track, running above the road and marked at frequent intervals by fortified towers and stone emplacements, was tantalisingly close. The steam train service to Landi Kotal was discontinued but it would have been absurd to have come to this far corner of the North-West Frontier Province and not traversed its most well-known feature.

The Khyber Railway was an engineering marvel and for a long time was considered an impossibility until its completion in 1925 proved otherwise. As well as steep gradients and heavy earthworks, there were thirty-four tunnels to be dug – a cumulative total of nearly 5 kilometres – and ninety-two bridges and culverts to be constructed. It swallowed up more than £2 million, a considerable sum of imperial funds but deemed worthwhile because the railway could rapidly bring up military reinforcements to a vital pass. The Khyber Railway was Britain's 'Forward Policy' rendered into iron and ballast.

General Musharraf had talked of reviving the line and extending it to Kabul, 200 kilometres away, but amid Pakistan's numerous and more pressing needs it was likely to remain just that – talk. Some things weren't talk, though. In the next day's edition of *Dawn*, a newspaper founded by Jinnah himself, I read that the general, in contravention of an International Labour Organisation convention to which Pakistan was a signatory, had slapped a ban on workers in essential services forming trade unions and negotiating wages and conditions collectively. The list of what were deemed essential services cast a rather unfavourable light on General Musharraf's regime. It included 'employees of the Bata Shoe Factory (supplier of footwear to the armed forces), Pakistan Security Printing Corporation, Pakistan Security Papers, the Mint, Pakistan Railway, open-line establishments, PIA [the national airline], seaports, airports, export-processing zones, watch-and-ward and security staff of oil refineries, gas and oil establishments, the Karachi Electrical Supply Corporation, and workers and tillers of the land'. This last category alone must surely have roped in two-thirds of the population. Who was not denied this most basic right?

Waiting passenger, Peshawar Cantonment Station.

The Quetta Express

OUTWARDLY, PESHAWAR CANTONMENT Station had all the administrative intricacy of a large Indian terminal, but the whole thing was an unused backcloth, a complicated stage set without actors. No one ever passed time in the First Class Ladies Waiting Room, no one bustled out the Lower-Class Exit or sauntered through the First-Class Exit – except at a few peak times. No one emerged from behind the door of the Head Clerk or of the Divisional Inspector (Special Ticket Examiner) or of the Commercial Superintendent (Commercial), each with its neatly painted signboard overhead. It had been no different the previous afternoon when I bought my ticket, and now the only souls about were three sweepers, unveiled old women, who made desultory dabs with their brooms down the length of the main platform. Alongside waited the Quetta Express, a diesel locomotive hitched to thirteen carriages which were painted in correct Islamic green and trimmed with red and yellow.

The day was dawning crisp and clear. It was also wonderfully still as the madly tooting circus machines, otherwise known as Peshawar's buses, had not yet got going for the day. Little by little men gathered in rings, each newcomer greeted with a prolonged bout of handshaking and ritual hugs. Pakistan was a country steeped in the rituals of greeting: the Chief Ticket Inspector himself, when we departed at 7.40 am, shook my hand as he came by. They were tall, heavy-set men in this northern corner of the subcontinent, with steady penetrating eyes and a vigorous handshake. Upon such men the tougher breed of British colonialist and army officer had looked with admiration, just as he regarded the slight Hindu of the plains with disdain.

When I ordered a glass of tea at a kiosk the proprietor subjected me to the usual inquisition about my religious leanings. 'You are a Christian?' he asked, to which I found myself saying, for convenience sake, 'Yes'. That drew an approving nod: Ahl al-kitab, People of the Book.

A man approached me and asked gleefully, 'Which is better, Pakistan or India?'

I thought for a moment, took a deep breath and said, 'In Pakistan, people are definitely more hospitable. More honest, too.'

His face brightened. I was always charged the local price and small change was scrupulously returned after every purchase.

Then the whistle went and in minutes we were off, travelling along a line that cut cleanly between the strict symmetry of the cantonment and the haphazard lanes of the old city.

First class, it turned out for me, meant a two-berth coupe with attached toilet and hand basin, a sliding lockable door for privacy (a greatly esteemed commodity in Pakistan), a mirror, collapsible table and wide green felt-covered bench seat with retractable arms. It was a very comfortable, if somewhat lonely, place from which to watch the North-West Frontier recede.

At nine o'clock I crossed the Indus a second time. The weathered melancholy hills across which cows and goats were foraging came to an end. The cultivable plains returned. And the heat. And the pewter-like haze. All about were hectares of cauliflowers, mounds of harvested maize and pencil-thin minarets protruding from rudimentary mosques. A shrunken pony hitched to a cart nibbled grass to restore its strength: all four-legged animals, with the possible exception of goats, looked to be on their last legs, and as soon as they took their final breath the knife was into them. Further on, smoke drifted lethargically from scores of brickworks, discolouring the sky with tall sooty smudges.

By 10.30 we were in Rawalpindi. Half an hour later the train drew out. At 1.15 we were at Jhelum Station, where all was quiet until a loudspeaker pierced the silence with its pre-recorded wail and a group of men who had been chatting lined themselves up obediently before the platform mosque. The disorderly Hindu way was not the Muslim way, which was the path of restraint, decorum and respect, the deeply ingrained forms of tradition. The distinction could be seen most clearly in prayer. The men on their knees in rows along the platform were prostrating themselves as one, dressed as one, were one. In Hindu temples, decorum consisted of little more than removing one's shoes; the rest was at the discretion of the worshipper. If, without straining an analogy, Hindu etiquette could be compared to the casualness of a Sunday brunch, then Muslim worship evoked the formality of a vice-regal banquet. There is sombreness, ceremony, strict separation of the sexes, a deep sense of occasion that one is separating oneself from the profane. For the Hindu, the business of worship was no more than an extension of life itself.

Throughout the afternoon the stations reversed themselves – Kharian, Lala Musa, Gujrat, Wazirabad, Gujranwala – as I stretched out, the sun pouring through my window, and skimmed my backlog of newspapers.

What astounded me most was the coverage of Kashmir. Sometimes I couldn't decide whether to laugh at the absurd bias or wince at the vitriolic language. 'India's nefarious and unprincipled attitude has once again stalled all peace efforts that were pushed ahead after the sincere efforts of Pakistan. This was stated by Chairperson of Kashmir Women Forum, Shamim Shaal, who said Indian atrocious activities have been increased on the whole occupied valley as daily 10 to 12 innocent Kashmiris are being martyred by the

Indian occupation forces. She added that on the one hand they are busy in genocide of Kashmiris and on the other they offer talks and peace process. In fact, these are tactics to hoodwink international community.'

For Pakistan, Indian troops did not kill terrorists, they martyred fighters – although in reports on the uprising in Nepal, Pakistan's media were happy enough to ascribe the bloodshed to rebels and insurgents.

Quite apart from the bias, there was also the question of veracity. Take this example; the italics are mine: 'Muzaffarabad: Two persons including an eight-year-old boy were killed and one wounded by Indian troops' *unprovoked* shelling across the Line of Control, police sources said. The Indian troops also *opened fire on civilian population* of Kairan, Titwal and Authmaqam sectors.'

Such reports, sadly, were commonplace. Never once did I come across a single mention of the machine-gun and artillery duels conducted almost daily across the disputed Kashmiri border, the so-called Line of Control, by Pakistani and Indian forces. The reader might easily have imagined that not a single shell or mortar round had ever been fired by Pakistani troops. The truth of this senseless killing by both sides was acknowledged some months later when the two rivals agreed to a formal ceasefire. In Karachi, I put these points to a seasoned reporter at *Dawn*, Shamim-ur-Rahman. He shrugged his shoulders: 'Indian side is also not reporting full story.'

❋

The Quetta Express rolled into Lahore, a sleek and modern thing against the makeshift surroundings of the city's suburban dwellers whose daily lives were laid bare before our passing gaze: the figures dozing outdoors on string beds among trash and smouldering fires, the men squatting to piss on the tracks, the youths playing snooker under footpath awnings or a tossing a cricket ball in railway sidings, the carter whose donkey collapsed before my eyes, unable to pull its load any further.

A little after four, the Quetta Express drew out of the echo-filled masonries of Lahore City Station. Signalmen cleared us through the minor stations with a flutter of their green flags. The conductor knocked at the door and asked for my ticket. Yes, the lower berth was assigned, but he did not know when the passenger would be boarding.

Soon night fell and cooking fires flickered on the plains. At each stop I listened to the passing footsteps. Would the occupant of the other bunk ever board? Invariably, when I peeked out the door, I saw a guard or conductor or one of the railway protection soldiers who drifted up and down the corridors.

When, by 9.30 pm, there was still no sign of the passenger who would share the coupe, I retracted the top bunk and went to bed, leaving the door unlocked. I slept long and soundly. Next morning the bottom bunk was still empty. I was baffled, for I knew I had obtained the last ticket in this coach.

Within half an hour we were approaching Rohri, an important railway junction on the Lahore–Karachi line. Having converged with the Indus and followed it south during the night, we now prepared to cross it and strike north-west for Quetta.

Rohri appeared to be a city of rubble. Some of it happened to be standing upright in the form of housing, but much of it lay in heaps on the ground, an impression compounded by its many burial grounds in which, as often as not, neat piles of debris doubled as gravestones. Standing among all this wretchedness, utterly dazzling in the rising sun, was the huge greenish-gold dome of the Akbari Masjid, a porcelain-tiled mosque built in 1583 during Akbar's reign. The dome gleamed with tremendous lustre, like a giant metallic orb, over the surrounding maze of ochre buildings.

Rohri was deserted at this early hour. When I clambered off to get some tea and fresh air a student called Aksar cornered me at a kiosk. Which was better, India or Pakistan? It was clear this was going to be a defining question. I rattled off my impressions and he said, 'I have spoken to many tourists and they all say in India there are many, many looters. If you put your bag down and look away it will be gone.'

'That's true,' I agreed, 'your belongings are safer here.'

'Yes,' he said, 'I am alone in economy class and I know my bag is safe there.'

Aksar was returning home to Quetta. He planned to do advanced studies in computer engineering but lamented the lack of jobs in Pakistan. When I suggested that he might go to India and work in Bangalore's big computer industry, he replied, 'That is impossible. Indian government is putting so many obstacles in the way. But our government is also doing same thing to Indians.'

The loco blew a warning toot and immediately began to move off. Departures were not the protracted business of India, and Aksar and I scampered off towards our carriages. In minutes we were crossing the Indus, which glowed like treacle in the morning light. The Ayub Khan bridge was a miniature of Sydney's harbour bridge, with a tremendous arch of steel and coiled wire ropes and fortified gateways at each end. Next to it was its predecessor, the Landsdowne, one of the great engineering feats of the nineteenth century, which closed in 1962 when it could no longer sustain the increased traffic load.

On the west bank of the Indus stood Rohri's twin city of Sukkur. It was a seamless transition because Sukkur, a sprawling place much troubled by dacoits, was as amply endowed with rubble and dirt as Rohri. Though about seven hundred years old, Sukkur was a place of little consequence until the British decided to build a barrage there to control the flow of the Indus: it was completed in 1932 after nine years of construction. One of the canals it feeds is wider and longer than the Panama or Suez canals. There are seven canals in all, totalling 650 kilometres, and they irrigate 2.5 million hectares of previously unusable hinterland.

Evidence of the barrage's transforming power was everywhere: rice, glistening as though with dew, grew uninterruptedly for an hour or more up the line. I breakfasted on peanuts and what several men described as 'sweet lemons', rather like small grapefruit, and watched the swathes of greenness go by.

Jacobabad marked the limits of the barrage's munificence. A few kilometres on, across the border in Baluchistan state, cultivation became a bitter struggle; the ground was hard and cracked, the crops of jawar stunted and intermittent. Villagers lived in mud huts rent by deep cracks; their cattle, children and women passed the day in stark compounds. Temperatures in Jacobabad were among the highest on the whole subcontinent, reaching 50 degrees in the shade. If such cruel heat were not enough, the town itself was as uninviting as any I had seen. Every building was low and drab, every courtyard entrance strung with a tatty sheet and sprinkled with runny-nosed children. The roads were largely the preserve of gaunt donkeys pulling tongas, the light, two-wheeled vehicles common in India.

The town, an administrative centre in colonial times, was named after the general who rid the region of the banditry then plaguing the region. Though a strict and uncompromising man, General John Jacob imposed order and peace, and for that he won much gratitude. He is one of only two Englishmen whose name remains attached to a town (the other town being Abbottabad). The anarchy existing in Jacob's time has gone, but much of Baluchistan beyond the main towns and highways is still a lawless place. Nature has not been kind to the Baluchis, whose burning wasteland the Pathans of the nearby mountains describe as 'the dump where Allah pitched all the rubbish left over from creation'. Banditry, understandably enough, must represent an attractive alternative to the toil and uncertainty of a farming life.

North of Jacobabad, the Quetta Express passed through the tiny station of Jhatpat, meaning 'immediately', the much-loved command of the British engineer responsible for its construction, and began the crossing of the Kachhi, a triangular-shaped desert of eastern Baluchistan at whose apex stands the entrance to the Bolan Pass.

For 140 kilometres the railway track ran in a dead-straight line. By ten o'clock the only consistent imprint of man upon this infinity of sand was a parallel road, strung with telephone poles, along which an occasional lavishly decorated lorry laboured. The emptiness exceeded anything I had seen before: a sprinkling of thorn bushes, small mounds of stones, some abandoned earthworks – and not a sliver of shade to be had anywhere. Miraculously, patches of barley pushed their way through the compacted ground from time to time. At even rarer intervals, the goats and tents of nomads flashed before my window and I realised that, stripped of the power lines, the scene before me could easily have belonged to the dawn of history. It was a life lived free of all modern conveniences and contraptions.

Sibi Junction marked the entrance to the Bolan Pass and the way up to Quetta, 1,676 metres above sea level. Four unneeded carriages were decoupled in preparation for the steep inclines ahead. A middle-aged man on the platform beside me mopped his brow and said Sibi rivalled Jacobabad for heat: in June and July temperatures often hovered between 45 and 50 degrees.

In twenty minutes I was staring at the beginnings of the Central Brahu Range. Without any preamble, a column of foaming rock and debris seemed to burst out of the floor of the plain, punching hundreds of metres into the sky. It was like a wave frozen at the instant before crashing down upon the shore. I slid open the compartment door and looked out the other side; it was just the same: a line of huge freakish rocks stretched away to the north, like a column of mute soldiers, blocking our way forward. But a breach materialised and the Quetta Express proceeded through what had moments before seemed an impenetrable barrier.

Behind this first defensive line of peaks arose another wave, and another after that, each forbiddingly jagged along its crest, strewn with boulders and slabs of broken rock on its abruptly rising easterly face, and yet, quite peculiarly, smooth and gently inclined on its westerly face, as though the whole range had buckled upwards before some vastly superior and suddenly applied tectonic pressure, rather than the usual grinding and locking of horns over millennia by two equal forces. The very air still seemed ripped and torn by the savagery with which this act of creation had been brought about.

Three tunnels brought us out into a wide, flat valley composed entirely of scree and boulders, after which we climbed into another amphitheatre of rocks, flanked all around by deeply eroded rock-faces. At the base of this amphitheatre was a stony river bed in which only a trickle flowed, but down which huge and sudden torrents have been known to flow, with devastating effect on man and beast. It was a place like nowhere I'd ever seen. To top matters off, nature had dipped its brush into the most extraordinary palette: there was bone-white, brown, ochre, grey, tawny yellow and, in the shadow-filled folds of the most distant ridges, crimson-blue.

Beyond the tiny deserted station of Panir the valley narrowed. Three or four more tunnels brought us out onto a ridge overlooking a colossal rock-strewn valley bounded to the west by a series of high ranges. Round we came, slowly losing height, until we were all but on the floor of the valley.

Visible high on a hill was a fortified tower, one of a series built by the British to watch over their railway line. The Baluchi tribesmen of the region were never entirely subdued to Britain's satisfaction. Forty years of trying to take control of Baluchistan had ended in a stalemate, and in 1876 treaties were signed acknowledging tribal autonomy, supplemented by subsidies, in exchange for the stationing of British troops at key points along the Afghan border and the use of supply lines leading to those points. The railway to Quetta and on through the Khojak Pass to the 3,895-metre Chaman tunnel, which emerges right on the doorstep of Afghanistan, was conceived with strategic considerations uppermost. Control of Baluchistan meant control of the passes by which invaders from the north might descend from the mountains of Afghanistan. And during the nineteenth century, the most feared invaders were the armies of the Russian tsar.

The present line up to Quetta was not the original. At Sibi it had turned north-east and looped around through Harnai, Khost, the Chappar Rift and Bostan. The Rift, a limestone gorge created by the separation of two plates during an earthquake, proved a terrific engineering challenge, and the iron girder bridge spanning this geological fracture was an extraordinary, if ultimately temporary, feat. Construction of the support pillars and the drilling of the tunnels immediately either side of the bridge were an almost impossible undertaking. In order to work against sheer cliff-faces, men were lowered on cradles. A drilling machine was drawn by elephants which were never again able to work. Flash floods swept down the defile.

The *District Gazetteer* described how work was carried out after men were lowered several hundred metres from the clifftops above:

> The first man down had to gain a footing by driving a crowbar into the perpendicular wall; after the first crowbar others were driven in, and then a platform was erected from which blasting operations could begin. So singular and difficult a piece of engineering has probably seldom or never been accomplished before. Six openings were made on one side of the cliff for one tunnel and six on the other, and galleries driven into them until points were reached from where the main tunnel could be constructed right and left, so that the work could be carried on by fourteen separate gangs; and in this way the whole tunnel was blasted out in a few months.

The flash floods ultimately proved the bridge's undoing, causing costly and difficult maintenance, and the line beyond Khost was abandoned. The railway builders certainly had no easy time of it when they began work on the present route. The track, laid originally along the bed of the Bolan, suffered the same flash floods as the more northerly route, and sections were realigned higher up out of harm's way. Gradients were exceptionally heavy, too – in places as much as 1:25. Between Sibi below me and Kolpur at the top of the pass, the line would rise from 120 metres to 1,798 metres above sea level through twenty tunnels, a distance of 96 kilometres of hard-fought railway engineering.

On we moved up the valley, shown on my map as one vast riverbed. Across this trackless waste I saw the first sign of life, two Baluchis pushing their bicycles, though from where and to where was impossible to guess. The down train was waiting for us at Abigum. This was no more than a few station buildings shimmering in the haze that flared off the ground. We had gained a few hundred metres or so in elevation, but when I stepped down, the heat that embraced me was still fierce. Among those stretching their legs there was not one female; they remained hidden on board, never to emerge until journey's end. With an extra locomotive hooked up at the rear, we chugged on at no more than 40 kilometres an hour, every half kilometre or so passing over a culvert where, if it could be imagined, flood water must sometimes have accumulated.

The township of Mach, clustered around the train station, smelt overpoweringly of coal. Labourers were digging away a hillside of the stuff and loading it, shovel by shovel, onto waiting lorries.

'You must be finding this hot,' said a passenger sipping tea beside me at the chai stall.

'Very,' I said.

The man, a retired army major now in business in Abbottabad, was on his way to visit friends in Quetta.

'You were a military man,' I said, 'so perhaps you can help me. The other day I read that fifty per cent of Pakistan's GDP goes on the military. But this morning someone told me it was eighty per cent. Which is the right figure?'

He turned a little sheepish. 'Forty, forty-five per cent,' he said, wobbling one hand from side to side a little, like old-fashioned scales in a grocery.

'That's a lot for a poor country like Pakistan.'

He gave a peculiar laugh and said, 'Not everybody, not everybody' before breaking off to rejoin the train. I followed suit, perplexed.

The major had said the climb would begin in earnest from this point, but we remained on the valley floor, still surrounded by monstrous brown rocky hills, the more distant of which were streaked ultramarine in their craggy shadows. The road to Quetta, on the far side of the valley, shimmered like a leaky trail of mercury in the burning sun.

Hirok Station consisted of a name-board on a platform. A short way on, the major's words were realised. The valley began to close in and the road and rail line were inevitably pressed closer together until the bitumen was alongside us, then curled beneath us, then re-emerged on our right. Scarcely 100 metres separated the two valley walls closing in on us, their rock-faces brutish and raw, a jumble of clefts and slips and overhangs and tremulous-looking chimneys. Via a series of bridges and tunnels, one following the other in rapid succession, we laboured ever upwards.

I stood at the doorway, quite alone, watching the drama unfold around me. The exhausts of the two locomotives reverberated in the valley. How at that moment I wished for company, someone with whom to share this spectacle. But every compartment door was closed to me.

Finally, at 3.20, we reached Kolpur and the top of the pass and began to bowl along the floor of the Shal Valley, at the northern end of which stood Quetta. The main activity on this desert plateau was brickmaking. Dozens of steeple-like chimneys belched smoke into the bright cloudless sky. The few Pakistanis to be seen on this vast canvas of plateau and range – a farmer on his cart or a cyclist making his lonely way home – were readily discernible by long columns of dust trailing in their wake.

Quetta appeared, low, unprepossessing, dung-coloured, a collection of mud and brick houses unfurling across the valley floor. We hardly seemed to check our speed entering the city, with the result that dust swirled up dramatically around the coaches, obscuring any view until we were crawling into the station, by which time, at 4.15, thirty-three hours to the minute since leaving Peshawar, all I could think of was getting off.

❂

'I have 400 acres,' Khudabux Bakhash said, loudly and unprompted. 'Near Jacobabad.'

'I see,' I replied after a suitable pause. 'And what do you grow on your 400 acres?'

'Some bananas, cane, wheat and cotton.'

'So it is not irrigated then?'

'Oh yes, from Sukkur Barrage.'

'Then your land must be valuable.'

Mr Bakhash said nothing but his swarthy features lit up with the pleasure of endorsement. He was, I guessed, one of the archly conservative landholders, or waderas, of the Sind upon whom so much blame was heaped for holding back progress in rural Pakistan. Such men as Mr Bakhash exercised power over everything affecting those directly or loosely under their sway, from whom they should vote for to whom they should marry.

Mr Bakhash was taking a rest from his numerous responsibilities. As he clutched his mobile phone and a packet of cigarettes in one hand, he explained, 'At this time I am living here at Bloom Star Hotel. This is best in town. It is the season for me in Quetta. When my family come we will go to my other house across town.'

'How many children do you have?' I asked.

'Well … nine.'

'Nine!' I exclaimed in mock astonishment. 'You have been busy. No wonder you need to come to Quetta for a holiday.'

'And you?'

'I have one.'

'Just one?'

'Yes, one. A son.'

'I wanted to practise family planning,' he said, a plaintive note now creeping into his voice, 'but my mother said to me, "You must have boys, four boys," so I kept trying for more boys. Number one is a boy. Number two is a boy, but number three, four, five, six, seven and eight are girls. Number nine is a boy, Ali.'

'Your farm, is it family-owned land?'

He nodded vigorously.

'So it is divided among the sons with each passing generation?'

'No, it is joint. It always stays joint.'

'That is good then. Your 400 acres will always stay together.'

'Yes,' he said simply, and I saw the tension drain from his face.

Land meant a lot to Mr Bakhash because in Pakistan land meant power. Earlier in the week the country had marked Poverty Alleviation Day with the customary high-faluting pronouncements by government ministers. Meaningful change was a distant prospect, though. According to one newspaper report, Pakistan's own experts estimated 84 per cent of farmers (in most cases haris, or share-croppers) were living at subsistence levels; failure to tackle land reform would allow 'feudalism', of which Mr Bakhash was the human face, to keep its stifling grip on the life of the country.

Procreation and matters sexual seemed to be a theme of my stay in Quetta. Next day I met Dr M. A. Asif. He was a sexologist. And though that was no particularly big deal in India where the shingles of sex experts were commonplace in large cities ('FIX ALL SEX PROBLEMS: Dr A. L. Patel (London trained)'), here in Baluchistan, the most conservative state in religiously conformist Pakistan, setting up shop as a sexologist was akin to an abortionist opening his doors around the corner from the Vatican.

Dr Asif was an assistant to Dr M. Aslam Naveed, who was absent in Colombo addressing an international symposium on alternative sex therapy treatment. I saw their sign, Yang Tian Sex Care Center, just off Jinnah Road and succumbed to my curiosity. I went in and laid my cards on the table: I was just a nosy foreigner looking for a chat. But Dr Asif, who wore a white shirt and tie and sat at a desk surrounded by framed diplomas and degrees in the manner of medical practitioners the world over, didn't quite understand me and kept motioning towards the seat opposite his desk.

'What is your problem?' he enquired with earnest eyes, once I was seated. 'Please, tell me, what is your problem?'

When, eventually, I made my purpose clear, he said, 'I am glad you have come to talk. You will take tea?'

And before I could answer he had picked up the telephone and ordered one of the few social lubricants permitted in Pakistan.

I had assumed Dr Asif would gleefully plunge into the most intimate discussion of sexual relations among his fellow countrymen and women. But he surprised me with his reticence. He had to be tickled like a trout to abandon his euphemistic language. When I first asked him about the most common sexual problems of his patients he talked repeatedly of 'too much congestion'. I kept seeing in my mind's eye engorged, unspent sexual organs. But with persistence the genial doctor made himself clear.

'The problem,' Dr Asif explained, 'is the great quantity of ignorance in this country. People have no awareness there is even a problem. In the villages, people live lives of complete ignorance. They have six, seven, eight, ten, twelve children. How are they to feed them? Income is very, very little. They believe they cannot say no to more children: "A gift from Allah – how can I refuse it?" they say to themselves. But the man, he is always thinking, how to feed all these mouths? And if they are girls, how to pay the dowries? One or 2 lakh rupees per daughter is common. All this stress, it is one reason for the torture of women—'

'Torture?' I interrupted. 'Surely not?'

'Torture there is. A great deal of torture – beatings, punchings …'

'Please, how many households do you think this is happening in?'

'The number I do not know exactly, but believe me, it is a great deal. Pakistan, I am afraid to say, is a deeply backward country. You must remember, this is still a country where many people think one book, the Koran, is all they ever need to read – what is revealed in the Koran and in the Prophet's own life. No more. It is like eleventh-century Europe.

'I have been to Sweden several times, and in that country there is much free love. It is good. I have tried. There it is a life. Here it is not. Sex, as I am sure you know, is a part of life. It is ….'

But he did not finish his words. An old bearded man entered with a tray on which were placed two cups and saucers of translucent porcelain containing chanaki, green tea. We each took a sip and he resumed.

'Here, men and women lead utterly separate lives: there is no meeting except among close family members. It is even true for husband and wife – they do not come together except in the bedroom, they remain strangers to each other throughout their lives.'

'Tell me,' I said, intrigued as to his professional opinion, 'how many couples have good sex lives? One per cent? Ten per cent? Fifty per cent?'

'Eight or nine per cent,' he replied unhesitatingly.

That struck me as an astonishingly precise estimate.

'And how many have okay lives? Neither good nor bad?'

He twiddled his ballpoint pen a moment: 'Fifty per cent.'

'So that leaves forty per cent with lives of abuse and no sex worth the name, yes?'

'Yes, that is fair.'

'In the West, the main problems for men would be erectile dysfunction and premature ejaculation. Is that true in Pakistan, too?'

'It is the same here.'

'And for women, what is the main problem?'

'I do not know. I deal only with men.'

'Are there sexologists for women?'

'Gynaecologists only. Mainly it is fertility problems.'

'Are men aware that women can enjoy sex also?'

Dr Asif, who struck me as a phenomenally cheerful individual in the face of all this ignorance, shook his head regretfully and said, 'Two or three per cent only. Maybe they have been to Europe. They have awareness. The rest, they know nothing. It is just this jiggy-jiggy.' He indicated the sex act by thrusting a finger in and out of the circled thumb and finger of his other hand. 'They know nothing of the different ways to have a married life, a sexual life. If they have awareness they can educate their wives. Or maybe their wives are educated already. My wife, I have put my beliefs into her mind, and we are having many ways to express our sexual life. At first she thinks it is not right to do it any time but in the evenings, in bed. "Pull the curtains, turn off the light! No, we cannot do it during the day. No, we cannot take off all our clothes – only the bottom half." All these things she was thinking. But now my beliefs are so in her head that she can enjoy many ways to do it.'

Dr Asif was now in full flight. 'What you must understand is that there is depression, a deep depression among women in my country. They are treated as though they are not part of the human race.'

Emboldened by his words, I said, 'How interesting you should say that, because walking here I saw a troubling thing. There was a bus waiting at the side of the road. Of course the women sat separately at the front. They didn't think they were being watched and they had their veils lowered. And every single face, from the prettiest and youngest to the oldest and most careworn, had the same deep, deep look of sadness. That was when I grasped what it must be like to be cooped up all day at home, never coming out except to scuttle from

A to B and back. I mean, husbands do not even walk alongside their wives in the street! They trail behind like perfect strangers.'

He gave a slow understanding nod.

I said, 'Tell me, do you think women should wear the veil?'

'No, I do not,' he said emphatically, 'it is a form of torture. How can there be shame in showing the face? But there are the mullahs, the traditions of Muslim peoples. For centuries there has been the veil and the mullahs preach against abandoning it.'

'And the reason they give for keeping the veil?'

'The reason is that if women do not wear it, men will be … will become aroused … they will make advances.'

'Are there people who oppose what you do?' I asked. 'I notice you have a security camera outside.'

'Baluchistan is a lawless place.'

'But there must be people who don't like what you do, surely?'

'Eighty per cent approve, twenty per cent don't.'

'And that includes the mullahs, I take it?'

He gave a slight smile in reply.

Dr Asif was too polite to end our meeting so I said, 'Sir, I have taken up too much of your time. I must let you get back to work.'

We rose, shook hands and I carried on down Jinnah Road, by which time it was after midday and the shop shutters were coming down as the town's menfolk drifted off to Friday prayers.

But that was not the end of my discussions about sex. I found a teahouse that remained open, and sat down. The waiter, a grizzled man with spectacles resting on a beaky nose, took my order for tea, which came in a battered metal teapot with separate bowls of sugar and milk and a chipped fine bone china cup and saucer. Teahouses were the one thing approximating public entertainment in Peshawar, and this was a typical example. It was high-ceilinged, ill-lit, its air everlastingly pervaded with the smell of cigarette smoke; some spindly wooden tables and chairs were arranged about a single large room whose floor was laid with small, beautifully coloured tiles, and wood-framed mirrors were fixed about the walls. In the far corner hunched a party of Afghans and Baluchis, wild-bearded individuals cloaked in an assortment of unlaundered costumes who spoke in furtive whispers, as though hatching some intrigue.

I jotted in my notebook, drank tea and was watched briefly by an Afghan wearing a flat woollen cap who sat directly opposite me and observed the movement of my pen across the page with all the awed intensity of a witness to the first true act of alchemy. After a time, he shook my hand, said 'Thank you' with a glorious smile and left, only to be replaced by a Pakistani who had not shaven in some days, wore an expensive wristwatch and whose opening line to me was, 'You are a journalist, correct?'

'Maybe,' I said, unhappy at being so easily pigeonholed. 'And you are?'

'A businessman.'

'What sort of business?'

He sat himself down and cast an eye about the room.

'Drugs.'

'Pharmaceuticals?'

'Yes,' he said, with a slight smirk, 'you could say pharmaceuticals. You are a Christian?'

'Yes,' I lied.

'What is the age of consent in your country? Between a man and woman, I mean?'

'Sixteen.'

'And to smoke?'

'The same.'

'And to drink?'

'Eighteen.'

'You have gays in your country?'

'Yes.'

'They do not hide? They, how you say, are out in the open?'

'Yes, well, many. Some don't.'

He lowered his voice. 'Here in Pakistan, they don't. Here they must keep hidden.'

But then he chirped up and spoke louder again. 'You saw the Pope today? On CNN? He was speaking against gays. In your country, people are against gays?'

'Some are, some are not.'

'But you follow the Pope? He is the Big One, is he not?'

I couldn't help laughing. 'Yes, you are right. He is the Big One.'

'You have a girlfriend?' he said, evidently tiring of the subject of gays.

'No, a wife.'

'Girlfriends, wives – they are all the same, yes? I have been to France. There they say, "She is my girlfriend" – it is like being married, the same thing.'

'Yes,' I said, humouring him, 'you have a point. Are you married?'

'I am,' he said grudgingly, as though I had wrung a confession from him.

'Any children?'

'Two.'

Soon, packing up my things, I left the teahouse. I had had enough sexual repression for one day.

There was a footnote to the day, in that morning's edition of Peshawar's *Frontier Post*. The paper carried a report about a conference on women's issues during which there were repeated references to the physical and mental torture of Pakistani women. There were also flowery words about government initiatives to rectify matters but nothing could beat this statement by Prime Minister Mir Zafarullah Khan Jamali, made to a 'delegation of lady Senators'. He said that 'women, being one half of the country's population, will have to play a proactive role in socio-economic progress of the country to accelerate the pace of overall development'. And this in a country where women could not go about the streets unescorted.

❁

Every night I ate at an eating-house in the bazaar where customers sat at benches and dined off Formica tables. At the entrance, kept warm by burning charcoal, was a row of aluminium pots, all identical in shape but ascending in size in perfectly proportioned gradations like a dismantled Russian doll. With a nod from a prospective customer, each lid was opened to display an oily-topped curry, ranging in brilliance from umber to cadmium-yellow to cherry to orange-red to molten steel, and containing either chickpeas, potatoes, lentils, beef, chicken or goat. The olive green of saag, or puréed spinach, stood alone among this fiery-coloured arrangement. Next to the pots, taking pride of place, was the tandoor, which two men worked ceaselessly to supply customers and passers-by with naans.

Eating there one evening, the hubbub of the laneway throng filling my ears, I met a Pakistani of thoroughly unconventional views. Ahmed Syall was a history teacher at Quetta's best private school, though the pay was still poor, and thus, like every other half-ambitious Pakistani, he was pursuing studies in computer science, which he hoped would lead to greater opportunities.

Mr Syall, whom I judged to be about thirty and whose hair and moustache were neatly trimmed in the Western manner, expressed views I had previously thought impossible of a Pakistani. The most audacious, which seemed almost treasonable, was that most Kashmiris did not want to go with Pakistan but with India.

'Yes,' he said, 'ten or twenty per cent want to join with Pakistan, indeed violently so, but nearly half want to go with India. The rest, they are undecided.'

In my surprise I never remembered to ask him how he arrived at that breakdown of opinion. My first thought and question was: 'Why would mostly Muslim Kashmir want to go with mostly Hindu India? We're all told they want to go with Pakistan.'

'That is easy. Because they have seen Pakistan and they do not want to be part of it.'

'Please, Ahmed,' I said, 'you had better explain yourself.'

'In this country, all the benefits go to perhaps a fifth of all citizens – the army and bureaucrats, the ISI* and such people. There is no democracy here, and these people, especially the generals, have so

---

* The ISI is the Directorate for Inter-Services Intelligence, Pakistan's foreign intelligence service and, according to some critics, the country's 'invisible government'.

arranged things that they are taking a bigger and bigger slice of the country's wealth. There are no brakes on them.'

'Is it true, then, that up to eighty per cent of the annual budget is going to the armed forces?'

'No,' he answered, as composed as ever, 'it is more than eighty per cent, I think. Their spending is hidden in all sorts of ways.'

I thought back to Mr Izmit on the Lahore platform and his bragging about the Air Force-funded school his children attended. That made me wonder about the possibilities for fudging the country's accounts.*

'Have you been to Islamabad, our new capital?' Mr Syall asked.

'No, I just passed through.'

'There you will find roads and apartments almost the equal of America and Europe. All the services and facilities are there. They want for nothing. They have no idea of what village people must endure. Do you know, a teacher friend of mine had a student who had come to Quetta for the first time in his life. He was twenty-five or twenty-six and he had never seen a train. "There are no trains in my district," he told my friend. "But you must have seen one on television?" my friend said. "No, we have no televisions in my village. We have no power." He had no idea of what a train was. A train!

'In many of the villages around Quetta they have no gas for cooking. They use firewood. And yet almost all of Pakistan's gas comes from Baluchistan. Sui district has one of the biggest gas deposits in the world. But these rural people are so uneducated, they know so little of the twenty-first century, that they are happy to get two meals a day and a roof over their heads.

'Why would Kashmiris want to become part of that inequality?

---

* According to the *Financial Times World Desk Reference*, spending on defence amounts to only 5.7 per cent of GDP (education is 2.7 per cent, and health 0.9 per cent). Where the remaining 90.7 per cent goes can be guessed at by the publication's comment: 'Members of the bureaucratic and political elite tend to be extremely rich, as are some of the top military.' The same publication puts India's defence spending at 3.4 per cent, education at 3.2 per cent and health at 0.8 per cent.

Look at India – it is far, far ahead of us. Its economy is booming, it is self-sufficient, it has growing exports, it has a sophisticated computer sector, it has a highly skilled English-speaking population. It has a well-established tradition of democracy. It has good relations with many countries. What do we have? None of those things! Not one. We have close ties with America, but who knows how long that will last. We are useful in its war on terrorism. That is all.

'People here say, "Oh, the Hindus treat Muslims in India badly ..." If you believe the Pakistani papers, Muslim Indians are living under siege. What nonsense! Yes, Muslims were killed in Gujarat after Godhra last year, but after Indira Gandhi was assassinated in 1984 people turned on the Sikhs and killed several thousand. It is terrible, this communal violence, but it is not a conspiracy against Muslims. It is India, imperfect India. Do you know that the president of India is a Muslim – Abdul Kalam Advani? He is the third Muslim president India has had since Partition. Our constitution forbids anyone but a Muslim from being a prime minister, deputy prime minister or president. Oppression of Muslims? I don't think so. And do not forget, there are probably more Muslims in India than in Pakistan.'

I expressed my doubts about India having any designs on Pakistan. Quite apart from having its hands full with problems of its own, it had everything to lose and nothing to gain. Did it really want to swallow 160 million disgruntled, impoverished and unwilling citizens? As long as Pakistan took no aggressive action on Kashmir, no Indian soldier would take a step on to Pakistan's soil. For once I found a sympathetic ear.

'India,' Mr Syall said, 'is held up as the bogeyman, the enemy we must always be on our guard against. Now we apparently have a dangerous Afghanistan, too: for the first time in fifty-six years we are deploying troops along the Durand Line. It is all a justification to keep taking the money from our pockets. Do you remember the Kargil incident? The Pakistani army on one side of this horrible, high frozen mount, the Indian army on the other, hurling artillery shells at one another, and for what? The mount ... what is it called?'

'The Siachen Glacier.'

'Yes, the highest, coldest battlefield in the world. It has no value. It is a terrible waste of life and money. A cup of tea, here it is 5 rupees, but we have learnt it is costing the army 45 rupees to supply a soldier with that same cup of tea 5,000 metres up in the ice. What a terrible, terrible waste. Truly no one is thinking.'

Earlier during the afternoon I had walked down Jinnah Road as far as Nabib Nala, a stream marking the northern limit of the city centre, where soldiers at a roadblock turned me back. The road led to the green spaces of the cantonment where people of privilege lived. Every decent-sized city had its 'defence housing colony', which was off limits to ordinary citizens. For me it was no particular bother, but what of the locals? How did they feel about being barred from a piece of their own country? After all, I said to Mr Syall, hadn't his taxes helped pay for a bit of that road through the cantonment?

'You must have a pass,' he said equitably. 'Otherwise you are turned back.'

'Doesn't that bother you? Hasn't someone demanded an official explanation of why a whole suburb is out of bounds?'

'Ignorance, lack of real democracy. No one knows the questions to ask.'

'What about the newspapers?'

'Yes, they have sought answers but it is all forgotten ...'

Forgotten. Yes, that was the Pakistani people. But they had not forgotten their duty of hospitality towards travellers. When I went to leave that very modest establishment I discovered some earlier customer had already settled my bill.

❁

I returned to my favourite haunt, the Café Regal teahouse, the following day. The grey-beards were there in force, sipping their chanaki, smoking and talking and talking ... and talking. Time was not a precisely measured element in Quetta. Motorists drove sedately – there were no hustling whiny scooters and motorbikes to speak of – and there was always time to adjourn for a tea at the least provocation. 'You will take tea?' I was asked on innumerable occasions. But I was happy to sit secluded in my teahouse where it was deliciously cool – even a little cold (it can snow in Quetta for three months of the year) – and watch the procession of gnarled and variously hatted faces pass by my window.

I had time on my hands before my next train, for Quetta offered little in the way of historic attractions. The earthquake of 1935 took care of that. It struck at 3.03 on the morning of 31 May, levelling just about everything and killing 23,000 people. The town was completely rebuilt, most structures being one or two storeys high out of fear of a repeat earthquake. As Baluchistan's provincial capital, it now housed the offices of various tribal leaders from surrounding districts. At one end of Zarghoon Road, previously Lytton Road, the administrative apparatus of the provincial government had moved into the quarters of the former British rulers. There, one official building followed another, each in the white stucco style of the period, each set back among substantial and immaculately maintained lawns and gardens, and each guarded by a smartly turned-out squad of soldiers.

The green, ordered perfection of this government enclave seemed surreal against the broader surroundings. The dusty valley floor on which Quetta sits is as flat as a snooker table. A short way off is a ring of bare mountains, all sloping sharply into a blue sky. There are impressive peaks among them: Murdar, Takatu, Zarghun and Chiltan. In the bright clear light, tantalisingly close at the end of any thoroughfare you care to look down, those barren peaks seem just a five-minute stroll away. Those views are majestic, and so are the hill men who march, with swirl of shawl and erect, deliberate bearing, through the bazaars. Now I could understand why the sahibs regarded this frontier post as one of the most desirable stations in their empire.

Brickmaking in Shal Valley, near Quetta.

The Baluchistan Express to Karachi

TOWERING EDDIES OF DUST corkscrewed down the Shal Valley, swift moving and unpredictable, like flashing scimitars. In the nearby brickfields figures, swathed against the wind, were loading the panniers of pony trains.

'How can they live there?' Dr Ahmad asked, more of himself than of me, as though wrestling with a troublesome conscience. 'No electricity, no water, no medical services.' He thought a moment, then added, 'But do you know what, they are happier than you or I.'

'That's possible,' I said, 'but I strongly doubt they'd say no to power and water.'

He pointedly said nothing.

Dr Ahmad was returning to Karachi after a three-month assignment at a charity-run hospital in Quetta – our coupe was bursting with his boxes of personal effects. In that time, he told me, he had performed 450 operations, most to remove cataracts.

'Basically government hospitals are not providing any services to the people. They are not functioning in any meaningful way. It is the same with the schools…'*

'And power and water and roads,' I interjected. 'The government is spending most of your money elsewhere.'

Dr Ahmad gave a grudging nod.

I knew it was an unnecessarily blunt remark but I couldn't help myself. What I didn't add was that General Musharraf had failed to deliver on law and order, too. On seizing power, he had promised to fix the country's criminal, ethnic and political violence, but the papers were full of examples of his failure in this regard: Shias setting off bombs outside Shi'ite mosques, politicians falling to assassins' bullets, banditry and murder day after day. The big cities as much as the remotest districts were subject to this violence. Only the day before I had read that dacoits in Baluchistan opened fire on a bus, killing two and wounding seven. The highwaymen fled and were not caught. But it was so unremarkable as to warrant just two sentences in the *Frontier Post*.

Two other dacoits, having been found guilty the same day in a Quetta court of murdering two security guards, were given the death sentence, a 29,000-rupee fine and fourteen years' imprisonment. In other words, the pair would forfeit the money, serve the jail term and then be hanged, the sanctioned method of execution in Baluchistan.

Dr Ahmad did not regard this as an unnecessarily drawn-out or cruel punishment. 'In Islam it is allowed. If you injure me, I am allowed to injure you.'

I studied Dr Ahmad out of the corner of my eye. He may have been a baby-faced twenty-eight-year-old but those words came off his lips with a chilling pitilessness.

The young doctor, after four years of additional training to become an ophthalmologist, was now undertaking further specialist training. Would he ever have time to marry, I asked.

He gave a boyish giggle of embarrassment. 'In two years, when my studies are complete. My mother, she has picked out a girl,

* The per capita availability of doctors in Pakistan is among the lowest in the world: one per 1,667 people.

informally of course, but she will not make me go with her if I do not like her.'

In that moment I saw, beneath his attempt at a good Muslim beard, a boy who had studied long and hard but tasted hardly anything of life.

The Baluchistan Express rumbled down into the Bolan Pass. The twisted mountain rubble had still not lost its power to awe. Dr Ahmad pointed to the dry riverbed. 'In the rains the water pours down here. Then the Bolan is a raging torrent. It is terrifying.'

At 6 pm we halted at Abigum, which means 'water is lost here'. The light was almost gone, and the sky and cold rock walls had dissolved into a swirling Turneresque amalgam of blues, yellows and oranges. Soon we were retreating across the desert towards Sibi, and in that last gasp of twilight the bitterly unrewarding plain was lent a veneer of softness.

Sibi, even at 8.30 in the evening, was gripped by a breathless heat. One of the locomotives was unhitched and we left. Dr Ahmad climbed into his top bunk and ate a chicken roll and some fruit. The catering service on Pakistan's trains was erratic and the food was poor so no one relied on it. I ate some biscuits with a cup of tea bought at Sibi and read the paper. The letters page exposed a controversy raging over Jinnah's intentions when he helped to found Pakistan. Some said he declared Pakistan would not be a theocracy but a liberal secular state. Others countered that he had given secret indications he wanted quite the opposite. The soul-searching stemmed from a television debate. When learned men were debating the intent of the father of the nation more than half a century on, then surely the country had lost its way. One thing was clear to me: if the state's defining characteristic was religious in identity, and Pakistan was carved out to protect the interests of those Indians who had believed in the Islamic faith, then it would be very difficult, if not impossible, for a secular outcome to result. Yet one letter writer would have had it no other way: for him the state and religion were inevitably inseparable 'simply because it is impossible to inculcate goodness of character without the support of religion'.

Quaid-i-Azam, or Great Leader, as the suave, ruthless Jinnah was referred to by his countrymen, had led the Muslim League through Partition talks, and he was driven as much by a fear and distrust of the Hindu-dominated Congress as by a desire for a Muslim homeland. Once, asked if there were any good Hindus, he snapped, 'There are none!' To him, they were untrustworthy, spineless, dirty and slovenly, and incapable of governing themselves, still less others. Muslims were a people apart, he asserted. 'We are a nation of 100 million and, what is more, we are a nation with our own distinctive culture and civilisation, language and literature, art and architecture, names and nomenclature, sense of value and proportion, legal laws and moral codes, customs and calendar, history and traditions, aptitudes and ambitions.' It was hardly surprising that Hindu–Muslim power-sharing talks became deadlocked.

Nothing better illustrates the lack of consensus over Pakistan's defining principles than the see-sawing constitution. Scarcely a year after Independence and with no constitution yet formulated, Jinnah died of tuberculosis. His deputy Liaquat Ali Khan assumed the position of prime minister. He, like Jinnah on the whole, thought Pakistan should be a secular democracy. Many religious leaders had a different view, and when Liaquat was assassinated three years later things stalled. It was not until March 1956, eight and a half years after its founding, that Pakistan could finally say it had a constitution. Pakistan became an Islamic republic with a parliamentary form of government. But two and a half years later, the constitution was gone. In a precedent-setting move, President Iskander Mirza, a retired major-general, declared martial law and abrogated the constitution, which he vowed to rewrite. President Mirza was followed by other military leaders, of which General Musharraf was but the latest example, who went on to seize power from civilian governments, and all inherited President Mirza's compulsion to fiddle with the constitution. General Musharraf's amendments were to dramatically strengthen the power of the presidency, formalise the role of the army in government and diminish the authority of parliamentary members.

Hyderabad Station, clean, whitewashed and vacant, fell away and in minutes we were crossing the Indus, a shadow of itself after so much water had been diverted into the hinterland by irrigation canals.

Then we were on a brown plain without sign of human or animal life. In the distance rose a line of flat-topped hills, like a collection of fezzes laid end to end, whose bands of plum-coloured rock glowed in the morning light. Here was the true Sind, the Sind without irrigation water pumped into it, the Sind as Sir Charles Napier found it in 1843 when he wrestled control of the region from the Talpur dynasty and telegraphed news of the unauthorised annexation to London with the single word '*Peccavi*' – I've Sind.*

Several factors motivated this seizure: the potential of the Indus as a trade route, the Sind's usefulness as a counter to perceived Russian expansionism through Afghanistan, though more than a few people suspected it was a bid to restore some pride to the British Army after the disastrous Afghan campaign. One commentator of the time likened the action to 'the bully who has been kicked in the streets and goes home to beat his wife in revenge'.

Dr Ahmad stirred late, although he had briefly risen very early to perform fajr, first prayers. For breakfast I had my last three 'sweet lemons' and watched the sandy Sind slip past.

Wasim whispered, 'Better we go somewhere else. Intelligence people are listening.'

Unlikely as that seemed, I nevertheless followed Wasim out of the Karachi bazaar and into a park. We crossed a lawn and sat beneath a palm tree. Wasim – he wouldn't disclose his last name – was a tank mechanic in the Pakistani Army. It rapidly became evident that what twenty-six-year-old Wasim really wanted to get away from was the

---

* One authority, Philip Mason, in his twin-volume *The Men Who Ruled India*, says the story of the telegram may be apocryphal, a Sind governor tracing its origins to *Punch* in 1846.

eavesdropping of devout Muslims. And his suspicion seemed well justified, because a lot of men sloped by, slowly and inquisitively, making Wasim stop in mid-sentence.

After the usual question about my religious affiliation, he said, 'I also believe in Jesus Christ,' his eyes darting among the passing men.

'Do you?' I said. He looked every bit the traditional Pakistani male. 'What is wrong with Islam?'

'When I die,' he whispered, 'I will meet Jesus, my saviour. Jesus said, "Believe in me and you will see me in Heaven." Muhammad said, "Be a good Muslim and you may go to Paradise." With Jesus Christ you are *sure* to go to Paradise.'

So Wasim was a sort of religious actuary who had calculated the odds and opted for Christianity.

I said, 'It's a very brave thing you are doing, but I don't think it really matters what religion you follow. Do your parents know?'

'They do.'

'And do they approve?'

'No. On Sundays I say, "I am going out." They know that means I am going to church to pray.'

Wasim had renounced Islam after joining a Christian group performing welfare work in Karachi's slums. 'My leader Saeed said to me, "Come and work for God and you will surely see his face when you die."'

'I don't really understand, Wasim. What exactly is wrong with Islam?'

'Muslims,' he said in a hushed voice, 'they are always fighting each other.'

'Christians do, too. In Ireland the Catholics and the—'

'I know, Catholics and Protestants. But the Muslims, they are *bad*.'

'Do Muslims treat women well?' I asked.

'Well?' he spat out. 'They put them so low – shut in one room all day. There is no trust. If you love someone you do not put her in chains, you let her go free.'

Wasim told me of his plans to marry his first cousin Khalida. She was very pretty and liked him a lot. ('She calls me every day at work.')

Her father, however, was opposed to the marriage because he earned so little: 2,700 rupees a month. But Wasim remained hopeful. 'She is not a good Muslim,' he grinned. 'She does not like to pray five times a day.'

❋

I walked past the Sind Secretariat, a favourite target of assassins and bombers, before coming to my destination, the National Museum of Pakistan. There, in the Freedom Movement Gallery, I found further expression of Muslim resentment at their thwarted ambitions on the subcontinent, of their bitterness at a destiny denied.

As expected, the gallery displayed many photographs of the Great Leader. Indeed, I might have been once more in Lahore's Freedom Movement Gallery. There was a tubercular Jinnah, all skull, eyeballs and brittle skin, meeting Mountbatten or Muslim League officials, or standing truculently beside Gandhi at some official gathering, or reclining aloofly with his devoted sister or his daughter whom he later disowned for marrying a Parsi-born Christian, although he himself married a Parsi half his age.

The aggrieved feelings bubbled to the surface in an introductory account at the gallery's entrance, which I copied into my notebook. My note-taking aroused the interest of a museum official, a tall heavy-set man with a drooping moustache.

'Any problems?' he asked.

'Well, now that you ask, there is one thing. It mentions here hundreds of thousands of Muslims being massacred during Partition, but nothing about a similar number of Hindus being killed.'

'Hindus killed?' he asked in surprise. 'Only a small number. It was the Muslims who had to move. They were the ones cut down.'

'A million killed. That's the figure most historians agree on. You're telling me hundreds of thousands of Hindus and Sikhs didn't die, too?'

He stood there, shaking his head slowly. 'It was the Muslims who suffered. They were the minority. The majority Hindus descended on them. That is the way: the big group picks on the little group.'

'So no Hindus or Sikhs died?'

'A few, sir. A few thousand.'

Three other men had by now drifted over to listen.

'What do you say if I tell you I've read that a roughly similar number of Hindus and Muslims died during Partition?'

'Then your book was written by a Hindu.'

'That, sir, is the saddest thing I've heard in Pakistan. But now you've said it, I'll tell you something. My impression since I've been in your country is that people feel there is a giant conspiracy against them, that every non-Muslim's hand is against them.'

One of the onlookers, who wore a Sindhi cap at a tilt just above the eyebrows, cut in: 'You are a Hindu sympathiser.'

'And you see conspiracies everywhere.'

'The West thinks we are all terrorists and attacks us.'

'You're wrong. Terrorists are mostly coming from Muslim countries. That does not make all Muslims terrorists.'

'What do you think of Osama bin Laden?' asked the onlooker.

'What do you think? You obviously have an opinion.'

'No, you first.'

'Well, I think he is an evil man because he is using violence to advance his aims. I don't care what his aims are. Same with the Americans in Iraq. How can a good result come out of bad means? Same with the Kashmiri terrorists …'

'They are not terrorists, they are struggling for their independence, for a homeland of their own, for self-determination.'

'They're high-sounding words, but here's the reality. Your freedom fighters, they sneak across the border, shoot up some civilians and vanish. Women, children, innocents dead. What do you call that if not terrorism? Right now, your General Musharraf is making a big fuss trying to get other countries to distinguish between terrorism and what he calls national liberation movements. He says that not all acts of terrorism are the work of extremists. What nonsense. People still die.'

The museum official said, 'You may not like Osama bin Laden and his kind but you will not get rid of them until you look at the causes of terrorism.'

'And what are they?'

'The persecution of Muslims.'

'Conspiracies again.'

'You may not know, sir, that the persecution of Muslims in India began under the Britishers. They favoured the Hindus. They set up the élite schools and allowed only the Hindus in. The Hindus learned English, they got the best jobs.'

'I think you'll find,' I replied, 'that Muslims often refused to send their sons to such schools. But in the end it was the Muslims who got the better deal under the British.'

I had read that, during the British colonial period, Muslims continued to get preferential treatment, at first in recognition of their former status as India's rulers and, towards the end of the Raj, as a counterweight to the mainly Hindu calls for self-rule, as articulated through the Congress Party.

'Sir, you are a guest in my country. You may say whatever you like, but I must go.'

And he turned abruptly and walked off. The trio drifted away as silently as they had appeared.

Continuing on through the museum, I came upon a huge painting depicting columns of Muslim refugees making their way on foot and by ox-cart towards the border and the safety of their fellow believers. In these kafilas, or human caravans, the Muslim refugees were depicted cowered and in flight, but never in the act of retribution. (A museum in the Red Fort, Delhi, portrayed similar scenes from the Indian perspective, also minus the acts of vengeance, which culminated in what was probably the biggest single massacre in history.)

In all the heroics about the creation of a Muslim homeland on the subcontinent, one thing was conspicuously absent from the official pictography: Bangladesh. East Pakistan, as it was known until the 1971 War of Independence, was the forgotten embarrassment, the dark family secret everyone was intent on brushing under the carpet. And with good reason: Muslim was killing fellow Muslim. The West

Pakistani Army, in its determination to suppress the uprising, committed atrocities on a massive scale.

Under General Tikka Khan, the Butcher of Baluchistan, West Pakistani troops began a systematic elimination of 'subversives', who came in time to include, in addition to the rebels themselves, students, Hindus, intellectuals, businesspeople and villagers supporting the insurgents. A million died in the ensuing raping, looting and slaughtering. Faith in the Prophet, hailed as the great unifying force among Muslims on the subcontinent, proved to be an insufficient basis for nationhood. The bonds tying East and West Pakistan quickly begun to fray under the sheer impossibility of 1,600 kilometres of 'enemy' territory separating the two halves of the country. The ummah, the community of Islam, could not smooth over differences in language, culture, history, national aspirations, economic wealth, customs and climate. The imposition of Urdu on the Bengali-speaking east was the final straw, igniting the uprising that put an end to East Pakistan.

But this absence of any critical assessment of history was perhaps no surprise in a country where it was a penal offence to suggest that the original basis on which Pakistan was created was mistaken. Pakistanis sang Jinnah's praises for saving them from the Hindus. But what had Pakistan ultimately achieved? It had created Muslim government in areas where there had originally been Muslim government.

❂

In Karachi's electronics market I heard something for the first time in Pakistan: music. The sugary squeals of Hindi cassettes rose through the laneways. And hanging on the walls of several shops were film posters of bosomy Indian movie starlets. The veil had made a grudging retreat in Pakistan's biggest city, and after Quetta it took some adjustment to look upon a woman's face without staring.

The blanket of religious conformity that cloaks Pakistan was lifted a little in Karachi. I met a bakery owner who was a Baha'i and I passed a Dar-i-Mehtar, a Parsi place of worship (though the gate was locked and a sign warned that trespassers would be prosecuted), and I saw church spires on the skyline (though extremists had a fondness for lobbing grenades at such places).

Karachi is not an attractive city, but Pakistanis still flock here in search of a better life. Many must have taken up jobs as guards, because an armed sentry stood outside every shop stocking half-way valuable merchandise. And police and paramilitary soldiers were posted on every corner, at every gate and outside every official and semi-official building. Their presence proclaimed in the flesh what the newspapers proclaimed in ink: the robberies, carjackings and murders were continuing unabated.

Downtown Karachi overflowed with ramshackle plazas tenanted by shops selling gold jewellery, Rolex watches and carpets. There were precious few places to eat at or parks to relax in, and for all its size, nightlife in Karachi was an oxymoron. Town planning was a theoretical discipline. One prominent developer boasted openly of building three plaza–apartment complexes in contravention of zoning rules and earthquake standards. Karachi's suburbs consisted of kilometre after kilometre of low, discoloured concrete blocks hastily thrown up to house the city's vast population. Nearer the city centre, the endlessly duplicated ugliness of the tenement blocks was partly disguised by hoardings and partly ameliorated by the bustle of traffic and crowds.

The total number of inhabitants, like that of the country itself, can only be speculated at: the best guess is between 10 and 13 million. Karachi is growing rapidly and no census has been conducted since 1981. The 1991 census was aborted by the president because it was so transparently flawed, and there were strong suspicions that it was deliberately made unusable. An accurate census in Sind would have resulted in a reassigning of electoral seats and national resources in favour of urban areas, a prospect deeply feared by powerful rural interests.

After three days trudging about in Karachi's muggy heat, never far from soldiers' searching gaze, I was happy to move on.

Badshahi Mosque, Lahore.

Calcutta! Calcutta!

YESTERDAY'S RUBBISH LITTERED the floor and the seats were a fakir's bed of nails, but at least the Shalimar Express left on time. Within an hour the sun was rising over the sandy plains north of Karachi. Lines of pylons receded towards an industrial plant, standing lonely among tussocks of coarse grass, the main stack of which emitted a column of smoke so vast it could have passed for a bank of clouds. It rose ashen, became unaccountably pearly-white and fluffy and, after a time, turned into a long brown smear.

The parlour car's passengers, mainly middle-aged males, wore Pakistan's equivalent of the Western suit: a beige or white salwar kameez. Soaped, scented, swaggering, flabby, they withdrew their mobile phones, fiddled with them, yawned, grew bored, pocketed them and dozed. A few plugged in headsets for the televisions mounted beside the overhead luggage racks. Only one passenger read. His great aquiline nose and clipped hennaed beard were buried in *A New History of India*. I longed to strike up a conversation but his forbidding appearance dissolved every flimsy pretext I thought up.

A little before ten, we crossed the Indus. With the exception of some green scrub on the high banks, the entire scene was one of shades of grey: pale-grey sandbanks, greyish-black country boats at rest, the river itself an opaque metallic grey, and finally the sky, a gritty, shifting grey all of its own. It was, for all its seemingly monochromatic drabness, an immensely beautiful view, and the iron latticework of the bridge captured it in a hundred fleeting frames as we crossed over to the right bank and stopped.

The city of Hyderabad, which can trace its distant origins to a Hindu ruler, is today an unremarkable industrial and commercial centre – and even that modest standing has been eroded by tensions between native Sindhis and the Mohajirs, the Urdu-speaking migrants from India. One day in September 1988 gunmen went on a rampage, killing one hundred and eighty-six people. Two years later police fired on crowds of Mohajirs, killing thirty-one. A two-and-a-half-year military clampdown has restored the veneer of calm to Sind.

The view from my window was certainly no inducement to get down. Hyderabad, like so many lesser Pakistani cities and towns, seemed a poor, sad, dusty place; the houses were decrepit and Spartan as army barracks; the potholed roads were the domain of clopping tongas and beeping jalopies; and the pavements were the preserve of solemn-faced men, with the rare interspersion of a woman, silent, silhouetted, shuffling.

While we took on more water for the toilets, I got down for a tea. And in so doing, I noticed a young woman seated behind me. A black headscarf encircled her pretty face. She looked glumly out the window, while her husband looked equally glumly out the opposite window — a reminder that the least sign of public affection, warmth or indeed mere acknowledgment between the sexes was discouraged.

This aloofness was perhaps not so strange when you understood that women were taught to defer absolutely to their husbands and male relations – a common admonition is 'a woman must not be heard outside the four walls of the house' – and that this inequality had been enshrined in law by military dictator General Zia ul-Haq, who imposed Pakistan's rigorous brand of Islamic fundamentalism, greatly approved of by many conservative Pakistanis.

One of Zia's most objectionable laws is the Hudood Ordinance, introduced through an amendment to the constitution and still in force. Among other things it dissolves the distinction between zina, or rape, and adultery and extramarital sex so a rape victim can be, and often is, accused of fornication. It deals also with the evidence of women in court. Their word does not carry the same weight as that of men, so that a woman, in order to prove rape, must produce four male witnesses, a next-to-impossible stipulation to satisfy and one reason so many rapes go unreported. There are also grave dangers in making an accusation of rape because if the victim cannot provide sufficient proof and the case fails, she is considered, by a perversion of logic, to have consented to the rape and becomes herself the accused.

Manipulation of the ordinance to suppress women's independence is common. To cite but one stratagem, it has become standard practice for parents disgruntled at their daughter choosing a 'love marriage' to lodge a complaint with the police, alleging kidnapping and zina by the husband. One such case in Hyderabad made the headlines. 'Faheem hailed from an Urdu-speaking family, while Hajira was an Afghani girl,' a report began. 'They got married without consent of their families. Police arrested the couple after a complaint of kidnapping was lodged against Faheem. After acquiring bail from the local court they were returning home when they were killed.'

Her death was the result of what is known as karo kari, or honour killing – male relations erasing what they regard as a stain upon their honour as a result of a woman's unsanctioned actions. Another honour killing made the newspapers while I was in Karachi. It followed a well-worn pattern. A man named Sarwar shot dead his younger sister for marrying a man of her choice. Police said his twenty-two-year-old sister Naureen had 'contracted a love marriage' four months earlier with a property dealer named Amanat Ali. The accused and his father Arshad were not happy with the marriage and pressed her to get a divorce, which she refused to do. 'Sarwar exchanged harsh words with his sister over the issue and opened fire on her at Arif Chowk in Green Town,' police said. 'She suffered serious injuries and died on the way to hospital.' The custom of honour killing, though outlawed, has great unofficial sanction.

From a legal perspective, the outcomes of the Hudood Ordinance could be plain bizarre. In one case, a fifteen-year-old named Jehan Mina was raped by her uncle and cousin and became pregnant. Her family filed a complaint of rape, but without witnesses the accused walked free. Yet her pregnancy was proof of extramarital sex and she was sentenced to 100 lashes in public, a sentence later converted to three years in jail and ten lashes. Zia's law also allows for the punishment of rajam, or stoning to death.

One man said to me that the thinking behind the ordinance and similarly oppressive laws relating to women had its roots in tribal attitudes which pre-dated Islam and for which Islam had become a convenient coathanger upon which to drape their ignorance and narrow-mindedness.

The ordinance has its proponents, however. They argue it is strictly based on the teachings of the Koran and Sunnah, the habits and religious practice of Muhammad as recorded by his family and companions and thus regarded as the ideal Islamic norm. Repeal, they maintain, is therefore impossible.

One such defender was Dr Fareeda Ahmed, a member of the National Assembly. She objected vigorously to changes recommended in a report by the National Commission on the Status of Women. She smelled a conspiracy. Reopening the issue 'was the handiwork of those non-government organisations which were getting huge foreign funds without any check'. She attacked the report's allegation that 88 per cent of women held in prisons were charged under the ordinance. The real figure, she said, was only 25 per cent. And to underline her argument that Pakistani women had nothing to fear from the ordinance, she explained that six categories of women were detained in jails: 'prostitutes, divorcees, second-marriage, runaway, rape cases or those convicted on their husband's accusation of bad character'.

Some estimate as many as 10,000 cases are registered each year under the ordinance. The exact number will never be known. But the questions of honour and the control of a woman's body run deep. What Dr Ahmed did not mention in her defence of the ordinance was that as many as three-quarters of women imprisoned for zina offences were routinely tortured and raped by police officers because they were perceived as immoral and dishonoured.

Considerations of honour crop up in the oddest places. A recent ban by the North-West Frontier Province government on male doctors attending to female patients had, according to one Peshawar academic, resulted in hundreds of deaths during childbirth because there simply weren't enough female doctors and technicians to deal with the workload. Nationally, 30,000 women die each year of pregnancy-related complications.

Provincial Secretary-General Maulana Gul Naseeb Khan defended the ban as in line with Islamic teaching. 'Men could derive sexual ecstasy from women's bodies while conducting ECG or ultrasound,' he asserted. 'Similarly, some women could lure the men under the ECG or ultrasound cover. In both cases, perversion could prevail.'

❂

At 10.15 we drew out of Hyderabad. Immediately the benefits of irrigation became visible. The sandy soil supported sugar cane, rows of mango trees, oil seeds, date trees, maize, cotton, banana plantations and rice. Cotton and onion pickers worked in the pitiless sun. After an hour we crossed the Rohri Canal, a principal feeder of the Sukkur Barrage, which terminates well south of Hyderabad. On and on grew sugar cane and rice beneath the enormous sky.

Back in the countryside after the town of Nawanbshah, trousered girls walked by the roadside, carrying on their heads long swaying bundles of firewood; cyclists came riding in from outlying villages in straggling companies; two bullocks waited stoically while a farmer loaded the wagon high with straw; another farmer ploughed his field as egrets descended in his wake in search of an easy lunch; a boy encouraged his donkey with repeated whacks of a stick; and an old man slept on a charpoy in the shade of a lean-to shack. It was a pattern that, except in a few details, had been going on for centuries.

The land around Khairpur, a city a little south of Rohri, provided a vivid example of the downside of the canal-building mania in Sind:

a raised water table, waterlogging and salinity. Though the area under cultivation during winter had risen fivefold, so had the prevalence of malaria. Rohri, second time round, rated just three words in my notes: 'Hot, fly-blown.' For an hour there was nothing to see but rice and a highway of trucks decorated in a rhapsody of chocolate-box scenes. On we went across this endless plain as it became steadily drier until cotton became the principal crop. My diary entries became cursory to the point of meaninglessness until we passed through Kanpour at 5.30: 'What an unexpectedly beautiful sight! Three camels pull trailers carrying home the day's cotton, each trailer's sides made higher by lengths of material fixed to corner poles to carry the huge but relatively weightless load. The white material is maybe 5 metres in height and billows like a ship's sail as the camels walk that slow dignified walk only they are capable of. Anywhere else this elaborate procession would look staged – here, a perfectly everyday improvisation.'

The coach's TV monitors, which were tuned to a state-run channel and which I had done my best to ignore, now broadcast a short promotion demonstrating the determination of Pakistan's armed forces to repel Indian incursions in Azad ('Free') Jammu and Kashmir, as Pakistan refers to its portion of the disputed region. As the film opens, Indian troops are firing artillery shells at civilians going about their daily routine in an idyllic valley somewhere in Azad J & K. Farmers, school children and helpless mothers are thrown in the air as the shells land indiscriminately in their peaceful village. Indian infantrymen descend out of the wooded hills, blasting away with small arms. More villagers fall, tomato sauce splatters their clothes. Some uninjured men commandeer a passing lorry to take the injured, predominantly women, to hospital.

But just when things look hopeless Pakistani soldiers appear through the trees. The sight of the carnage makes them really angry. They counter-attack with tanks, stopping many of the invaders in their tracks. In slow motion, the bullets rip through the bodies of the Indian soldiers, who crumple and fall.

Meanwhile, the Air Force scrambles jet fighters and these bring down some intruder helicopters. The Pakistani Navy goes on high alert. A convoy of frigates alters course sharply and heads at full speed towards ... somewhere unknown.

Finally, back in Azad J & K, Pakistani soldiers are mopping up the remaining Indians, hitting them with artillery, rocket-propelled grenades and machine guns. A young Ranger raises Pakistan's flag and gives a quivering salute, concluding the presentation.

Nine o'clock, Khanewal. The Shalimar Express halted for fifteen minutes so passengers could perform isha, the day's final prayers. Large mats had been laid out in advance along the platform. Religious obligations fulfilled, we trundled northwards into the darkness of the Punjab.

By now the journey had turned into an endurance test of quite unexpected proportions as 11 pm, our scheduled arrival time, came and went and still we were several hundred kilometres from Lahore. There was no way to sleep in these infernal chairs, though God knows it didn't stop a few passengers from contorting themselves in search of a sleeping position. I sat in exasperated exhaustion, unable to sleep and too tired to read, until, at 2.30 next morning, the train entered the forbidding arches of Lahore City Station and I stumbled off in search of a room for what remained of the night.

At the Wagah border crossing I witnessed dried-figs diplomacy (no relation to ping-pong diplomacy). A stream of Pakistani coolies, each with a green jacket over his salwar kameez and two crates of figs balanced on his head, moved towards a line demarcating the Indo-Pakistan border. There, beneath the unswerving eye of soldiers from each country, this human conveyor belt shifted its load on to a mirror-image chain of Indian coolies, who were distinguished by a blue jacket over their regular clothes. In a picture of perfect co-operation, each Pakistani shifted his two boxes into the waiting grasp of an Indian before turning back to the truck discharging its cargo a little way distant.

The Indian coolies, meanwhile, padded off towards a cargo agent's shed where, one presumes, after sufficient time and paperwork had been expended, the figs would be loaded onto an Indian truck to resume their journey eastwards towards the heart of the enemy and the destination stamped on each box: Delhi.

A Hindustan Ambassador taxi took me along the ruler-straight road to Amritsar. It was a very elderly example of a very elderly design and when the Sikh driver threw the steering-wheel one way, which he did often because he overtook often, the front wheels deigned eventually to follow suit and the car made a lurching shift in direction. It was the lazy, undulating ride of a ship, but one whose captain was a frustrated racing car driver.

For all my bracing against possible crashes, however, a previously unremarkable sight caught my attention as though I were witnessing it for the first time: there were women about. Not occasional pairs of black burqqas darting furtively in the shadows, but women in numbers, moving about freely and in bright clothes that now and then suggested the contour of a thigh or outline of a breast or exposed an upper arm, a midriff, a face. They were smiling, talking, serving in shops, going about on scooters. I saw a woman riding pillion on a motorbike, her hand resting casually on her husband's thigh. To long-cloistered eyes, this was an audacious display of intimacy. What's more, there were cows on the streets, not on the menu, and the streets sang with lightness and life.

At Amritsar Junction Station I bought a ticket on that evening's Golden Temple Express and then went off to see the train's namesake. The Golden Temple as a place of worship is without equal on the subcontinent by reason of its combination of water (the temple is built around a tank), sound (the singing of verses from the Sikh's holy book, the Granth Sahib, fills the air almost round the clock), light (the reflection of the copper-gilded temple itself, in the centre of the tank, ripples like molten gold and makes you rub your eyes in wonder) and cleanliness (visitors must remove their shoes and wash their feet, making the marble-tiled walkways clean enough to eat off, which is what many in fact do in the community kitchens where meals are provided free). I joined the faithful circling the tank, sat awhile in one of the cloisters and left.

Outside, my accumulated calm ebbed away in the commotion that filled the old city's web of laneways. As expected, there was around me a confusing similarity in business names in this Sikh city: Singh Tailors, Singh & Sons, Singh Batteries, Singh Suitings and Shirtings, and Singh & Singh Stationery Agents.

My train left at 9.30 pm, so I climbed straight into bed and fell into the deep dreamless sleep of someone returning home after a long absence. Everything was familiar to me: the hubbub of the platform, the punctual departure, the neat pile of sheets, blanket and pillow at the foot of my bunk, the courteous inspector who asked for my ticket. And when I woke at seven, twenty minutes from New Delhi Station, a licensed vendor's voice, drawing nearer down the aisle, droned out the magical mantra: 'Chai, chai, coffee, chai.'

✿

The New Delhi Howrah Rajdhani Express is not an atmospheric ride. The Indians who book a berth wish to get to Calcutta with all possible haste (there are just five scheduled stops) and can afford the steep fare. The mustard-and-red coaches are the modern-day counterpart of a royal palanquin. They do not touch on the lives of ordinary Indians. Passengers shelter behind their tinted windows, borne along at speeds of up to 130 kilometres an hour, as the express makes its eighteen-hour eastward dash. But having crossed the country's north twice already, that suited me fine.

At dusk, Delhi flickered with oil lamps and strings of light bulbs in celebration of Diwali, the noisiest festival in the Hindu calendar. Day and night the capital's streets had reverberated with exploding firecrackers. Around Connaught Place traffic had slowed to a crawl as residents searched out gifts and sweets, much like last-minute Christmas Eve shoppers. Old Delhi had been more congested. Chandni Chowk, the bazaar's main thoroughfare running west from the Red Fort's Lahore Gate, was a long thin rectangle of madness. Not one square centimetre of space was unoccupied by a merchant, his merchandise or prospective customers. Into the swirling mass of pedestrians was added every sort of human- and animal-drawn cart, plus the everyday torrent of delivery vans, scooters, cyclists and auto-rickshaws. One advanced through the mayhem as though a boxer in the ring, weaving, bobbing, ducking to dodge the protruding handles of a trolley, or a porter's load of bobbing plastic pipes, or a mongrel snapping at the heels of another stray, or perhaps the vendor's mound of marigold garlands, stacked to within a hair's breadth of grinding cart-wheels and the relentless press of feet.

Darkness left me nothing to look at but my companions, two Bangladeshi doctors and an Israeli tourist. Like me, Dr Huq and Dr Haq were bound eventually for Dacca. Dr Haq, the older at thirty-two, had been to Delhi to collect visas for a tour of the Continent, making him, by Bangladeshi standards, exceedingly well off. For all his wealth, however, he had unsavoury habits, burping loudly and often and chomping open-mouthed on his food.

Dr Huq, a devout reserved Muslim who retreated at the prescribed times to his top bunk where he donned his skullcap and prostrated himself in prayer, said just one thing to me: 'You must go to Sundarbans, to Mongla. There you will find the jungle and sea meet.'

I hadn't the heart to tell him Mongla was a long way from any train line.

Anan Buzy, a professional photographer, made up the foursome. Mr Buzy had been in Kashmir for six weeks making a natural history documentary. 'It was so beautiful there,' he enthused. 'So close to nature!'

Mr Buzy was something of a natural wonder himself – a human walrus; a blubbery, bumbling hairy giant with a straggly beard like a nineteenth-century Russian peasant. At the earliest possible opportunity, he stretched himself out on the lower bunk, supporting his tremendous bulk on one elbow and forcing poor skinny Dr Huq to perch one buttock on the edge by the aisle. Mr Buzy appeared to need a lot of rest, dozing at every opportunity and producing a sonorous, faltering snore that filled the carriage.

Later, after dinner and another of his naps, Mr Buzy told me of the delights of staying in a houseboat on Dal Lake. His had featured a drawing room, two dining tables to seat fourteen guests, a spacious master bedroom, hand-carved furniture, a family who would cook anything he wanted – and the whole shebang cost 400 rupees a day.

'That's cheap, 400 rupees!' he said, the memory momentarily shaking him out of his torpor. 'Not even 100 US dollars a month.'

There had been one snag. Banks in Kashmir would not advance cash against credit cards. He had to buy goods in Srinagar's bazaar, for which merchants would advance a roughly equal amount of cash. But it had pained him to buy goods he didn't really need in order to get cash.

Still, he was off to Thailand for a month where it was just as cheap to live. 'Good food, always parties and music. And the women!' Their alluring shape he indicated with a curving sweep of his hands.

'Do you know how much a ticket is to Bangkok?' he asked.

'No, I've no idea.'

'Seven thousand rupees, return. That's cheap!'

I turned in, reading some more of Gandhi's autobiography, *The Story of My Experiments with Truth*. It was proving a trial. Of course he had a great many qualities, all well known, which made him deserving of the title Mahatma, Great One, but behind the saintly demeanour was a steely determination to impose his beliefs and mode of living upon those close to him. He probably should have trained as a doctor rather than a lawyer. He had many quack remedies for ailments, hip baths being a favourite: these could apparently fix everything from constipation, from which he often suffered, to nervous collapse. His dietetic dilemmas were frequent and interminable. In the end I found myself bored by them. The question of diet was interwoven with the course of his life, and he readily acknowledged his relentless enforcement of his beliefs upon his wife Kasturbai, his children and his friends. In matters of food, as in so many other things, he was incapable of taking no for an answer, and by sweet and inexorable argument demolished all opposition.

Every illness or moral doubt, it seemed, could be solved by an ever more severe food intake. There was ethical uplift in a vegetarian diet; fasting was another subject in its own right. His own list of permissible foods shrank eventually to a fruit-and-nuts regime which would not allow even milk.

In one recollection, he described his quandary when Kasturbai's doctor urged him to allow his wife, then gravely weak, to take a meat broth to help restore her strength. This produced an interminable bout of self-examination and moral justification. In the end, of course, Kasturbai had to recover unaided.

He pleaded human frailty but never did, or omitted to do, anything that might warrant regret or remorse by the standards of an ordinary human being. The sole exception was in the raising of his sons, whom he deprived of a normal education and upbringing.

Nonetheless, Gandhi was at heart an intensely likeable individual. The half-naked fakir who would attempt to parley on equal terms with the representative of the King-Emperor, as Winston Churchill once thundered, was nothing much to look at. But this small, wizened man had an exceedingly sharp mind and was a very eloquent and droll writer. Some of his observations of India could have been written yesterday. I was sympathetic to his disappointment after a visit to the Vishvanath Temple at Varanasi. After the noisy commercialism around the temple and the 'stinking mass of rotten flowers' inside, he approached the Jana-vapid (Well of Knowledge).

I searched here for God but failed to find him. I was not therefore in a particularly good mood. The surroundings of the Jana-vapid too I found to be dirty. I had no mind to give any dakshina. So I offered a pie.* The panda in charge got angry and threw away the pie. He swore at me and said: 'This insult will take you straight to Hell.'

This did not disturb me. 'Maharaj,' said I, 'whatever fate has in store for me, it does not behove one of your class to indulge in such language. You may take this pie if you like, or you will lose that too.'

I took the pie and went my way, flattering myself that the Brahman had lost a pie and I had saved one. But the Maharaj was

* The lowest-value coin in India before the introduction of decimal currency. It was one-twelfth of an anna, sixteen annas making a rupee.

hardly the man to let the pie go. He called me back and said: 'All right, leave the pie here. I would rather not be as you are. If I refuse your pie, it will be bad for you.'

I silently gave him the pie and, with a sigh, went away.

❀

I woke at Dhanbad, the last stop before Calcutta. Wet and intensely green, with drooping palms and slippery muddy footpaths and mildew-streaked huts and rice growing between knobbly hills, it made a contrast to the dust and granite-hard maidans of Delhi. Mist curled through the trees and around the station walls, and every depression in the ground was marked by a brown puddle. Then we were off, speeding south-east, flashing through a good-sized town without my even catching its name, before once more returning to rolling hills and rice.

Breakfast was handed out. Mr Buzy, still half-asleep, growled at the bearer, 'All right!' and lifted himself upright to take the tray from his hands. He peeled a banana and ate it with his eyes still closed. Then, putting the tray on the fold-out table, he flopped back down and immediately resumed his gurgling snoring. Each sway of the coach made his belly wobble. A little later, he woke with a start, grabbed a roll of toilet paper from his carry-bag and hurried off along the aisle.

By mid-morning we were deep in the immense plain of ripening rice that was West Bengal, ticking off the towns but never stopping. At each station platform men huddled beneath black umbrellas, shoulders hunched against the rain, while trees with big buttressed trunks cast their dripping murkiness over red-brick walls made greasy with the perpetual dampness.

By eleven we were cantering into Calcutta, which never looks enchanting on even the brightest day – and on an overcast Sunday morning looked positively glum. Through the empty marshalling yards we crept, coming to a halt at Howrah Station.

Dr Haq shook the sleeping Mr Buzy by the arm and laughed: 'He has no tension.'

Calcutta has a bad name but it wasn't always so. The capital of British India until 1911, it was once a city of fine colonial architecture where a lady, with a parasol in one hand, could cross the street without fear of soiling her hem. The climate might have been filthy for most of the year, but pomp and grandeur abounded: it was known as the City of Palaces, though also the City of Stinks on account of the native quarters' rudimentary sewers. Today, those Victorian mansions are but rotting, verminous corpses. Saplings sprout from their gutters and cracked masonry, slime grows thick upon walls where downpipes have long been blocked, and shutters hang drunkenly on their hinges. Here and there, splattered on a façade, are the faded remains of a hammer and sickle. None of this, of course, prevents their full and continued use: they are subdivided a hundred ways, each balcony and window ledge supporting a flagstaff for saris and singlets and underpants to dry on. It was the same stern law of necessity that applied to Calcutta's anachronistic taxis, which still clog streets laid out in the time of hand-drawn rickshaws – and rickshaw-wallahs who, washing their hands of the new-fangled bicycle versions introduced elsewhere in India, still ply their trade here.

Calcutta has its staunch defenders: a city of poets and singers and intellectual ferment, they say; a city with an artistic soul. Several tourists, with perfectly straight faces, declared to me that it was their favourite Indian city. But I saw more of the peculiar argumentativeness and obduracy of the Bengalis.

The misshapen taxi queue I joined outside Howrah Station was a perfect example. Men and women pushed and shoved and squabbled and berated one another interminably over the tiniest matters. 'Move that suitcase,' barked one man. 'It is in my way.'

'Why should I?' retorted another.

One fellow got a jab in the ribs. 'You are jumping the queue,' said someone behind him.

'Good gracious no, sir,' the interloper replied, 'I am minding this place for my friend.'

And off they went, jabbing their fingers at one another as the argument raged on. I was tearing my hair out to get away from it all but the pre-paid taxi queue moved with maddening sluggishness.

Almost an hour passed before I reached the grilled window and had in my hand a 40-rupee chit to Chowringhee. That was not to be the end of my teeth-gritting. When I climbed into the next waiting taxi, the driver was indignant.

'Give me 20 rupees more,' he demanded. 'On the meter it is 60 rupees. I am losing 20 rupees on this fare.'

Since the whole point of pre-paids was to protect visitors from such fleecing drivers I refused. As he got out and rebuked the clerk in the booth I sat in the back seat, perspiration trickling down my face, waiting for the argument to subside.

The driver returned, slammed his door and we jolted over the Howrah bridge. The pavement squatters with their desperately pathetic worldly possessions camped out in the open. The lucky ones had an awning for shelter, perhaps a black plastic sheet or some gunny sacks draped from a graceful columned wall. On this quiet Sunday, crows and mangy dogs outnumbered pedestrians. My driver swerved to avoid a double-decker bus, then overtook two ancient trams which clattered painfully over the cobblestones like a pair of rheumatic old ladies.

Calcutta, it seemed, was a city incapable of helping itself; indeed was unwilling to help itself. The most glaring civic deficiencies had the appearance of unalterable features of the landscape. It did not help that the monsoon which, in India's countryside, enriched the earth, here rapidly turned buildings a mouldy colour that seemed to presage ruin and collapse. Dampness seeped from the newest brickwork. Confronted with these forces, the Bengali put on a mask of impassivity.

As the taxi neared the maidan the sky roared with peal after peal of thunder and then rain fell, growing heavier and more violent until it seemed impossible so much rain could fall at one time. The grey sky and the grey buildings became one. The gutters, unequal to the task, overflowed. Brown torrents streamed over the bitumen.

The taxi stopped.

'Kyd Street,' yelled the driver over the din.

I climbed out and ran for cover. Even Calcutta's beggars had perfected the art of the extreme. A man lay on his stomach on the pavement, stripped to a dhoti and flapping in the air two stumps where arms should have been, like a performing seal clapping its flippers. His ploy worked: he had caught my attention, and I gave him a coin.

Peak-hour rush, Kamalpur Station, Dhaka.

The Mahanagar Provati
to Chittagong

THE FARE WAS NOMINAL, the queuing was not. Shoved and elbowed by a hundred impatient Bengalis, I wriggled free after an hour with my 17-rupee ticket and ran for the 5.55 am to Bangaon. Minutes later, the commuter service departed from Sealdah Station in the rain.

Dawn broke as we paused at Dum Dum Junction where the snack sellers came aboard, treading on everyone's toes as they pushed their way along the carriages. The rain had not relented as we trundled off again, forcing a man by the door to open his umbrella before his legs to keep dry. From my wooden seat I could see housewives trying to get their spluttering fires going for breakfast.

At the little stop of Durganagar, a woman led aboard a man with a scarf wrapped floppily around his head, drooping to a point just above his eye sockets, which were shrivelled hollows. He began to sing in a strong haunting voice. He made quite an impact: fifteen passengers dropped a coin into his outstretched hand as his helper guided him along aisles and through the rubber coupling booths to the next carriage. There he resumed earning his livelihood. It was a long time before his voice was overwhelmed by the noise of the train.

Barasat Junction, forty-five minutes on, turned out to be the end of the decaying city. Before long, rice grew beyond the rows of shanties thrown up on railway land, and every murky-green pond brimmed with rainwater.

At Habrah, the driver enquired through the window: 'You will come and sit with me? I have some questions.'

I happily complied and took a seat before a bank of controls whose functions he briefly explained before concluding with a warning about entering the power-room immediately behind us: 'If you go through the door you must first turn off this switch. Otherwise the electricity will suck your blood.'

We pulled out of the station and the speedometer lifted smoothly to 70 kilometres an hour.

It soon became apparent Mr Samir Das wasn't so much looking to ask me some questions as seeking an audience for his views on the world's ills. The most strongly felt of these was that Muslims were bent upon world hegemony, but that Hindus and Christians outnumbered them and with luck would be able to forestall their designs. Muslims were not the minority they used to be, he said, having resolutely ignored family planning measures taken by other communities. I nodded with as much sympathy as I could muster, though it plainly wasn't enough.

Mr Das took his duties seriously, at each stop noting the time on a clipboard to verify he was keeping to the timetable and making up any shortfall with a little extra speed. We reached Bangaon Junction, near the Bangladeshi border, at 8.25, right on schedule.

But such punctuality was in vain, for me at least. Border formalities swallowed up three hours. Officials on both sides twiddled their pens, vanished from their desks, exchanged jokes with colleagues and put my passport to one side to deal with the hordes of Indians and Bangladeshis who passed through – anything, in fact, but put the required stamps in my passport.

The Indian immigration official repeatedly girded himself, but each time he lowered his stamp, he laid it to one side and subjected another page of my passport to the closest scrutiny. Protest, I knew, was futile. I waited in silence. Outside, truck drivers revved their engines to get some traction in the sea of mud encircling the immigration post. More travellers clutching tattered bags stormed through. Then, miracle of miracles, I had my stamp.

The Bangladeshi side was a replica of shabby buildings, recalcitrant officials, money changers' sheds, soldiers with lordly ways, a wide straight muddy road and mulling travellers, together with hangers-on, pickpockets and unscrupulous-looking types whose eyes were everywhere. The one unique feature on the Bangladeshi side was the bicycle-rickshaw riders who lined the road in pestilential numbers. They were the most visible manifestation of Bangladesh's biggest problem: too few real jobs.

One official said I might just have time to catch the train to Jessore – my map certainly showed a railway line leading there – but without exception everyone else laughed at my naivety. Train service? Ha! My anxiety grew. I remembered the Bangladeshi I met on my first day in India, at Chennai Central Station's reservations office. He frowned when I told him of my plans to travel about his country by train. 'You must go by bus, everyone else does,' he warned. 'Bangladesh is a country of many rivers – the trains must make long detours. Take my advice, catch the buses.'

A more careful look at my map showed there were few railway lines in the western Kulna district and none running in anything remotely resembling a direct line to Dhaka. It could be done by train with a long detour north using a series of locals and probably as many buses to plug the gaps. The difficulty was indeed rivers. Bangladesh had so many of them, and wide ones too, that a decent bridge-building programme would probably be forever beyond its means – the country had, after all, been beset by one economic disaster after another since its inception – and what railway lines and bridges existed were built during British times. Bangladesh had contented itself with roll-on, roll-off ferries.

So I resigned myself to taking a bus. There were plenty plying the

Dhaka route and I boarded the first to come along. It was an unlucky choice, but no more than I had expected. The driver was reckless, but not uncommonly so. We suffered two punctures – no surprise, as all the tyres were bald. The air-conditioning failed, and the windows could not be opened. I had a back-row seat, so every bump – and there were many – felt as though we'd hit a landmine. The curtains were all drawn, leaving me only a view down the aisle to all the oncoming buses and trucks flicking their lights and tooting their horns at us because we were on their side of the road in the middle of some madcap overtaking manoeuvre.

On the plus side, I arrived in one piece.

There was an interlude of sanity. For forty-five minutes I was able to relax as we crossed the Brahmaputra on a ferry. Before very long the riverbank receded from view and it was easy to imagine you were on a tremendously big lake, or even the open sea. The brown, debris-laden torrent of Assam had become an immense slab of blue slate, as tranquil as the cloudless dusk sky. It was only near our bow that any features revealed themselves: a few sandbanks and a string of flagged buoys marking our course.

Once on the other side, the bus driver's deadly antics began afresh.

❁

The moment I clapped eyes on the stark, modern outline of Kamalpur Station from my taxi I smelled a white elephant. And once inside, I was proved right. There was scarcely a soul to be found among the expanse of walkways, the soaring concourses, the platforms two or three football fields long.

For all the lofty concrete, just two trains stood in wait: my inter-city to Chittagong and a frightfully dilapidated local; out one window of the latter an old woman leaned in a coma of fatigue, and out one doorway a naked boy urinated. Below them, goats cropped the grass between the tracks.

I boarded my coach which, like most, was nearly empty and waited, hungry and parched, for the train to leave. Not even a cup of tea could be had. It was the second day of Ramadan.

At eight o'clock, the Mahanagar Provati pulled out. Packed hard against the tracks were the meanest, flimsiest hovels I had ever seen, sometimes no more than scraps of cloth and plastic laid over wobbly bamboo poles. Better-off squatters could claim ownership of something resembling an A-frame tent. Washing hung from barbed-wire. Children in rags and with shaved outsized heads were everywhere, playing in the rubble, howling for attention, swatting flies from their mouths and tugging at the saris of their mothers, who were stoking cooking fires into life. There was one thing to be said for an early-morning passage through a tropical slum: it was a fail-safe way to put one's own cares in perspective.

Behind the shanties were more liveable quarters, bare concrete apartment blocks, and at every level crossing waited a tidal wave of bicycle-rickshaw riders, nine out of ten without a passenger. Past timber yards we clanked, past garages, past a glassworks, then more dismal tenement blocks whose occupants leaned languidly against doorways, dulled by the prospect of another long hot day of inactivity.

Cramped and underemployed lives so many might have lived, but they were joined each year by countless others from the countryside who possessed little besides misplaced hope of a better life; misplaced because at least half of the city's residents lived below the poverty line. Dhaka was growing at an uncontrollable rate and was well on the way to becoming one of the biggest cities in the world. No one knew its population. Maybe 10 million, maybe 12 million. Every flood, every disaster brought another influx to add to the strain. Some predicted it would reach 19 million within two decades.

What enthusiasm I had for visiting Dhaka's sights ebbed away in the more or less continual gridlock that besets the streets. The city's 600,000 bicycle-rickshaws have become an acute impediment to the flow of traffic. The legions of auto-rickshaws have added to the congestion and poisoned the air to an alarming extent: Dhaka's air pollution is among the worst of any city in the world.

So I was relieved to be leaving aboard my train, and my spirits lifted further when the apartment blocks began to thin out and we wove between waterways and ponds bisected by fishing nets and edged by huts perching on stilts. At the suburban stop of Biman Bandar, hawkers with baskets of plump little fish were pounced upon by customers, proof of the fondness Bengalis, whether in West Bengal or Bangladesh, have for fish.

Men moved along the platform, stripped to the waist in checked lungis that revealed their slight, boyish builds and gave them the languid shuffling step that put in my mind the gentle rhythms of nearby South-East Asia. Women had a more relaxed dress code, too. Their Muslim sisters in Pakistan would have been shocked, or maybe envious. Yes, many covered their heads with scarves, but concealing the face was almost unknown. Indeed, the gulf between Bangladesh and Pakistan struck me anew as so vast that I realised only the madness of politics and religion could have blinded anyone to the impossibility of these two regions forming one nation.

Off we moved at last, and it was clear I would have the sleeper to myself. But I was not really alone. The train was plodding along at such a leisurely rate, and there were so many villagers pulling in fishing nets or digging about in vegetable plots or paddling flimsy-looking canoes, that I always had someone within sight of my window. And since spare time seemed to be one thing available in abundance here, there were always adults and children lazing about in ink blots of shade.

Bangladesh was proving to be a surprise, and a pleasant one, too. The railway track, built on top of a high embankment, was never out of sight of water and with a clear sky the land sparkled – the ponds, the estuaries, the paddy fields and the marshlands whose boundary between water and dry land was never entirely clear. Hyacinth grew profusely and what looked like solid land might just be soggy weeds. The Bangladeshis in their shallow-draught wooden canoes punted from one open passage of water to another as though in command of amphibious craft, working with a grace and dexterity to rival the most flamboyant gondoliers of Venice.

But of course the high embankment was not some elongated viewing platform for the convenience of passengers. During the monsoon, huge stretches of countryside were routinely under a metre or more of water, making the long straight band of railway track the only thing visible for hundreds of kilometres, the only link able to defy the rains. And the rains were always bad in Bangladesh, so routinely bad that even when scores or hundreds of people drowned the news seldom made any impact in the outside world. It was just one more disaster for an incurably unlucky country.

By late morning we had reached Bhairab Bazar, a sizeable town disguised among a thick collar of palm trees crowding both banks of the Meghna River. Freighters and barges moved across its placid surface, as did stately country-made boats propelled forward by sail and the peculiar twisting, sculling action of the boatmen. In the skyline above the sea of fronds rose banks of power pylons and what looked like a huge cement works, but it was no more than a trifle next to the mighty Meghna, which we now proceeded to cross via the one railway bridge to be found anywhere along its length. That done, we were in a position to reverse our north-easterly course and turn south for Chittagong.

Very soon we were back among the sparkling ponds, paddy fields and marshlands, and still my stomach rumbled. Ramadan, I was discovering, was a curse for the traveller. Yes, Islam exempted travellers from the requirement to fast, but where could one buy anything to eat? With my meagre supplies of nuts and biscuits exhausted, I went in search of the pantry car. The cooks and assistants, all eight of them, lay asleep in orderly rows beneath the tables. Ramadan had made their services redundant for a month. However, a bearer found me a tea-bag, some hot water and condensed milk. It was a far cry from the elaborate preparations I had come to take for granted on Indian trains.

Ramadan had one consolation: tickets were easier to secure as Muslims preferred not to travel during this time because of the general inconvenience. A man on the Dhaka bus, a stationery shop owner named Bishwajit Deb, told me there was no compulsion to fast. 'In Islam, you do not *have* to do anything,' he said of what I had always regarded as a fairly prescriptive religion. 'No one will say anything if you don't. It is between you and Allah alone.'

Mr Deb knew the precise moment at which the fast could be broken that day – 5.25 pm – and when that time arrived the bus came alive with the rustle of food wrappers, the snapping open of tins, the gurgle of thirsts being quenched and the steady munching of mouths. The feeling of relief was palpable; until that moment even a sip of water was forbidden to fasters.

Back in my compartment, the air-conditioning, which had only ever worked in a grumbling sort of way, was now dead. I complained to the conductor. He moved me to another compartment. The three men stretched out asleep each opened a resentful eye and did not move until one, the nearer to me on the lower bunk, was obliged to raise himself up to give me somewhere to sit.

I swung back the curtain. They gave me a hostile look. 'It's daytime,' I said. 'I wouldn't mind seeing something of Bangladesh while I'm here.'

Silence. They watched me scribble, grew incurious and went back to sleep, the fellow beside me having to do so sitting upright.

The station at Brahman Baria, where we halted at eleven, was, like every other, in a terribly neglected state. Even the smallest had separate men's and women's upper-class waiting rooms, but they had long ago been padlocked against use. The instant the train drew to a stop it was besieged by beggars – shaven-headed children in rags along with a miscellany of bedraggled adults. I bought some bottled water and shrank back to my coach. It would not be long before I came to dread the stops with their mobs and their unremitting cry of 'Baksheesh! Baksheesh!' and the tugging at your clothes and the cupped outstretched hands.

But, given the opportunity, Bangladeshis seemed an industrious and inventive lot. To catch the fish they were so fond of, they had evolved a variety of intricate nets, which dotted their watery landscape. No pond was too small for their attentions, whether a simple stick fence barrier with a net in the centre or an elaborate contraption resembling the Chinese-inspired nets of Cochin, which could be raised out of the water.

On we laboured across a vast region of paddy fields and hamlets snuggled among palm groves, coming after midday to the town of Comilla, three hours from Chittagong. The three old men, woken and rested, now rose as a single body and readied themselves for asr, third prayers. One by one, they repaired to the toilet to wash their hands and faces, then each took his turn on the other bottom bunk. I might have been inside a mini-mosque, so intimate was the setting and so solemn the atmosphere. I tried to resist staring, but couldn't: the unceasing sameness of this ritualised praying, which I had witnessed a hundred times before, still held an inexplicable fascination for me.

As the afternoon wore on, the compartment became so stuffy I began to wonder if the air-conditioning was failing a second time. And when, on my way to the toilet, I passed the open door of a much bigger compartment, my suspicions were aroused. The guards had installed themselves there, and it was as cold as a freezer. A wall-mounted air-conditioning unit hummed away merrily, and extra seats, all occupied, had been improvised. Perhaps today was no one-off failure. When I recounted this to one of the trio in my compartment, an army colonel on his way to take up a posting in Chittagong, he answered quite nonchalantly that the cabin was probably accommodating chair-class passengers prepared to pay the guards some baksheesh.

And there, I imagined, the matter rested. I watched jungly hills encroach on our left, funnelling us down a strip of coastal land abutting the Sandwip Channel. But then the conductor happened to come by and one of the other two, a thin, erect man with a lavish beard and rather stern pale eyes, accosted him over the air-conditioning. He evidently got no satisfaction because his companion said glumly to me: 'Everything is about money in Bangladesh. They cheat us – they are taking our money but they are not giving us facility.'

'If these people can't deliver, they should refund some of our money,' I said.

Bearded One clearly understood my words because he gave a loud huff, as if to say: such arguments carry no weight in this corner of the world. Emboldened by this breaking of the ice, he then began to harp on about George Bush and the invasion of Iraq. 'Bush was a terrorist. Did Americans back him over Iraq?' he asked.

'Many did,' I replied, 'but many didn't.'

'Then why don't the American people do something about it? Get rid of him!'

'For the very same reason you don't take your complaint about the air-conditioning any further.'

'What nonsense you are talking,' he spluttered.

'You don't make an official complaint because you don't think it will make any difference. The American people don't agitate because they don't think they can change anything either.'

'He is right,' said his companion, who introduced himself as Mr Karam.

But Bearded One shook his head.

Added Mr Karam, 'I am thinking George Bush will go down in history as a bad president.'

'Clinton, I think, was a better president,' I said.

'Clinton *was* a good man,' Mr Karam concurred.

His agreement startled me. Maybe there was hope the Muslim world might distinguish between good and bad American presidents, good and bad American foreign policy.

Chittagong's outskirts were now upon us, along with the customary quota of bicycle-rickshaws jamming the streets.

Mr Karam, gesturing towards some shacks beside the track, said: 'That is a slum.'

'Yes,' I said, 'I've seen those before.'

'These people have no land, no money, no jobs.'

Bearded One spoke up: 'Fifteen lakhs of homeless are living in Dhaka. There they have a chance of work. In this place there is nothing for them.'

The train stopped. We filed out into the waiting throng of beggars who looked truly destitute and desperate, unlike many of India's alms-seekers who pricked your conscience with horrifying disfigurements and diseases.

Chittagong Station was a scaled-down version of Dhaka's Kamalpur Station – big, new, austere and underused. I emerged onto the street and into the clutches of the bicycle-rickshaw men. It was impossible to take ten steps without being shadowed by some hopeful pedalling his floridly embellished three-wheeler in search of a fare. The law of supply and demand seemed all out of whack. How many, I wondered, earned anything approaching a living? But what else was there to do? They could, I suppose, take some consolation in having the apparent means of employment, the illusion of work.

I walked about the city's broiling streets looking for a decent hotel. Every room looked like an Asiatic prison cell. I was not prepared for this clapped-out country. I had thought India could not be beaten for poverty, but I was wrong. No wonder the Bangladeshi consular official in Calcutta had asked with more than a hint of suspicion in his voice, 'What is the purpose of your visit?' And no wonder he had looked unconvinced when I replied, 'Tourist.'

The same look of disbelief was written on the face of everyone who heard me say blithely, 'I'm a tourist. I just want to look at your country.'

Finally I understood their scepticism.

❋

'Are you fasting for Ramadan?' I asked.

'Fasting?' Shikha Akram laughed. 'Why should I? I'm a Christian. Only the silly Muslims fast.'

A giggle rippled through the men standing nearby. But I was taken aback by the rashness of his remark. In this overwhelmingly Muslim country where Islam was the official state religion, matters of faith were taken very seriously. Mr Akram seemed to realise his error, too. He became suddenly very circumspect and suspicious.

'Come,' he said, taking me by the elbow, 'come away from all these ears.'

We moved along the footpath a little way. 'I dress like a Muslim, it's easier,' he said, indicating to his lungi and long-sleeved shirt.

Mr Akram was a teacher, although he worked nowadays as a

private tutor. He was between lessons, he explained, and passing some time on the street corner, which, it had to be said, was not an especially pleasant place to stand about aimlessly. Chittagong struck me as an incredibly congested, noisy and undistinguished city, made doubly trying by the suffocating humidity.

Mr Akram was something of a rarity on the subcontinent: he and his wife had deliberately chosen to have only one child.

'This country has too many people,' he said, a claim that was beyond dispute. After a few city-states like Singapore, Bangladesh was the most densely populated place in the world.

'Muslims here are having five or six children. How are they to feed, clothe and educate them properly? They cannot.' *

Mr Akram was acutely aware of his minority status in a country where almost 90 per cent of people were Muslim and the balance Hindu, with only the tiniest smattering of Buddhists and Christians.

'BNP is good for minorities.' He was referring to the Bangladesh Nationalist Party, then the leading member of a four-party coalition ruling the country. 'You write that – BNP is good. Our prime minister, Mrs Khaleda, she is good. She knows how to look after the minorities. Not like the Awami League – they are very ...'

'Pro-Muslim?'

'Yes.'

He looked about at the gathering crowd, all po-faced young men, and murmured, 'They are always listening, these damn Muslims,' and once more we shuffled along the footpath and out of earshot.

The previous evening I met a Buddhist and a Hindu, and these two young men also talked of lying low. Most of the friction among communities, they told me, arose over religious festivals.

I asked the Hindu, a Mr Chowdary, 'Have you been celebrating Diwali?'

'No.'

---

* Bangladesh's population of about 130 million has been growing by up to 2 million a year, although the average number of children per family has fallen from more than six a quarter of a century ago to about three today.

'Not at all?'

'No.'

That staggered me. Diwali was the most boisterously celebrated religious event of the year. What would it take to stop Hindus erecting images of their ten-armed goddess Durga in the streets and blasting the neighbourhood with music from public address systems? Fear was the only thing I could think of.

Mr Chowdary and his co-religionists congregated in the shops and laneways around their temple. The temple's appearance was telling: it was a no-frills building, half hidden behind a brick wall, that rose hardly two storeys. Mr Chowdary was set upon leaving Bangladesh, but to where he hadn't yet decided.

Mr Akram had similar intentions. He felt besieged. 'The Muslims are always trying to grab our things,' he said.

When I asked him to explain, he said his father had been murdered two years before, seized by unknown assailants from his home and never seen again. Then difficulties had arisen over the transfer of the family land from his father's name to his own. He could not prove title, which was being contested by some Muslim claimants.

'It is in the courts now,' he said, motioning towards an office block on the other side of the intersection.

His solution, like that of so many Bangladeshis, was to emigrate – or try to. Several hundred thousand slipped across the Indian border illegally each year. His sister worked at the British High Commission in Dhaka. His teaching qualifications were sound: 'Even the Muslims send their children to me.' Who knows, maybe he would be lucky.

As we parted, he urged me once more to visit the Zia Memorial Museum, formerly the Circuit House, where President Zia Rahman was assassinated in 1981 during a military coup attempt: Bangladesh's generals share the same propensity as Pakistan's top brass for usurping civilian power.

'You will see his bloodstained clothes there,' he added, almost by way of inducement.

But I was no longer interested in going – I had, in a sense, already been there, thanks to Mr Akram's first-hand account of Zia's killing. Quite by chance he had been standing across the road at the time. He was eighteen. The sky that day, he remembered, had been black as ink. Thunderclaps crashed overhead. Mr Akram had been gazing up at the sky when he heard the first crackle of machine guns. He looked down just in time to see Zia fall, and to see the killers themselves gunned down by loyal soldiers.

As I listened to Mr Akram's words, the smell of paan on his breath, the commotion of passing vehicles in my ears, perspiration dripping from me as the sun beat down out of a tropical sky, I felt I was almost there myself that day.

Chittagong has one saving feature, its port, Bangladesh's main shipping gateway. Anchored in the turbid Karnaphuli River or beached on its mudflats can be found every sort of craft, from the smallest open-hulled tubs to caravel-shaped timber fishing boats, steel trawlers, barges laden with hardwood logs, becalmed dhows with a graceful sweep of hull, sampans, launches, rusty freighters by the score, blistered tramp steamers and a lesser number of container ships berthed well upstream and half invisible in the haze.

I spent a morning wandering about the mudflats, shoes in hand. A man walking down a pathway of planks to a rowboat called out a greeting. Mr Imam, impeccably dressed and carrying a briefcase, could have been an office worker. In fact, he was the captain of a stinking fishing boat riding at anchor a little way off. He was about to sit his first-class skipper's ticket and this, he explained brightly, would secure him enough points for a New Zealand or Australian visa. Mr Imam's youngest brother was studying computer science in Sydney. Inshallah, God willing, he would soon add his own name to the roll-call of skilled and motivated Bangladeshis fleeing their country.

I was killing time until my next train and, reluctant to spend it in the city, went off to a cricket match. Bangladesh was playing England. The idea had never interested me before, but the prospect of a cool green oval, a shady seat and nothing noisier than the polite clapping of the crowd won me over. I bought a 50-cent ticket and found exactly what I had been hoping for.

Farmer in marshalling yards, en route to Sylhet.

The Paharika Express
to Sylhet

FINDING THE TRAIN TO SYLHET was easy: it was the only one in the station. My first-class compartment was empty and in precisely the state I had come to expect. The lights didn't work, the seats were lumpy, the floor was filthy, the ceiling fans barely stirred a breeze and the toilets down the corridor had no water. But as dilapidated as my cabin was, I was happy to be on the move once more, to be quitting this town.

The Paharika Express rattled out of Chittagong and into the vegetable plots and paddy fields beyond.

For the first time a conductor moved through the carriage checking tickets. Mr Abedin was solicitous. 'You are happy? There is any service I can do for you?'

No, I said, everything was perfect.

Feni Junction revealed hawkers selling a pathetic assortment of goods: a single bunch of bruised bananas, a handful of boiled sweets, a single bottle of mineral water. The sound of passengers clearing their throats and spitting rose above the idling diesel loco.

The unblemished green of the countryside returned. Every hamlet was shrouded in the cool shadows of bamboo and creeper-entwined palm trees. Every hamlet was also wisely built on a high bank or mound as a precaution against the annual rains and flooding. Bangladesh derives its name from bangala, an ancient term for the region meaning 'the people who live on mounds'.

By late morning we were firmly back in rice-growing territory. Men and boys, the latter mostly naked, were busy repairing dykes or clearing blue-flowering hyacinth from waterways. A few old women were stooped over in the fields, their sun-toughened skin hanging in folds from their backs. In the hamlets, very young girls in frocks stood by hut doors. Of the females between those two extremes of age there was none to be seen. They were presumably stuck indoors in purdah – and in this region temperatures ranged from the merely warm in winter to the ferociously hot in summer.

This countryside, I concluded, had to be among the most exquisite of any on the subcontinent – all those luxuriant groves rimming the paddy fields, the succession of streams and rivers to add interest, the castled clouds soaring overhead, and not a trace of a slum or an industrial wasteland anywhere. It is from this lush landscape that Bengali culture has drawn so much of its inspiration. The national anthem, in verse adopted from Nobel Prize winner Rabindranath Tagore, pours out the Bengali's love of the land: the springtime fragrance from the mango groves, the full-blossomed paddy fields in autumn, the quilt spread at the feet of banyan trees and along the banks of rivers. For all its distantly observed beauty, however, rural Bangladesh was no paradise for those living there. It offered hard work and few conveniences but at least it was tranquil and clean, unlike the cities.

At Akhaura Junction we drew alongside an Army train. Soldiers were stacked to the ceiling like loaves in bakers' trays. Mosquito nets and mounds of kitbags filled the remaining space. One soldier sat cross-legged on his bunk while a barber lathered his face in preparation for a shave. The rest, stripped to white singlets, reclined in oriental positions with the numbed expression of opium den smokers. From somewhere among the shoulder-to-shoulder mass of soldiery arose a smell compounded of curries, gas burners, perspiration and cheroots. Altogether, it was not a persuasive advertisement for the military life.

The wait at Akhaura was considerable. So was the onslaught of free-loaders. Having filled the corridors, they began clinging to the sides of the carriages and clambering onto the roofs. The guards were quite uninterested in evicting these ticketless travellers. The only way I could keep them out of my compartment was to bolt the door. Soon battle was joined on another front, the window, where beggars congregated. They were so prolific and unrelenting I was reduced to shuttering the window and waiting in the slatted gloom. But once we were moving again, I raised the shutter and stretched out to enjoy the jungle flashing by my window, along with a succession of ponds, paddy fields, banana plantations, huts, village mosques as small as garden sheds and meadows cropped as low as short-pile carpet by scrawny cows.

Finally, in the middle of the afternoon, we passed through a tract of hills and tea gardens and, still clinging closely to the Indian border, as we had been doing all day, negotiated a marshland of lagoons and streams and broad reaches of water. On my map, flecks of blue were sprinkled across this eastern bulge like handfuls of confetti. The boats on these waterways were as graceful as slippers, with slender rounded hulls drawing to a point at either end. At dusk, the boatmen's lamps glowed inside the flaxen enclosures, dimly illuminating the bamboo fishing-rods that overhung bow and stern. Bamboo was put to an almost infinite variety of uses in these parts, for everything from dainty footbridges to picket fences around vegetable plots (each picket as narrow as a stalk of rice) and complicated-looking fish traps.

It was after dark by the time we reached Sylhet, a provincial centre straddling the Surma River. The town resounded with the jangle of bicycle bells as rickshaw riders ferried their customers about the unlit and otherwise deserted streets. They made an attractive sight, gliding by with lanterns fixed to the rear axles in compliance with municipal regulations. But that was the only attractive or interesting thing about Sylhet. For my purposes, it lay at the end of the line. The next day I bought a ticket out.

❁

The poorest of the poor were drawn to Sylhet's station to cadge a living. They camped on the tracks and under derelict freight wagons and spent the day importuning waiting passengers. They had to compete for alms with the professional beggars – the lame, the blind, diseased, disfigured, limbless and homeless – as well as the naked children who were merely perpetually hungry. Whole families squatted on their haunches, faces blank, bodies filthy, clothes ragged, scratching themselves, coughing and spitting.

The Joyenteeka, the inter-city service to Dhaka, was supposedly the fastest train to Dhaka, but it took us three hours to reach Srimangal, 80 kilometres away. Mr Das's commuter service to Bangaon would have made better time. Hard as it was to believe, my first-class cabin was more beaten-up than the last. A third-class local in India would have matched it for cleanliness. Nothing worked, everything rattled, except the public address system which enjoined passengers to pray at the prescribed times throughout the day. It also broadcast religiously inspired programmes and, with delicious irony, ended each transmission with a reminder to enjoy the ride aboard Bangladesh Railways. The instrument of religious and state propaganda was in fully functioning order; the fans, which we could sorely have done with, were not.

For the return journey I had company of sorts: a young man rather nattily dressed in Western clothes who was returning to Dhaka after visiting his parents and who slept the whole way; a middle-aged Hindu man of very stern disposition with the doleful unblinking eyes of a frog; his teenage daughter, in a pink-and-green salwar kameez, who uttered not a single word to anyone all day and looked miserable; next to me, a man who regularly spat wads of paan out the window; and finally, his son, a lad of eleven or twelve, new to train travel, whose mouth was agape all the way to Dhaka. Later his father took his place by the door and began to spit onto the corridor floor. When the Hindu man climbed into the top bunk to sleep, the paan-chewing man, a devout Muslim with a skullcap of the hadj-returned tucked into his shirt pocket, stared with undisguised lechery at the girl. Much later in the day, fed up with the discomfort he was causing her, I snapped at him to stop. He didn't understand the words, but he understood the tone of voice. The ogling ended and she glanced my way for the first and only time, which I suppose amounted to a thank you.

So there we were, a merry little lot, making our way south at a mournful pace. The two old men napped on the top bunks. The young man slept on, head propped against the cabin wall, without waking once. Normally on such a train, going all day, people would be eating and reading, but in Bangladesh there was nothing to eat and no one seemed much interested in reading.

At each halt, there was much shouting as more people clambered onto the roof and clung to the doorways as though magnetised. A conductor checked our tickets but ignored all those around us riding free. It was not until early evening, tired from nine hours of sitting, that I arrived back in Dhaka where, in a city of undernourished millions, I counted three substantial mosques under construction.

✿

One night I had the good fortune to meet Hossain Chanchal. I was at a downtown Chinese restaurant and he beckoned me to join him. Mr Chanchal was candid about the difficulties facing his country, though he still loved it dearly. He didn't live in Dhaka but in a nearby town because he worried for his children's health in a city so chronically polluted. He certainly had the money to afford a house in a good suburb because he skippered ocean-going bulk carriers and had worked in Britain and the United States.

I asked him how he found the traffic jams.

He shook his head slowly. 'It can take an hour to go around the block. Of course, the problem is the rickshaw pullers.'

'Why not get rid of them? Ban them from central areas?'

He gave a hearty laugh, no doubt at the extent of my foolishness. 'If you did, there would be a very big employment problem.'

'But they do so little anyway. In fact, they're simply in the way.'

'There was a plan to retrain them once ... but nothing ever came of it. The real problem, you know, is political disturbances.'

'Disturbances? What kind of disturbances?'

'Each government is undoing all the work of the previous government. Then the previous government gets back in and undoes that government's policies. We could be a rich country – where else can you throw a seed on the ground and without any effort something pops up twenty or thirty days later? But bad politics and too many people, that is our undoing.'

I said women were better off in Bangladesh than Pakistan. They went about unescorted and regarded the sari as sufficient to protect their modesty.

'In Pakistan they are too fundamentalist. They will never progress while they put half the population to the chador and say, "Stay at home, you know nothing."' He chuckled and added, 'Pakistan are number one crazies and we are number two crazies.'

'I think you exaggerate,' I protested.

'It is true we are not forcing people on matters of religion. Force does not work. Some fundamentalists tried it here, but they were put in their place.'

Bangladeshis, it seemed to me, had avoided the identity crisis still bedevilling Pakistanis. Nine out of ten citizens might be Muslim, but their constitution defined the country as a secular democracy and that seemed to satisfy most. Certainly, Islam had been the official state religion since 1988, but the clergy held no sway in national politics.

'You are not tempted to emigrate?' I asked. 'Every Bangladeshi I talk to wants to leave.'

'I am too old.'

'How old is old?'

'Forty.'

'That's not old.'

He smiled. 'It's not just age. I have friends, family ... yes, I could be well off in Britain or America, but I would be alone. And I like my country. You can have a peaceful life here. In America everyone is always rushing, rushing to make money. Always it is about money. I don't want that. So I stay.'

Bangladesh, he agreed, would be better off as part of India in some ways. A realistic way forward might be a sort of European Union with an exchange of ideas, capital and labour. Bangladesh could only benefit from better relations with its bigger neighbour. But politics had spoilt that, too. One party was antagonistic towards India, the other repaired the damage, then the first spoiled relations again.

'Hindus, Muslims, we are all the same – same skin, same land, same traditions, same religion.' That made me raise an eyebrow, but more in delight than doubt. 'This line Jinnah put through Bengal is a nonsense. The flow of people across that border, legal and illegal, is too great to stop. So why try? India I have great respect for. It is self-sufficient, it will never buy abroad unless it must. Look, it even has nuclear power stations. Old Russian designs maybe, but it has still made nuclear power on its own. And us? We are still clogging up our capital with rickshaws.'

Mr Chanchal perplexed me. He hardly sounded like a Muslim, so I asked, 'Are you fasting?'

He affected a mocking tone: 'I'm not, but he is,' he said, indicating his friend who now joined us. 'He's a good Muslim – I'm not.'

'I think you're being too modest.'

He shrugged off my remark. 'I'll tell you this. Fasting is good for you, good for your body – it gives it time to regenerate – and good for the spirit. Even before the Mohammedans, I think, it was something people were practising.'

Although this worldly sea captain might not have observed the outward forms of a good Muslim, I had no doubt the finest instincts of Islam were present in him. He seemed to me the face of how Islam could be: progressive, tolerant, outward-looking – and still perfectly true to the spirit of the Prophet's teachings.

Politely, Mr Chanchal expressed himself a little incredulous that I had come as a tourist to Bangladesh. 'There is nothing to see here – only lots of people and lots of water.'

I said it deserved more tourists. But I also said it was hard to reconcile how a country could be at the same time so beautiful and so poor. And apparently so corrupt. Was it as corrupt as was claimed?

'Of course, top to bottom.'*

'Even your prime minister Mrs Khalada Zia?' Mrs Zia is the widow of the assassinated former president.

'Especially her. You cannot get to the top otherwise. Mrs Zia is not clever. There are a thousand, ten thousand women in Bangladesh smarter than her. But she has her family connections and political cunning. Next to a Tony Blair or someone of his ilk, she is nothing, a nobody.'

❂

'Bangladesh is a poor country,' one Bangladeshi after another said to me. It was not a prelude to begging or a prompt for sympathy. It was a simple expression of fact, like remarking casually, 'Haven't the floods been bad this year!'

But some Bangladeshis did very well out of poverty by milking the aid industry. At the Benapole border post I had a long talk about aid with Haruki Taniguchi, a PhD student who had spent three years in the country. We had plenty of time to talk because the Bangladeshi officials were especially difficult that morning, and they were aided by soldiers who kept the snaking queues in order with liberal use of their lathis.

Mr Taniguchi reckoned officials and politicians siphoned off more than half of all aid.** There was even enormous money to be made legitimately. His department head, a well-known professor, was a frequent consultant to Japan, one of Bangladesh's biggest donors, on poverty, gender bias and other vague and ungraspable matters. For his troubles, the professor received US$150 a day. His academic

---

* A British survey of businesspeople and academics found that Bangladesh was rated as having the most corrupt public sector of the 133 countries in the poll. Nigeria and Haiti came second and third respectively.

** Bangladesh is estimated to have received $US36 billion since its creation in 1971. Half of its citizens survive on a dollar a day.

salary was 20,000 taka, or US$400 a year.

Mr Taniguchi had a great regard for Bangladeshis and their culture, but he had never come to terms with the rudeness of officials. And there was a twist. The higher an official's standing, and that included everyone from the humblest policeman to the chief of customs, the haughtier and more intimidating that person became. Curiously, it was sometimes a signal to the intimidated individual to proffer a bribe.

Back on the bus, a man sitting next to me said he was taking his sixty-five-year-old father to Calcutta for treatment of a heart condition. It turned out many Bangladeshis made the same journey to get surgery. Bangladesh's hospitals, he told me, had the equipment but not the doctors. At least, not doctors with the right attitude and training. Most were there in body only: their preoccupation was with their private practices.

'Would Bangladesh not be better off as part of India?' I asked.

'It is an open secret that Bangladesh is totally dependent on India.' Then he added, with a note of irritation, 'But India is always taking, taking – never giving anything back.'

'I don't understand.'

'It takes our money but does not buy anything in return.'

All the vehicles on Bangladesh's roads were Indian-made, as were many of the goods in shops.

I asked, 'What does Bangladesh make that India would want?'

'Well, there is tea …'

'Yes, but India makes some of the best tea in the world – Darjeeling, for example – and it exports a lot of what it grows.'

'Then there is rice and garments.'

'India has all it needs on that score, too,' I suggested.

He fell silent.

Mr Chanchal was right. It was a silly line the mapmakers had drawn.

Roadside shrine, Madras.

The Coromandel Express to Madras

THE COROMANDEL EXPRESS, all twenty-three coaches long, thundered south throughout the afternoon and by the time it made its first stop, at Kharagpur, at 4.30 pm, most passengers had already drawn their compartment curtains and taken to their beds.

Thankfully, Major Wala chose to remain up. We strolled along the platform, the sky a blaze of dusky saffron, while a diesel locomotive was attached for the non-electrified section ahead. Kharagpur had just one distinction and we were walking on it. The platform, at 833 metres, was the longest in the world and could accommodate three train services simultaneously.

For an army man, the major had very magnanimous views about Pakistan. 'J & K problem has been stirred up by Pakistan's army leaders so they can stay on in power. They paint India as the enemy. Without that they cannot continue.'

'In power, you mean?'

'Of course. Pakistani people are wanting good relations with India at all levels. At all levels! It is their generals who are spreading poison.'

There could be no doubt an external 'enemy' was infinitely more straightforward for the military mind than the internal enemies of poverty, illiteracy, overpopulation, an economy in a coma, communal violence, rampant crime and ethnic conflicts.

The Coromandel Express resumed its marathon sprint down the length of the Coromandel Coast. All that night I tossed in my bunk when I should have slept soundly. There would be no more dream-filled nights broken by the screeching rush of passing trains, the hissing of brakes or the banging of luggage as passengers descended into grainy puddles of light at anonymous stations. But my relief was tinged with regret. Part of me could have rolled on indefinitely in this twilight existence, a day here, two days there, scribbling my notes, drifting through the cavernous railway waiting rooms that had become my home, the only imperative being to choose my next destination.

At 4.30 am I woke once again. Movement stilled me, and we were not moving. I peeped through the curtain. The signboard read: 'VISHAKHAPATNAM'. We had reached Andhra Pradesh state's big port city. I wrestled with sleep, and at 6.30 the bearer, Mahesh Kumar, brought me tea.

Major Wala got down from his bunk in a talkative mood. He had been in the Kargil operation, the world's highest battleground.

'Terrible conditions for men. Supplies up by horse and on men's backs. Terrible. Mobility was restricted. But flexibility and simplicity there must be – to change an order and go this way instead of that.'

Four tours in Kashmir, he said, had convinced him all the soldiers in the world would not solve the problem. 'It is the same with nearly all wars. Solution is mutual understanding. Each side must fully appreciate the other's point of view. It is by talking, by diplomacy, that J & K issue will be solved.'

When I asked him what shape that solution might take, he adopted the attitude of a professional soldier: 'That is a political matter. I am a soldier. Diplomacy is for the politicians.'

The major vanished, off to join colleagues in another carriage for the remainder of the journey, and I sat alone as the Coromandel Express entered Rajahmundry, an important city on the Godavari. Passing a ghat-side temple devoted to Siva, a shrine that would have looked spectacular to any new arrival to India but which now joined the ranks of commonplace marvels, we proceeded out across what was, at 5 kilometres, the longest rail bridge in India. It seemed to take forever to cross the Godavari and rejoin the paddy fields, those endless reaches of greenness traversed by chorus lines of areca palms. And in Andhra Pradesh's coastal belt, every colour was acute: the shoulder-high rice was a bottle-green, the sky a luminous blue, the swooping egrets a lustrous white, the field-workers a coal-black.

The city of Vijayawada made but a fleeting interlude. I stretched my legs and came upon a Railways police post where a notice-board displayed, under the words 'TRAVELLING PUBLIC – BE CAREFUL', a line-up of railway rogues. Their mug shots were arranged by category: Doping Criminals, Criminals of Suitcase Lifting, Snatching Offenders, Lady Criminals and Inter-state Criminals. Every last one looked deeply untrustworthy.

On we continued across this unchanging landscape of rice. Dulled by it, I opened my copy of *Patanjali Yoga Sutras*, which I had bought from a platform bookstand at Howrah. Patanjali was a great Indian sage, about whom hardly anything is known, including exactly when he lived (somewhere between the fourth century BC and the fourth century AD). His work was a reformulation of Hindu ideas about yoga in its fullest sense; not merely the limb-bending exercises Westerners associate with the term, but the pursuit of spiritual union with the Godhead, the Reality, the Atman.

As aphorisms, they are pithy almost to the point of abstraction, so it is the commentary that makes them either accessible or unintelligible. This edition was as down to earth as it was possible to get on a subject so esoteric. For instance: 'When Patanjali speaks of "control of thought-waves", he does not refer to a momentary or superficial control. Many people believe that the practice of yoga is concerned with "making your mind a blank" – a condition which could, if it really were desirable, be much more easily achieved by asking a friend to hit you over the head with a hammer.'

Maybe, I thought, such a book might offer some clues into the Hindu mind. But the gulf was too wide for me. Patanjali argued the mind had to be stilled of so-called 'good', 'pure' and 'truthful' thought-waves. 'This may at first seem shocking to a student who has been trained in the Western approach to morality,' explained the commentary. 'But a little reflection will show him that this must be so. The external world, even in its most beautiful appearances and noblest manifestations, is still superficial and transient. It is not the basic Reality. We must look through it, not at it, in order to see the Atman. Certainly it is better to love than to hate, better to share than to hoard, better to tell the truth than to lie. But the thought-waves which motivate the practice of these virtues are nevertheless disturbances in the mind.'

The mind of the truly illuminated man, it went on, was calm 'not because he is selfishly indifferent to the needs of others, but because he knows the peace of the Atman within all things, even within the appearance of misery, disease, strife and want'.

As I read on, the realisation came to me that however long a Westerner might spend in this country, however much of its culture he might absorb, he must always remain a stranger, an outsider. I put my book to one side, defeated.

Finally, at 2.30 pm, after exactly twenty-four hours aboard the Coromandel Express, we reached Nellore. Gudur soon followed, but we didn't stop. A street sweeper stood with one hand on a hip and the other grasping her brushwood broom, chin tilted like some heroic communist worker immortalised in bronze, as she watched us hurtle past. We rounded Pulicat Lake where fishing boats with mutton-chop sails were making their way downwind, their canvas aglow in the late-afternoon sun. Madras was only an hour away. And in no time the red-brick mass of Chennai Central Station, with its 40-metre central clock tower, rose into view.

✹

Returning to Madras disquieted me. The Nilgiri Express to Ooty had seemed an eternity ago. Yet I wasn't ready to leave. A restlessness, elusive and ill-defined, stirred inside. After a few days of inactivity I decided to walk off my unease. I tramped the length of Anna Solai Road, formerly Mount Road, with its shopping arcades and designer-label stores. I trooped off up Wallajah Road to Marina Beach and the Bay of Bengal, passing on the way Moghul buildings formerly part of the palace of the Nawabs of the Carnatic and now the neglected offices of minor government agencies; passing also the Senate House of the University of Madras, in an equally depressing state of disrepair but sheathed by scaffolding as workmen undertook restoration work; past the beachfront Anna Square Park with its superabundance of marble; across the snaking Cooum River whose stagnant waters had the colour and consistency of used motor oil; past the naval officers' quarters and the Victory Memorial, built in honour of those of the Madras Presidency who served during the Second World War and now encircled by a busy roundabout outside the main Chennai Port entrance; northwards further still past the colonial administrative building and its modern additions, which house the government of Tamil Nadu; past Fort St George, the site of the first settlement of the East India Company in South India; past the Orwellian-looking Reserve Bank of India tower; past the destitute families squatting in burlap huts along a wide treed verge next to the Chennai Port boundary wall, a strip designated 'a green belt in the abatement of pollution'; past women riding scooters who gave me the once over or a smiling, shouted hello and who made me grin stupidly in delight at their boldness; past the traffic speeding efficiently along four-lane Kamaraj Road parallel to the beach (as a Calcutta man on the Coromandel Express said to me, 'The South is so *organised.*'); past the Port Trust Administrative Office high-rise (notice on the gate: 'NO BRIBE PLEASE'); now finally turning inland past the sprawling red-brick Indo-Saracenic High Court complex on Parry's Corner with its plethora of onion-shaped domes (said to be the world's biggest judicial building after the Courts of London); past the chauffeurs flicking dust off Ambassadors while their employers were engaged on court business; past the 'Sulabh pay-and-use urinal complex', a stinking single-room dunny built against the High Court perimeter wall and amply demonstrating Indians' fondness for attaching grandiose titles to the most mundane of things; past the monolithic insurance and bank towers; past the Moghul-inspired YMCA, its exquisite façade mutilated by hoardings; before eventually my frantic pacing gave out in the narrow streets of Georgetown, Madras's old port district.

And there, hot, tired and covered in grime, I heard the long, plaintive hoots from nearby Chennai Central. I felt comforted. That sound beckoned me no more. I was free to go.

Glossary

asr afternoon prayer recited by Muslims

babu clerk, generally in government service
bhuja savoury snack
bustee shanty town, slum

chador full-length semi-circle of cloth worn by Muslim women and
  held shut by the hands or teeth
chai tea
chappals sandals or slippers without a back strap
charpoy rope bed
chatty earthenware water-pot
chhatri cupola
churidar tight-fitting trousers worn by men and women
crore 10 million, or 100 lakhs

daba tin used to hold lunch carried by daba-wallah
dacoit armed bandit, usually a member of a gang
darshan audience with, or offering to, a holy or important person;
  viewing of a god
dhaba roadside eatery common in North India, much favoured by
  lorry drivers who avail themselves of the charpoys to rest on
dhoti ankle-length white cloth worn by men, like a lungi, but pulled
  up between the legs
dosa thin pancake made of fermented rice flour and dhal, served
  with various condiments

fajr dawn prayer recited by Muslims
fedayeen literally, one who is ready to sacrifice his life – a Muslim
  fighter

ganga Ganges River

gurdwara Sikh temple

hari share-cropper
hartal closing of shops and offices as a mark of protest or sorrow

idli rice dumplings, a South Indian speciality
inshallah Muslim exclamation meaning, 'If God wills it'
isha evening prayer recited by Muslims

jawar tropical cereal grass sorghum
jheel swampy area, lagoon
jizyah tax once imposed on non-Muslim adult males
jnana-marga in Hinduism, one of the three principal ways of
    achieving salvation. The term means 'way of knowledge'. The
    other two paths are bhakti-marga (salvation through faith and/or
    love) and karma-marga (salvation through acts)

kachh short drawers worn by Sikhs
kafila caravan
kakkar one of the five marks of an orthodox Sikh
kanga wooden comb worn by Sikhs
karo kari practice in Pakistan of honour killing, most prevalent in
    the Punjab, Sindh and the North-West Frontier Province
kesh practice in Sikhism of not cutting one's hair
khadi coarse, homespun cotton Mahatma Gandhi urged all Indians
    to wear
kirpan short sword carried by an orthodox Sikh
kurta loose-fitting shirt worn by men

ladoos sweetmeats, usually balls made with sesame seeds or nuts
lakh one hundred thousand
lassi yoghurt drink often flavoured with salt or sugar and essence of
    rosewater
lathi long wooden or bamboo stave meant for use as a weapon,
    hence a lathi charge by police to break up a mob

lungi loose garment, similar to a sarong, worn by men and reaching from waist to ankle

maidan open grassy area in a town or city used for relaxation or sport

masala dosa dosa, but with the addition of spicy potato filling

masala movie formulaic film containing all the ingredients for a box-office smash, including song and dance, fights, romantic interludes and coarse comedy

masher fourth daily devotion in Islam

moksa liberation of the spirit; salvation; escape from cycle of reincarnation

naan bread made from plain flour and cooked in a tandoor

paan mixture of betel nut, lime paste and spices, wrapped in a betel leaf and eaten as a digestive or mouth freshener

pakora fritter of gram flour and spinach or another vegetable

panchayat traditional village council of elders

poya full-moon day when practising Buddhists in Sri Lanka visit temples for the rituals of worship

puja Hindu religious rite

puri deep-fried bread

ramadan ninth month of the Muslim year when strict fasting is observed during daylight hours

roti generic term for bread, used interchangeably with chappati, to indicate the most common variety, which is unleavened and is cooked on a hotplate called a tawa

rupee monetary unit of India, Pakistan and Sri Lanka (and also of neighbouring Nepal)

saarg spinach, often used to describe any leafy greens

sadhu holy man, sage or ascetic

salwar kameez baggy trousers and loose shirt worn in North India and Pakistan

sambar spicy vegetable and lentil stew

suttee Hindu custom, now all but gone, whereby a widow burned herself to death on her husband's funeral pyre

swadeshi self-sufficiency, entailing a boycott of foreign goods during India's struggle for independence from British rule

thali large metal dish with upturned sides, usually of stainless steel, on which as many as a dozen or more dishes are served

tiffin light meal or snacks eaten during the day; also, the stainless steel carrier, usually with three or four compartments, to hold lunch at work or meals on long journeys

tilak forehead decoration, once of religious significance, but now more ornamental in the case of women

ummah in Islam, the community of the believers and thus the whole Islamic world

uppma pilaf-like dish made with semolina

uttapam dish similar to the pancake-like dosa

varna the concept of caste

wadas deep-fried lentil rings

wadera conservative landholder

zina in the Muslim code, fornication